Sociology of the Family with a View to Islamic Sources

Written by :

Hossein Bostan (Najafi)

Translated by:

Somaieh Rahimzadeh

ISBN-13: 978-1517265441

ISBN-10: 1517265444

TRANSLATOR'S FOREWORD

Islam puts down some specific rules for family life and also lays the foundation of a normal family on religious thoughts. In that spirit, the main objective of this work was transferring the valuable views of Islam regarding family and marriage into English. Conferring with cultural and scientific centers in other countries, the Center of Organizing Translation and Publication of Islamic Sciences and Humanities in Iran has identified some suitable and valuable Persian books for being translated into other languages among which this book figured as a worthwhile one. Fulfilling this goal was the second objective of the translation.

Alhamdulillah. Thanks to Allah whose grant gave me the opportunity to complete my translation. I would like to express my deepest gratitude to my family, especially my sister, Samira, and my cousin, Leila, for their cooperation, encouragement, constructive suggestion and their full unflagging support for the completion of this work, from the beginning to the end. Also thanks to Dr. Bostan, Dr. Hadidi , Dr.Sabouri , Mr.Ghassabi and my dear friend Miss Sima Pooryeganeh, and everyone who helped me along by supporting my work and helping me out in various ways to the last moment of it.

Somaieh Rahimzadeh

June 2015

AUTHOR'S PREFACE

Being the smallest social institution, family has attracted the attention of social thinkers due to the special significant place it occupies. On the one hand, the mutual effect between family and other sections of society, and on the other hand, its survival throughout ages and centuries have driven many thinkers to study it using different approaches. Apart from the religious, ethical, philosophical and legal approaches dominant in the past, there has been a growth of historical, anthropological, psychological and social approaches to family since the 19th century.

According to common definitions, sociology is a theoretical science which attempts to describe and explain social interactions and institutions by using various experimental methods. The application of this scientific discipline comes to manifest itself in policies and strategies which are presented by the experts in order to improve social conditions. On the other hand, since Islam intends to present an all-embracing and comprehensive plan for the personal and social happiness of humans, it has revealed its stance on different issues concerning family in an extensive series of Quranic verses and narrations sometimes in the form of descriptive phrases and often in the form of normative phrases.

Therefore we can expect to find many overlaps between the phrases concerning the family in this comprehensive religious plan and the phrases in the discipline of sociology about family and this will provide a proper ground and the necessary motivation to embark on interdisciplinary studies by integrating religious and sociological approaches, because these type of studies play a significant role in extending the boundaries of knowledge in the field of humanities. In fact, such works will pave the way for achieving two main objectives in this field; first, the establishment of the idea of humanities and Islamic ideology and specifically the paradigm of Islamic sociology in academic settings the need for which is felt in recent years more than ever. Second, the localization of the human sciences which attracts more supporters in comparison with the first objective due to the fact that today the shortcomings of the non-native human sciences have been revealed even further.

Particularly in the field of the sociology of family, a considerable part of the topics includes those which do not fit the general setting of the Islamic societies, even though they might have pervaded some Westernized groups and social strata in these societies, these topics may include: romantic love, cohabitation, homosexual families, and the conflict between love and parenting. On the other hand, the family in Islamic societies is facing numerous issues that the sociology of family has not yet engaged in a deep study of them which includes the functions of alimony, zeal, *hijab*, the restrictions on the relationship between the men and women, the Islamic upbringing of the children, temporary marriage, polygamy. Since social realities are the result of social values to a great extent, and given the differences of social values of different societies, it is quite natural that the sociology of the family as a new and budding science in the Western world should concern itself with the ideal Western family and be specified to resolving the issues and problems emerging in the Western culture and the Western family, while it should also be noted that these problems will most probably not be considered as problems and issues at all in other societies.

Furthermore, even when a sociologist is engaged in studying the non-Western societies, he usually employs the same concepts and theoretical frameworks of the Western sociology and this is also an important obstacle in gaining a true understanding of the realities in these societies. For instance, when the sociologist of the family uses some of the concepts originating from the Western culture such as patriarchy and sex discrimination to analyze the family relationships in Islamic societies, this problem emerges.

The current book is the abridged form of and at the same time a complement for the book Islam and the sociology of family which its first edition was published in 2004.The discussions of this book are organized in five parts and fifteen chapters; the first part deals with the subject of marriage, in the second part the structure of the family, and in the third part the functions of the family will be explored, the fourth part is specified to important subjects in the area of the pathology of the family and the ways to strengthen it and finally the fifth part will present some theoretical discussions in the area of the sociology of family.

The method followed in presenting the topics involves first doing an overview of the topic from a sociological perspective and referring to the theoretical views and the current experimental findings, and then presenting phrases and points available from the main Islamic texts, namely Quran and the narrations quoted by the Prophet (pbuh) and the Immaculate Imams[1] related to that topic.

Here I would like to express my gratitude and appreciation for the authorities, colleagues, and the respected staff of the Emissary and University Research Centre who provided help and support for the accomplishment of this project. I ask for God's help and blessing for all who endeavor to be in the service of dear Islam.

Hossein Bostan (Najafi)

December 2011

---

1. The twelve Imams of the Shiites

CONTENTS

PART I

MARRIAGE

PART I

MARRIAGE

The institution of marriage and the formation of family are considered as universal institutions. Yet, various patterns of this institution have been demonstrated by historians, anthropologists and sociologists in the past and present that these varieties diminish its conceptual clarity. Therefore, before proceeding with further discussions it's necessary to have a short conceptual survey regarding the concept of marriage.

Marriage has taken on a variety of definitions .Here are three of them:

- "Marriage can be defined as a socially acknowledged and approved sexual union flanked by two adult individuals".[1]
- "Marriage is a process of interaction between two people, a man and a woman, who have fulfilled some legal requirements and arranged a ceremony for establishing their marital life and generally their action has been approved by law and considered as marriage".[2]
- "Marriage is a bargain and pursuant to an agreement whereby, a man claims the right of sexual access to a woman. This right precedes and is dominant to already sexual access rights by others as well".[3]

Such definitions generally focus on four important features- physical relationship, sex difference, endurability and social contract. According to these definitions, in order to fulfil the marriage, developing a bond between two opposite sexes based on enduring sexual relationships is necessary; thus, a relationship between two people of the same sex cannot be called marriage, as the unstable sexual relationships would not be marriage. Moreover, marriage is subject to a social contract that can bring legitimacy to physical relationships; this means, to fulfil the marriage, we should have the approval of the society as well.[4]

In an overall evaluation, due to the variety of marriage patterns and contradictory valuations regarding any of these patterns, presenting a comprehensive definition of marriage is very difficult or impossible. Issues such as the legitimacy of polygamy in many societies, the legitimacy of temporary marriage in Islam, the approval of same-sex marriage by some new movements and Western governments and the advent of sexual communes in some societies open the door for further doubts regarding the comprehensiveness of marriage definitions. Even some tend to include cohabitation, man and woman living together as partners without getting married, in the concept of marriage. Usually this definition is set forth as a pattern opposite to marriage. They set forth the claim of the change in the concept of marriage by adducing to the idea that cohabiting couples usually have a long- term relationship with each other and they have gradually come to enjoy spousal rights in recent decades. Therefore, the impact of diverse cultures and varied value perspectives concerning the definition of marriage

---

1. Giddens, *Sociology* , p185.
2. Sarokhani , *An Introduction to Sociology of the Family*,p23.
3. Fox(ed.),*Family Patterns, Gender Relations*,p.5.
4. Sarokhani , *An Introduction to Sociology of the Family*,p23.

seems inevitable and as a result the concept of marriage will be surrounded by a kind of relativity.

Thus, the following definition can be presented according to Islamic law (from the Shiite viewpoint):" Marriage is a legal contract which creates a bond between two opposite-sexes, usually adults, and legitimizes establishing a permanent or temporary sexual relationship between them."

In this section, the subject of marriage will be reviewed in three discussions; age of marriage, the rules of mate selection, patterns and customs of marriage.

CHAPTER 1

AGE OF MARRIAGE

Chapter 1

Age of marriage

Learning objectives of chapter 1

Getting familiar with sociological perspectives of age of marriage and Islam's overall point of view in this regard

Based on stage objective of this chapter, the learner is expected to achieve the following learning objectives and be able to:

1. distinguish between the discussions of legal age and actual age of marriage;
2. state the factors increasing the age of marriage in recent decades;
3. offer some solutions for decreasing the age of marriage based on Islam's point of view;
4. explain the factors shaping the norm of age gap between the spouses.

Introduction

After discussing the concept of age of marriage, factors increasing the age of marriage in recent decades including economic problems, higher education, sexual freedom, values and customs will be reviewed and then the norm of age gap between the spouses and its origin will be mentioned. Moreover the view of Islam regarding these two subjects is going to be discussed.

1-1 Legal age of marriage

The interpretation of marriage age is sometimes used in the sense of legal age of marriage which rests on two independent legal rules: a rule regarding the minimum age of marriage and another rule regarding full competence age of marriage. First rule, i.e. minimum age of marriage, refers to the age before which individuals are not allowed to marry and this age limit has been determined to be concurrent with sexual puberty or a short while before or after it in many contemporary legal systems. The second rule refers to the age of legal maturity at which a boy or a girl enjoys full competence age of marriage. In many Middle Eastern countries, based on two above-mentioned rules, the marriage of people having the minimum age of marriage but short of the full competence age of marriage is permissible only with the permission of the court and often with the consent of the girl's guardian but marriage before sexual puberty has not been absolutely recognized by them. [1]

Separation between two mentioned rules had been included in laws of Iran before Islamic Revolution but the rule of full competence age of marriage was revoked under the laws made after Islamic Revolution and based on the rules of Shiite jurisprudence, as marriage before maturity was allowed with the permission of the guardian and when

---

1. Lawson and Garrod , *Dictionary of Sociology*, p.146.

deemed advisable [1] and this also means revocation of the rule of minimum age of marriage.[2]

From the perspective of jurisprudence and due to the fact that the marriage of children is permissible in Islamic legal system provided that their interests be protected and their parents can marry them off, we can conclude that no minimum age of marriage has been set by Islam.

Undoubtedly, the permission of the marriage of children in Islam does not imply the permission of satisfying sexual desires in childhood but it has taken place merely for supplying the possibility of fulfilling other functions of marriage such as support and care of the child, the transfer of legacy and maintaining of camaraderie between families and tribes which bears more importance particularly in traditional societies. However, due to the lack of powerful sexual and emotional attraction between children and low possibility of their getting deeply attached to each other, no positive attitude is adopted by Islam toward marriage of children, especially younger ones. According to an authentic narration, one of the Imams was asked to express his opinion regarding marriage of children. He replied:" If they have been entered into marriage in childhood, it's unlikely to get intimate with each other." [3]

Regarding the second rule, Islam has regarded sexual puberty as well as maturity as a criteria for full competence of person for marriage while sexual puberty is not determined only based on the age of puberty; that is because reaching the age of puberty is one of the several signs for maturity that has been established in Islamic jurisprudence and there is no age limit for maturity. So, it can be concluded that no certain age criterion has been set by Islam regarding full competence of marriage.

1-2 Actual age of marriage

Actual age of marriage refers to the age at which the individuals actually enter into a marriage. The necessity of human nature is that whenever he reaches sexual puberty he takes a step to satisfy his sexual desire, but since marriage, as a normal way to satisfy this desire, does not have only biological dimension and as other human issues is influenced and directed by culture, sexual puberty is not usually a sufficient condition for marriage and social and economic maturity should be considered necessary as well. Sexual puberty almost relies on age, climate and nutritional conditions. Economic maturity is achieved when a person is capable of providing the expenses of his life and his family's. Social maturity means obtaining enough knowledge of social rules and norms and being able to make decisions if the situation requires in such a way that a person be able to accept the responsibility of his commitments to others.

Since societies are growing in level of sophistication, the transition from childhood to adulthood has become more difficult and rendered it necessary to acquire more

---

1. Anderson, *Law reform in the Muslim World* , p156.

2. According to Article 1041 of the Civil Code amended in 2000, "Marriage of girls before the age of 13 full solar years and boys before the age of 15 full lunar solar years is contingent upon the permission of the guardian and upon the condition of the child's best interests as determined by a competent court."

3. Horr Ameli,*Wasael al-shiah*, Volum 14, p.72

education and skills. Moreover the gap between sexual puberty and socio-economic maturity has become more marked and manifested itself in elongation of teen years and

increase of marriage age. In every society, the age of marriage is determined based on climate, economic, social and cultural conditions peculiar to that society. Not only is the age of marriage different in various societies but also in the same society it does not remain stable over time and it increases or decreases according to the above-mentioned conditions.

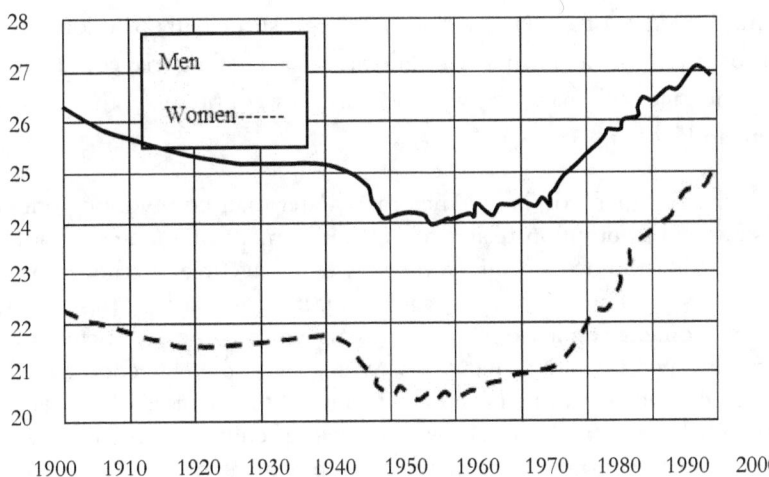

Diagram 1: the average of the age at first marriage in the U.S, for each sex

www.u.s.bureau of the census

1-3 The factors contributing to the increase in the age of marriage in recent decades

Various factors have caused the increase of marriage age in recent decades which some of the most important ones will be mentioned in the following.

a) Economic problems

In many societies, accepting the husband's role means that the husband is committed to provide the expenses of the newly established family. In fact such requirements are determined in advance by tradition, Sharia or law. Financial expenses of a family includes a wide range and are varied and diverse: housing expenses, food, clothing, medical care ,entertainment of family members , children's education, transportation costs, etc. It's clear that full covering of such expenses is only possible in the case that the men have access to sufficiently paid jobs. Otherwise they will be forced to live a poor life after marriage or not to get married at all as long as they get a suitable job. Many people turn to choose the second option.

According to the diagram (1-1), in 1956, the average age of marriage in the US reached its lowest level (22/5 years for men and 20/1 years for women) and its most important reason was that the economic growth of this country after war (World War II) enabled the men, especially young ones, to get a suitable and sufficiently paid job in order to support the family. Since 1960s, the age of marriage increased. The main reason was that the salary of young men dropped, especially the ones those who were poorly educated. This conclusion has been confirmed by the research studies conducted in other countries including Japan and India.[1] Generally, it can be said that if the economic structure of a society cannot provide a sufficiently paid job for the youth at the age of marriage, in normal conditions the age of marriage will increase and conversely the age of marriage will decrease by improving the conditions of employment and income.

Due to the fact that working women marry later than non-working ones, it's clear that the mentioned assumption relates to the employment of young men and does not hold true for the employment of women, whether we regard the employment of women as a factor of increasing the age of marriage or accept this view that two mentioned phenomena result from another trend which is more difficulty of access to the expected lifestyle for new generations. Whatsoever, merely economic explanation of the correlation between women's employment and the increase of marriage age does not seem compelling. Hence, focusing on the role of cultural elements, theorists have declared that since economic advantages of employment provide more security and personal satisfaction for western women than marriage, they attribute priority to the employment objectives and delay marriage.[2]

b) Education

In traditional societies, technique and skill training used to begin from childhood and informally and when the children reached the age of adolescence, they had usually acquaintance with career skills and after maturity it was not necessary to spend years in order to learn the techniques and skills required. But modern societies have become so complex that it is necessary to pursue a long term education in order to have an acceptable life and a life conforming to the societies' expectations.

An academic degree has the potential to bring social and economic prestige to individuals and improves their employment prospects in administrative centers and factories; therefore, the youth are forced to spend the third decade of their life in school in order to enjoy economic and social status. Education rules out the possibility of marriage for the youth because the youth with modest means cannot afford to meet the expenses of the family while pursuing their education. But higher education has become more important for women mainly because it enhances their social

---

1. Mitchell, *Sociology of Family and Marriage*, p146.
2. Wilkie ,"Marriage ,Family Life, and Women's Employment", *Marriage and Family in Transition* , p.145.

status.Women with a higher education can marry the men enjoying higher socio-economic status.

c) Sexual freedom

Due to the fact that sexual desire has always been the most important motivation for marriage, if a society lets its members establish a sexual relationship with each other without getting married and undertaking its responsibilities, finding a sexual partner cannot be certainly the first motivation for marriage. So, avoiding getting married, a large number of youth will satisfy their sexual desires by resorting to low cost ways. That is why, Western societies in which marriage has relatively preserved its social value yet in parallel with cohabitation growth, we are witnessing the increase of age of marriage in recent decades. In 1960, 439,000 households consisting of unmarried man and woman lived in the US while this number reached 4 million and 236,000 by 1998. Moreover, seeing congruity and adjustment tested through time are among the reasons many cohabiting couples who get married later set forth for delaying their marriage.[1]

d) Values and customs

Undoubtedly, the culture of a society is one of the most important determinants of marriage age in that society and the aforementioned factors have also a close relationship with cultural changes of societies. The values approved in a society determine a set of norms for marriage such as appropriate age of it.

In this regard, it's necessary to mention the customs and encumbering rituals that sometimes prevail among people. For example in Iranian society, factors such as heavy *mehrieh*,[2] breastfeeding price, backbreaking dowry, expensive wedding ceremony, high expectations from the groom regarding job, house, car, etc, usually prevents young couples from marrying at a desired time; since they themselves and perhaps their parents will be forced to spend a lot of time working in order to meet the requirements and provide their expenses. In Western countries, despite relative welfare enjoyed by many people and considering the fact that some of these customs are not as important as they were in the past, exorbitant cost of wedding is among the reasons to which lots of youth refer for delaying their marriage.[3]

Furthermore, new cultural values arisen from the prevalence of individualistic and liberalistic thoughts have also played a significant role in reducing the youth's motivation for marriage. Since marriage is still considered as a social value in Western societies and most of the people turn to marrying at last,[4] so instead of witnessing the

---

1. McRae," Cohabitation or Marriage? Cohabitation", *The sociology of the Family*, p.184.
2. In Islam, mehriyeh is defined as a mandatory payment, in the form of money or possessions paid by the groom, or by his father, to the bride at the time of marriage that legally becomes her property.
3. Ibid, p.180.
4. For instance, in Britain most people still form a nuclear family for part of their adult life and 9 out of 10 people eventually get married. In 1981, just 6 per cent of women and 10 per cent of men had never been married in 35 to 44 years (Abbott and Wallace, *Introduction to Sociology of feminist attitudes*, p172-173).Also, the review of data derived from fifty surveys conducted between the years 1968 and 1988 in France indicates that the people of this country still believe

fading of the tradition of marriage, we have been facing an increase in the age of marriage.

e) Analysis and evaluation

Two points should be reminded in analyzing the issue: first, men and women's age of marriage should be investigated separately; because the increase of men and women's age of marriage does not occur in parallel and this implies the existence of some different factors which distinguish the increasing trend of marriage age in them. In Iran, for instance, in 1956, the average age at first marriage stood at 25 years for men and 18/4 years for women, but in 1986, it reached 23/6 years for men and 19/8 years for women. In1996, it increased by 25/6 and 22/4 for men and women respectively. So, it reveals the fact that the rise of marriage age has taken place in women more than men; because unlike women's age of marriage, which has been increasing in the past decades, men's age of marriage has increased a little after a temporary slowdown. There is no evident increase in men's average age of marriage in 1966 in comparison with that of in 1996; however, a four-year increase can be seen in women's age of marriage.[1] Probably, the latest statistics will show the continuity of this increasing trend. So, it seems that in a society like Iran, among the aforementioned factors, it should be focused on the increase in women's education level as the most important factor of an increase in their age of marriage.

The second point is that it seems a large number of family theorists consider the increase in the age of marriage as inevitable and as one of the essential demands of the urban life in developed or developing countries. Issues such as the tendency of the teenagers and youth towards the continuation of education to higher levels, economic difficulties, the problem of population growth, the outcomes of girls' early pregnancy and teenagers' social and deficiencies in the psychological and social growth of teenagers in younger ages have been considered as the factors of compulsory increase of marriage age by family theorists. But Islamic value system seems to be incompatible with such passive approach and given the negative consequences of delayed marriage for youth and society as a whole, the orientation of Islam is toward reasonable decrease of marriage age.

It seems that two mainstays of economic and cultural organization should be focused on in order to provide a solution tailored to the Islamic point of view for this problem. On the evidence of other countries, it can be predicted that a dramatic decline will take place in the age of marriage by improving the status of people's livelihood. In addition to government's support and other responsible governmental organs, the financial supports provided by parents, relatives and acquaintances can pave the way for youth to a large extent. However, the role of cultural elements should not be ignored. Undoubtedly, the culture of every community interferes to a great extent with the definition of words such as "economic welfare", "livelihood" and "poverty line". By changing minds and public attitudes and promoting simple austere lifestyles, new

---

the family is a fundamental value and an inevitable reality (Refer to : Le Gall, "Family Conflict in France through the Eyes of Teenagers ", *Multidisciplinary Perspective on Family Violence*, p.80.)
1. WWW." Statistical center of Iran" and "The management of household socio-economic statistics".

definitions of these words will be approved by society which can be effective in the decrease of the age of marriage. Also, by a carefully planned and persistent cultural work, we can take a step toward changing or adjusting problematic customs such as specifying high mehriyeh, expecting heavy dowry and demanding breastfeeding price.

Although narrated hadiths from the Holy Prophet and Infallible Imams (AS) and their practical behaviors provide obvious evidence for their efforts on accelerating the marriage of young people, in short, regarding Islam's point of view, it can be said that no specific age for marriage has been set by Islam. According to some narrations, one day the Holy Prophet (pbuh) said in the masque:

> O people! Gabriel came to me from the threshold of God and said: virgin girls are like the fruits on a tree; when they ripen, they should be plucked. Else they will be spoiled due to exposure to the rays of the sun and scattered about due to the blowing of the wind. When girls mature and feel sexual inclinations, there is no remedy for them but a husband. If they do not get married, they are not secure from corruption and making mistakes since they are human.[1]

In another narration we read: One of the rights of offspring over father is to marry him off when he reaches the puberty age.[2] Therefore, it can be concluded that Islam in its ideal pattern considers the lower age of marriage as the superior norm. Meantime the compatibility of this norm with contemporary social conditions can be scientifically proved; because it seems that the problems arising from early marriages are not inevitable and they can be tackled to a large extent by expanding educational, health and cultural programs as well as by improving people's economic situation. The results of Winch's experimental studies conducted in the American society are partly consistent with this orientation. He says:

> The problem of early marriage is not necessarily a problem by itself, but originates from the lack of preparation for taking on marriage obligations and the roles related to it. Therefore, early marriages are completely satisfactory in two states: 1.When teenagers are ready for accepting the roles of adults, like the members of lower strata in American society engaging in unskilled or semi-skilled jobs. 2. When teenagers are not supposed to accept such roles, like the members of upper strata who usually are financially supported by their parents; but when the youth are expected to be economically independent at the beginning of their marriage, and in the cases that contraceptives are not used properly and long term training is conventional, early marriage has the potential to bring negative effects.[3]

Therefore, in social policy-making, it cannot be agreed on the view of the individuals those who recommend delaying in marriage by adopting a quasi-deterministic attitude toward above-mentioned problems and ignoring sexual problem of the youth, or at least they have a favorable opinion toward increase of marriage age. They make the argument that decrease of marriage age will cause negative

---

1. Horr Ameli , *Wasael al-Shia*, vol 14,p39
2. Ibid, Vol 15 ,p200
3. Winch, *The Modern Family*, pp.602-603.

consequences such as the increase of women's fertility period and consequently population growth.

1-4 Age gap between the spouses

Although most human societies do not legally consider the man and woman's age difference as a barrier to their marriage, there are usually norms regarding age gap between the spouses which individuals strongly require themselves to conform to. These norms differ from each other in terms of desirability or prohibition. In many countries, for example, an old man can legally marry a newly-matured girl, but it hardly happens; that is because the social norms, particularly the modern norms, do not approve of it. And the opposite of this assumption is that, although the marriage of an elderly woman with a teenage son has not a legal restriction, it almost never happens because it is considered quite unacceptable in public norms. It's clear that such norms should not be restricted to being approved or not being approved by norms; because the impact of other factors such as the difference in social and economic status of both men and women and even their different natural tendencies in shaping these norms can be easily indicated.

However, one of the important norms which relates to the age of the couples and is established in most societies is that the woman should be preferably younger than her husband. The universality of this norm is seen in most Eastern and Western societies, but societies vary in terms of the extent of age gap and even the same society undergoes changes over time regarding this matter. For example the age gap between Iranian spouses reached from 6/6 years in 1966 to 3/2 years in 1996.[1] Refer to previous diagram in order to observe the changes taken place in American society over a century regarding age gap between the couples.

The norm of age difference between the wife and husband has rooted in various factors which two of the most important ones will be mentioned here:

1. Biologically, females lose their fertility ability a few years earlier than males and sexual desires abate in men later than women.
2. In almost all societies men are considered as being mainly responsible for meeting the financial expenses of the family; Therefore, since the shaping of culture is inextricably linked to biological, environmental and social needs of human, marital norms have typically been established according to biological, economic and social requirements.

Probably for these reasons, the girls had to marry a few years earlier than boys in order to have a husband from the early period of sexual excitements and fertility ability and then to terminate sexual activities at the same time as their husbands. Also, the men's economic responsibility had made them not to get married until they found themselves ready to meet and handle economic needs of the family. Just in specific cases which the parents shouldered the responsibility of financial provision of their

---

1. WWW." Statistical center of Iran" and "The management of household socio-economic statistics".

offspring's newly established family, the men could get married; but there was no such an economic requirement for girls, so they could get married immediately after puberty.

However, due to the growth of individualistic and equalitarian values in many contemporary societies, we are witnessing the fading of this norm and the decrease of age gap between the spouses. Even according to the research conducted in some socialistic countries, the number of women who marry younger men has greatly increased. The results of these studies suggest that the proportion of such women between 1920 and 1960 reached from 12/5 percent to 33/5 percent in urban areas and from 13 percent to 30/5 percent in rural areas.[1]

Tending toward the facilitation of marriage, the general orientation of Islam has resulted in adopting a flexible approach towards the mentioned norm in this discussion, and hence, no emphasis on denying or proving the norm is seen in the Islamic texts. However, natural bases of this norm should not be forgotten and accordingly it can be claimed that the decrease of age gap between the spouses or the increase in women's marriage with younger men has a root in specific social causes and factors that has led to the increase of women's age of marriage. It seems that if the ideal norm of Islam as the lower age of marriage is fulfilled, due to the faster maturity of girls than boys, a multi-year age gap will be made between couples.

o **Abstract**

- Legal age of marriage rests on two independent legal rules: a rule regarding the minimum age of marriage and another rule regarding full competence age of marriage. Actual age of marriage refers to the age at which the individuals actually enter into a marriage.
- A set of factors including economic problems, higher education, sexual freedom, values and customs have resulted in the increase of the age of marriage in recent decades.
- Solutions tailored to the Islamic point of view regarding the increase of the age of marriage are based on two principles of economic and cultural organization.

o **Self- Test**

1. Islam has permitted the marriage of children merely for supplying the possibility of fulfilling other functions of marriage such as …
2. Why does the issue of the increase of men and women's age of marriage need to be investigated separately?
3. Analyze and criticize the deterministic approaches of some sociologists towards the increase of the age of marriage.

o **Research topic**

- Research the relationship between the age of marriage and the growth of economic in the country.
- Research the outcomes of early marriage in Iran or your province.

---

1. Mitchell, *Sociology of Family and Marriage*, p1477.

CHAPTER 2

RULES OF MATE SELECTION

Chapter 2

Rules of Mate Selection

Learning objectives of chapter 2

Getting familiar with sociological analysis of the rules of mate selection and Islam's point of view in this regard

Based on stage objective of this chapter, the learner is expected to achieve the following learning objectives and be able to:

1. state sociological theories of the rules of *mahramiyat* [1], endogamy and exogamy;
2. explain the parameters of homogamy rule;
3. state Islam's point of view regarding the mentioned rules.

Introduction

In all societies, there are diverse rules which determine explicitly or implicitly the range of mate selection. Some of these rules are universal; while others are specific to some societies or historical periods. The difference which exists between cultures and societies in this regard rests on the extent of this scope, the degree of severity and consistency of the aforementioned rules and also the level of their explicitness.

In some societies, the individuals of a group are only allowed to select partners from a specific group, while in others this scope is so broad and no specific group is identified to require people to select a partner from its members. The strictness of rules related to the scope of mate selection is also different; For example, the strictness of "caste" rules in India which forbids the marriage of two people from two different castes was so extreme that people could not even dream of such a thing. Of course, in many societies there are less strict rules which[2] do not approve of the marriage of a man from lower social class with a woman from upper social class. However, violation of this rule is possible under certain circumstances. In terms of the degree of the explicitness of the rules, it is stated explicitly in some tribal societies of Africa or caste system of India that it's not possible to select a mate from a certain group! While there is not such an explicit prohibition in the range of mate selection in many societies.

In this chapter, we are going to review some of the most important rules which determine the scope of mate selection, i.e. mahramiyat , exogamy, endogamy and homogamy and state Islam's point of view in this regard.

2-1 Mahramiyat

In almost all cultures and societies establishing sexual relationship between some close relatives is prohibited. The extent of this prohibition which is called mahramiyat varies in different societies but in most cultures father and daughter, mother and son, brother and sister are regarded as mahram and their marriage is considered illegitimate. The criterion for mahramiyat in principle is blood close kinship .The more this kinship is

---

1. In Islam, mahramiyat is defined as a rule in which two people who are mahrams cannot marry each other and their marriage is illegal.

closer, the more the emergence possibility of mahramiyat relationship will be. But in some tribal societies, all men and women of the tribe on the grounds that they are deemed to be of the same generation (real or imaginary) and consanguineous are regarded mahrams and cannot marry each other. In such societies, men are obliged to select their wives from other tribes with whom they are not consanguineous and of the same ancestor (exogamy rule). In some cases, blood kinship is generalized to people who are not naturally placed in the circle of blood kinships; for example, in many cultures, stepfather or stepmother and stepbrother or step sister are considered mahrams since they are placed in the position of real father, mother, brother and sister.

Mahramiyat is not only limited to having common parents or ancestors; in some societies, foster mahramiyat is created between two or more people who have suckled milk from one women's breast which prevents them from marrying each other in future. Foster mahramiyat is not specific to sisters and brothers. It also applies to other close kinships and family ties as Islam has forbidden the marriage with mother, daughter, uncle, aunt, foster aunt and uncle. Mahramiyat by marriage is another kind of mahramiyat and it occurs when two people become kinship through marriage; for example when two people marry each other, mother –in –law with groom and father-in – law with bride become mahram.

The range of mahramiyat by blood varies in major religions like Islam, Christianity and Judaism. Among these religions the narrowest range belongs to Judaism and the widest domain range to Christianity. In Judaism, just the marriage with brothers, sisters, parents, offspring, grandparents and grandchildren is prohibited. In addition to these, in Islam, the marriage with uncle and aunt is also prohibited and unlawful; but in Christianity, along with the cases prohibited in Islam, the marriage with their children is also illegal. [1]

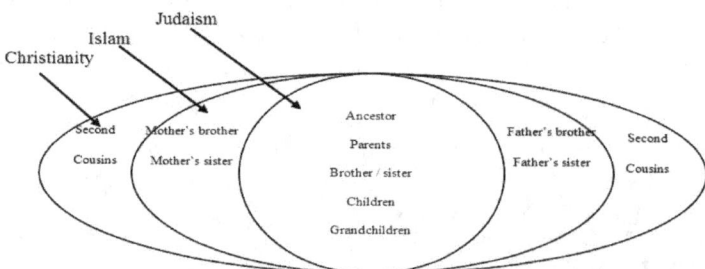

Diagram 2 : Blood mahrams in major divine religions

1.In Islam, the marriage with three classes of women is prohibited: 1. The women who have a blood relationship with him like mothers, grandmothers, sisters and their daughters, father's sisters and mother's sisters; 2. The women who have a foster relationship with him like foster mother, foster sister and the like; 3. The wife's mother and daughter in law who are mahrams with son-in-low and the husband's father respectively. The wife's sister bears a conditional prohibition, it means the man cannot marry a woman and her sister at the same time but in the case of divorce (after the termination of *iddah*) or the death of his wife he can marry her sister.

A natural question to ask at this point is why do human beings despite having so many cultural and environmental differences avoid marrying close relatives? To explain this issue, diverse theories have been set forth which generally can be classified in two classes: one of them focuses on the role of instinctive and innate factors and the other on the role of social factors. Theories which have considered instinctive and innate aspects as involved in mahramiyat rule have adduced to natural aversion of humans to marrying close relatives and believe that some factors such as the life of people with each other during childhood which is not compatible with the incidence developing mutual love and also the harmful effects of marriage of consanguineous people with each other have led to the emergence of this natural and inherent aversion and this could explain the generality of the rule.[1]

This set of theories are faced with some challenges; for example, in the past there were diverse societies in which the marriage with close relatives was a normal and common thing ; For example, the Zoroastrians over the centuries, considered marriage of sister and brother legitimate and did not abhor it. In Ancient Iran, the marriage with close relatives took place even among members of Shah's family to prevent mixing of the royal blood with the blood of other classes.[2] Anthropological evidence of contemporary periods also shows various cases of marriage with close relatives [3] and these are irrespective of the statistics derived from the expansion of incest phenomenon, particularly in industrial countries. As a result, at least inherent nature of the rule of mahramiyat will be thrown into doubt. Freud goes beyond it and not only fails to regard marital relationship with close relatives as an inherent thing but also based on psychoanalytical experiences believes that the first manifestations of sexual desires of teenager are adulterous in terms of nature[4] and according to some psychologists, he means incest.[5]

Many theorists do not accept instinctive explanations and regard social functions of the rules of mahramiyat as the main root of it. In the meantime, some theorists like Levi Strauss believe that in primitive societies, human exchanges are governed by a series of equal exchange rules and the prohibition of marrying or having sexual relationship with mahrams is regarded as a part of the bartering system of exchange[6]. The origin of this rule goes back to early human's inclination towards expansion of kinship relationships through exchanging women between families, groups and tribes. It's clear that if someone wants to marry other man's sister, he should be ready to marry his sister off to that man; otherwise this exchange will not take place. A conversation between a Rapsh tribesman with an imaginary person who wants to marry his own sister can explain this theory well:

> What's wrong with you? Do you want to marry your own sister? Don't you like to have a brother in law? Can't you understand if you marry someone else's

---

1. Kleinberg, *Social Psychology* ,Volume 1, p 167.
2. Hejazi , *The Woman by the Suspicion of History: The Woman's status in Ancient Iran* ,p 87.
3. Kleinberg, *Social Psychology* ,Volume 1, p 166 & 169.
4. Freud, *Totem and Taboo* , p 204.
5. Kleinberg, *Social Psychology* ,Volume 1, p 173 & 174.
6. Mitchell ,*Sociology of the Family and Marriage* ,p 42

sister and the other person marry your sister, you will have at least two people as wife's brother and brother in law? While if you marry your own sister you will have no one? Whom will you go hunting with? Whom will you have to see him? [1]

Other groups believe that the cause of prohibiting marriage with relatives is that such marriages throw the relationship between family members into turmoil. Montesquieu can be regarded as one of the forerunners of this theory; since although he considers this rule as a natural law and talks about natural disgust, as an argument he places greater emphasis on social functions and benefits of the mentioned rule. He explains separately the prohibition of marriage between son and mother, daughter and father, brother and sister, groom and mother-in-law, bride and father –in-law. Regarding first case, he argues:

> The marriage of sons and mothers is naturally illegal and based on natural law is prohibited, because this marriage disrupts the natural order of things, because the boy should respect his mother and he should know obedience to her as his assumption and if the mother and son marry, this marriage will disrupt the obedience principle, and on the other hand, natural laws will put forward the partition date and the time that man can produce children will roll back, and now if mother and son marry, when the boy comes of mature age and can produce children, the woman has lost her partition talent and such marriage is contrary to natural laws. [2]

Although these theories have proposed explanations which deserve consideration, given violation evidence [3] as well as due to the fact that they don't provide compelling explanation regarding the universality of this rule, the theories are controvertible. Thus, in an overall evaluation, it seems that a complex set of environmental, psychological, social and even religious factors is involved in the prohibition of marriage with close relatives and the reductionism of the theories that have emphasized just one class of these factors cannot be defended.

It can be said that not enough attention has been paid to the role of religion in this regard by researchers; as in other similar discussions, the role of religion is usually overlooked. However, the possibility that in the beginning periods of the appearance of human race (Adam and Eve period or Noah period), that is, when the people of the earth lived in a single community and had not been separated into diverse communities, conditions and specific requirements could have been offered regarding marriage and other subjects by Prophets of God should be taken into account.

2-2 Exogamy and endogamy

In primitive societies where group has a definitive dominance over the individual and his/her benefits, the possibility exists that all of the group be considered as a family and its members as sisters and brothers. This means the generalization of the rule of mahra-

---

1. Mendras and Gurevich , *Foundation of Sociology*, p 236.
2. Montesquieu, *Spirit of Laws* , p741
3. Kleinberg , *Social Psychology* , Volume 1 , p 173.

miyat to all members of the group. In totem tribes,[1] since all members of the tribe are deemed to be of a common generation and ancestor having sexual relations inside the group may be regarded as taboo. In this case, the scope of the rule of mahramiyat will embrace whole of the totem group and all members of the group would be regarded mahram with each other even if they have a more distant degree of kinship, and they will be compelled to turn to other tribes in order to find a mate who does not belong to their totem ancestor. This kind of marriage is termed exogamy in sociology and anthropology.

What is the origin of exogamy rule? In other words, why do close relatives as a primitive subject of the rule of mahramiyat give way to the whole group of blood relatives? Freud believes that the expansion of mahramiyat rule to all of the blood relatives has arisen from strong aversion and obsessive caution of totem tribes to incest. He states:

> Totemic exogamy and the prohibition of sexual intercourse between members of the same clan, appears to have been the appropriate means for preventing group incest; a means that became established in that age [period of group marriages]and persisted long after its raison d'être had ceased.[2]

But according to Levi Strauss, exogamy as a broad social term of incest prevention, demonstrates a pattern of equal exchange in primitive societies and indicates the desire of the

group to form alliance with others and to ease loneliness. He says:

> Exogamy confirms and proves the existence of social fellow man and forbids inter-group marriage not because marriage with consanguineous people is biologically harmful but to create alliance with other family group; since exogamy brings social benefit.[3]

This view, as an explanation of exogamy rule, which emphasizes social functions of it such as camaraderie in time of war, cooperation in the hunting time and other economic and ceremonial activities, has been confirmed by other anthropologists too.[4]

As very strong group tie can lead to exogamy, it may sometimes lead to endogamy too whereby individuals are compelled to select their partner only from inside the group. In some cases where a group sees a strong and unique distinction between itself and other groups, it may prohibit its members from marrying the members of other groups. For example, in caste system of India, the members of two upper and lower castes not only were not permitted to marry each other , but also the members of caste

---

1. Totem is as a rule an animal (whether edible and harmless or dangerous and feared) and more rarely a plant or a natural phenomenon (such as rain or water), which stands in a peculiar relation to the whole clan. In the first place, the totem is the common ancestor of the clan; at the same time it is their guardian spirit and helper, which sends them oracles and, if dangerous to others, recognizes and spares its own children.
2. Freud, *Totem and Taboo*, p 28.
3. Mitchell, *Sociology of the Family and Marriage*, p43.
4. Kleinberg ,*Social Psychology* , Vol 1,p171

" untouchables " were not even allowed to socialize and be in contact with the members of other castes.

Other factors can also be a basis for endogamy among which religion is the most important one. Religions claim exclusive legitimacy of their own; therefore, they try to decrease the risk of the tendency of their followers to other religions adopting other religions by setting boundaries in their relationship with others. Definitely, marriage establishes the closest and most intimate relationship between two people and that is why religions have paid full regard to it. In this regard, Holy Quran prohibits believers from marrying pagans:

> Do not marry pagan women unless they believe in God [though you be obliged to marry slaves]; since a believing slave girl is better than a free idolater one, even though the beauty and other privileges of her may attract you. Do not marry women off to pagan men unless they believe in God [even though you be compelled to marry your daughters off to slaves]; since a believing slave is better than a free idolater, even though property, status and beauty of him may attract you. Those call you unto the Fire; and God calls unto Paradise, and pardon, by His leave.[1]

In addition to prohibition of Muslim marriage with a pagan, the marriage of a Muslim with followers of other religions as well as the marriage of Shia with the enemies of Ahl al- Bayt are illegal except in case of emergency.[2] In one of the narrations, concern about religious future of the children has been considered as a reason for the prohibition of Muslim marriage with none- Muslim.[3] Of course, the possibility exists that the focus of Islam on religious endogamy is partly because of preventing possible conflicts of such marriages.

2-3 Homogamy

Theorists generally concur in homogamy rule as being the common rule for mate selection in different societies.[4] Based on this rule, people who intend to marry, usually select a person who has the highest level of homogamy and similarity with them. On the other hand, the more striking differences, the less willing the people will be to marry.

Even the theory of complementary needs which sometimes is regarded as a challenger for the theory of homogamy, indeed does not aim to deny this rule and just regarding psychological characteristics, it sets forth this claim that a person in the stage of mate selection chooses from among those who are within the range of choices available to him someone who promises the prospect of fulfilling his needs in the highest degree. For example, someone who is in need of others' help more likely will be attracted to a person who possesses a mental need to help others. Similarly, extraverts

---

1. Surah Baghareh ,221
2. Horr Ameli ,*Wasael al-shia* ,Vol 14, p410-435.
3. Ibid ,p 411
4. In family studies, homogamy is sometimes discussed as a descriptive concept and sometimes as a normative concept which this discussion rests on the first concept.

and introverts and submissive and domineering individuals are more likely to be attracted to each other.[1]

Parameters of homogamy between wife and husband may vary in different societies but the necessity to establish some kind of homogamy is an accepted rule in many societies. Even in industrial societies where the freedom of individual choice has reached its highest level and sometimes completely random mate selection has been proposed,[2] establishing at least some similarities is regarded as a necessary condition for mates selection. Here, the most important types of homogamy will be mentioned.

a) Age homogamy

In previous periods when young boys and girls played an insignificant role in mate selection, it happened many times that the parents due to family interests married their young or even immature girl off to a man who had a long age gap with her and this was regarded as a common affair in many cultures. But today, in most societies, marriage takes place between the individuals who have not a considerable age gap. Age homogamy is usually more obvious at first marriage and it decreases in next ones.[3]

b) Residential homogamy

Geographical factor plays a significant role in mate selection; the more the residence of boy and girl be closer, the more the possibility of marriage between them in equal circumstances will be raised. According to a study conducted in France, 75% of the spouses were in the same neighborhood before marriage and 81% of them were from the same province.[4] Within a broader view, the factor of residential homogamy can be generalized to homogamy in educational and occupational environments and the like.

In explaining the influence of geographical factor, it can be said that firstly, geographical proximity increases the communication between the youth and provides the ground for their familiarity. Secondly, people who live in the same geographical areas, typically have more cultural resemblance and belong to the same class.

c) Religious homogamy

Many religions do not legitimize the marriage of their own followers, especially women, with followers of other religions. Since religion, as an important cultural difference, causes incongruity of people from different religions, even those who are not bound to religious duties marry their own coreligionists. Of course, the more religious devotion, the greater the possibility of marriage with a coreligionist will be. The content of religious teachings has a great impact on this matter. Some religions create more negative attitude towards other[5] religions in the minds of their own followers. The research suggests that Jews avoid marrying non-Jews more than others. Among Christians, Catholics are more likely to turn to inter-group marriages. Hollingshead's study conducted in the US at the beginning of the second half of the twentieth century

1. Goode ,*The Family* ,p.38
2. Mendras and Gurevich, *Foundations of Sociology*, p 237
3. Goode ,*The Family* ,p.34.
4. Sarokhani , *An Introduction to Sociology of the Family* , p65-66

showed that 98 percent of Jewish men and 100 percent of their wives married their own coreligionists. Protestants with less percentage and reverse difference between men and women (79 percent of men and 74 percent of women) married their coreligionists.[1]

It is noteworthy that social status of the followers of a religion in a certain society, such as being a minority or not, can probably have an influence on their attitudes towards other people of that society and consequently on the rate of their marriage with the followers of other religions.

d) Ethnic and racial homogamy

Although in today's world racism is less formally confirmed, race is still one of the discrimination factors and more importantly, ethnocentric attitudes have also a lot of influence. Ethnic and racial differences are often accompanied by bigotry and prejudice and the existence of such negative stereotypical ideas prevent associating people from two different ethnic or racial groups with each other and consequently, inhibiting the establishing of marital relationships between them.

e) Social homogamy

Max Weber defined social class based on three factors: wealth, power and prestige. Each of these three factors has a great impact on the formation of social distinctions. Hence, each social class has its own specific life style and norms that make it difficult to establish intimate relationships between people from two different social classes. These distinctions which are usually accompanied by geographical distances, influence the mate selection and strongly decrease the possibility of marriage between heterogamous youth. Assuming the division of society into six classes, Hollingshead's survey in one of the American cities showed that in 58 percent of marriages, both couples were from the same class and 83 percent of marriages were taken place between the couples who were from the same class or adjacent class.[2]

f) Educational homogamy

Today's world is the world of knowledge and information and usually those who possess greater knowledge get more social and economic privileges and facilities. Since education requires tolerating deprivation and many expenses, it is regarded as a valuable commodity. People who enjoy high education see themselves as being different from those who enjoy less of it. Highly educated people have different insights and attitudes compared to others; so, they prefer to establish a relationship with those who are at the similar educational level. According to a study conducted in France, in 66 percent of marriages the couples had the same educational level and in 88 percent of marriages, they had similar educational levels.[3]

Aside from the mentioned kinds of homogamy, other instances of homogamy rule can be identified, although they play less significant role in the process of mate

1. Goode ,*The Family*,p.35
2. Sarokhani , *An Introduction to Sociology of Family* ,p60.
3. Horr Amelli ,*Wasael al-Shia* , Vol 14 , p44

selection. Including are mental or intellectual homogamy as well as homogamy in physical characteristics such as height and weight.

Putting emphasis on the principle of "being well-matched" in marriage, Islam has expressed its agreement with homogamy rule in its generality although based on its value principles, it has not presented a specific definition. In a narration we read "A believer man is the well-matched of a believer woman and a Muslim man is the well-matched of a Muslim woman."[1] Likewise, according to another narration the Prophet (pbuh) in response to a question about well-matched people says that: "Believers are the well-matched of each other."[2] The concise substance of these narrations is that Faith and Islam are both necessary and sufficient conditions to fulfil the condition of being well-matched.

From the first perspective, it can be said that Islam does not consider the non-Muslim man or woman as the well-matched people. In other words, it considers them as people who lack necessary conditions for marriage. But, Islam, in addition to formal faith and Islam, concerning some tremendously important religious duties, implicates the person's practical commitment to faith in the state of being well-matched. In this regard, the Holy Quran has introduced the evil and adulterous people inappropriate for marriage. Likewise, in some narrations the probity and integrity of man have been included in his well-matching [3] and other narrations have considered being a drunkard man as something depriving him of qualification for marriage.[4]

From the second perspective, other different narrations confirm that faith and Islam are sufficient conditions to fulfill being well-matched. Therefore, if this criterion is in place, other criteria of homogamy could be ignored. In a Hadith, the Prophet (pbuh) said: "if someone whose faith and manners you take a liking to and approve comes to you for matchmaking, agree to their marriage." And when he was asked: "Even in terms of ancestry and blood, he is a lowly person, should we give away to him our daughter?" The Prophet repeated the above command, adding: "If you don't do so, great intrigue and corruption will occur on earth."[5] In this regard, we read in a narration that a person wrote a letter to Imam Javad (AS) wanting to know Imam's comment on his daughters' marriage and the fact that he does not find anyone similar to himself in station. Imam wrote in the response to his letter thus:

> We learned of what you had to say about your daughters and the issue that you don't find a person for your daughter alike in station; but- God bless you – do NOT tie up your daughters' marriage to this matter; for the Prophet (pbuh) said: "If someone whose faith and manners you take a liking to and approve comes to you for matchmaking, agree to their marriage. If you don't do so, great intrigue and corruption will occur on earth."[6]

---

1. Ibid ,p 39
2. Surah Nour ,3
3. Horr Amelli ,*Wasael al-Shia* , Vol 14 ,p 51-52.
4. Ibid,53.
5. Ibid, p52.
6. Ibid ,p 51

Also there is a story about Jobeir, a young black man, gaunt, strange and poor who married Zolfa a pretty girl of aristocrats of Median and this marriage was conducted by Prophet's ordering and mediating. The marriage of the Prophet (pbuh) with Safieh, his handmaid, and the marriage of Imam Sajjad (AS) with his freed slave that led to reproving letter from the Caliph and Imam's harsh reaction to that letter[1], provide further evidence in support of the above claim.

Consequently, it can be said that Islam, instead of adopting conservative approach and coming to terms with wrong preconceptions such as the necessity of ethnic, racial and class homogamy of man and woman, has proposed amendatory approach and tried to introduce and replace a new pattern for homogamy.

However, from the beginning up to now, the mentioned pattern was faced with challenges in practice. Of course, challenges to this pattern in contemporary Islamic society are less of a[2]racist, ethnocentric or similar nature but to a large extent arisen from profound cultural and structural changes which have influenced the family institution. As a result, even many people bound to Islamic values on the grounds that cultural and economic heterogamy in most families and even in religious families has the potential to lead to conflicts , consider faith and moral homogamy just as a necessary condition for marriage not a sufficient one; that is because faith and piety of both spouses are less fulfilled in their favorable form and in the case of their realization, the negative effects of factors such as expectations of relatives and friends cannot be ignored. Hence, Muslim families have felt the need to take more similarities into account in mate selection and avoid making do with homogamy in faith and Islam.

o **Abstract**

- The rules of mate selection exist in all societies irrespective of the extent of the scope, the degree of strictness and consistency and also the level of their explicitness.
- Diverse theories have been set forth to explain the rule of mahramiyat which generally can be classified in two classes: one class focuses on the role of innate and instinct factors and the other one on the role of social factors.
- Main kinds of mahramiyat include mahramiyat by blood, mahramiyat by marriage and foster mahramiyat.
- A complex set of biological, psychological, social and religious factors have been involved in the prohibition of marriage with close relatives.
- Pursuant to homogamy rule, a set of age, geographical, religious, racial, ethnic, class, educational, mental and physical homogamy, more or less, influences mate selection.
- Putting emphasis on the principle of "being well-matched" in marriage, Islam has expressed its agreement with homogamy rule in its generality although based on its value principles, it has not presented a specific definition.

1.Ibid, p44-50.

o **Self–Test**

1. Review and evaluate the theories of mahramiyat.
2. Review and evaluate the theories of exogamy.
3. Does theory of complementary needs contradict the homogamy rule? Explain.
4. What relationship does exist between the Islamic rule of being well-matched and homogamy rule? Explain.

o **Research topic**

- In the Islamic resources, some hadiths have been stated regarding the marriage of Adam and Eve's children. Do a research in this regard.
- Research the rule of religious endogamy in different religions.
- Research homogamy rule in one of the country's regions.

CHAPTER 3

PATTERNS AND CUSTOMS OF MARRIAGE

Chapter 3

Patterns and Customs of Marriage

Learning objectives of chapter 3

Getting familiar with the patterns of mate selection and customs of marriage from the sociological and Islamic point of view.

Based on stage objective of this chapter, the learner is expected to achieve the following learning objectives and be able to:

1. explain the difference of mate selection patterns according to different societies;
2. explain ideal pattern of mate selection from the Islamic point of view;
3. analyze the most important marriage customs from the sociological perspective;
4. explain Islam's point of view regarding the most important customs of marriage.

Introduction

In this chapter, after examining the patterns of mate selection and marriage in different societies, we will review the most important customs of marriage including marriage proposal made by men, marriage contract, wedding ceremony, paying mehrieh to the woman by man and providing dowry by the woman's family.

3-1 Patterns of mate selection

Historically, there have been three main patterns of mate selection: dominance-based pattern which marriage by capture was one of the most prominent examples of it in the past; the pattern of marriage by arrangement and the pattern of free-choice mate selection.

Although marriage by domination was not a conventional practice, in many cases the men were used to doing it, especially in societies where women were looked at as a property. For example, in cases where a man was in love with a woman but was not able to pay mehriyeh to the woman's family or they didn't approve his marriage. It is still seen in some cultures the traces of the customs of marriage by capture in wedding ceremony. While the marriage is arranged in advance, the husband pretends to seize the bride by force and the bride pretends to resist.[1]

Since the mentioned practice is not formal and popular, sociologists divide societies into two classes based on two other patterns: collectivistic societies and individualistic societies. There are two main differences between these societies which are important from the sociological point of view: the first difference is the role of parents and other relatives in selecting a mate for the youth and the second one is

---

1.Ingoldsby," Mate Selection and Marriage ", *Families in Global and Multicultural Perspective* ,pp.133-134.

related to the attitude of these societies towards the role of love in marriage.

In collectivistic societies in which the pattern of arranged marriage is practiced, parents and heads of the family usually play active roles in matchmaking and mate selection for the youth; it is highly likely that the wishes and desires of the youth who want to marry are not taken into consideration quite so much. This practice can be found in societies in which the pattern of extended family is prevalent and marriage can probably affect socio-economic status of the bride and groom's family. In such societies, marriage is indeed a transaction between two kinship groups and consequently, mutual love between young couples in marriage does not figure here or does not have any pivotal role, rather Western thinking about love marriage is rejected as it is only after marriage that the couples will fall in love with each other or probably come to hate each other. In such societies , the heads of the boy's family , especially his parents , select a girl taking different considerations into account and then go to her parents or heads of her family and ask for girl's hand in marriage based on specific rituals which exist in many societies. In selecting the bride it is focused on characteristics such as morality, obedience, housekeeping skills, religiousness and physical appearance. The girl's family, for accepting marriage proposal, considers the socio-economic status of the groom's family, educational level of the young man and his ability to earn money.[1]

Individualistic societies which contemporary Western nations are prominent examples of them, have presented the pattern of free-choice mate selection. Considerable decrease of the parents' role in supervising and decision making on youth's mate selection is the main feature of this pattern. In comparison with previous periods, the decreasing trend in parents' role and the increasing one of children's independence in mate selection have continued at a speedier rate from the first half of the twentieth century up to now. According to a research conducted regarding parents' supervision on youth's mate selection in the late 1940s on a group of married and educated women in Ohio, 31 percent of the first generation of these university graduate women reported that their parents did not agree on the man with whom they got married; 45% of the second generation and 55% of the third generation have reported their parents' disagreement.[2]

Another feature of this Western pattern is that mate selection and marriage have been based on "romantic love" in general public opinion. Undoubtedly, there existed romantic crazes in all societies throughout history but they occurred occasionally and did not play a significant role in most marriages.In contrast, since love as a precondition for marriage has gained popularity in contemporary Western societies, and established a specific pattern and particular cultural meaning, romantic love can be considered as a new phenomenon.[3]

---

1. Taylor et al, *Social Psychology* ,p.251
2. Shorter ,*The Making of the Modern Family* ,pp.162-163
3. Hendrick & Hendrick , *Romantic Love* ,p.24

In 1967, in a research conducted focusing on love and marriage, 1000 American male and female students were asked "Would you like to marry a boy or a girl if he/she had all your ideal characteristics but you don't feel any love to him/her?" Other researchers asked new generation of American students the same question in 1976 and 1984. The results of these studies shown in figure 1-1 indicate increasing and comprehensive growth of feelings and romantic attitudes among Western youth, especially girls, so that in 1984, about 85% of men and 85% of women answered the aforementioned question "No" – with insignificant difference.[1]

Table 1: the rate of love marriages among American college students.

	1967		1976		1984	
	Women % Men		Women % Men		Women % Men	
Yes I'm not sure	11/7	4	1/7	4/6	1/7	3/6
	23/7	71/7	12/1	15/4	12/7	11/5
No	64/6	24/3	86/2	80	85/6	84/9

The norm discussed, i.e. love marriage, can be evaluated based on its positive and negative functions. Its positive function is that in modern Western world which marriage is not considered as the only way of satisfying sexual desire, romantic love may seem necessary to capitulate people to marriage. An American sociologist says:

> In the modern world, people have a wide range of options in marrying or not marrying. A contract which obligates an individual towards another person is not necessarily a tempting suggestion; it looks rather more like chains or fetters than a bed of roses. Without a feeling of heady and romantic love, many people may not have any motivation for marriage.[2]

Probably that is why romantic love is advertised by all mass media such as books, magazines, tapes, movies and films.

Negative aspect of romantic attitude towards marriage is its impact on the family's disintegration and the growth of divorce rate. Most researchers acknowledge that although romantic love can create strong mutual attraction between young man and woman but this love lasts just for a while and when initial passion goes away , it can be expected that a marital relationship built upon such love could become unstable and fall apart. Therefore, romantic love cannot guarantee the continuity of conjugal life at all.[3]

Findings of comparative studies clearly indicate the extent of prevalence of these two patterns (free choice mate selection and marriage by arrangement) in different societies. According to a research conducted on 40 societies in 1960s, utterly free

---

1. Taylor et al, *Social Psychology* , p.249.
2. Petersen, *An Introduction to Sociology* , p 323
3. Taylor et al ., *Social Psychology* ,p.251

choice mate selection was prescribed just in five societies; in other six societies the youth was allowed to select their mate by parents' supervision; in other twelve societies there was mixture of marriages by arrangement and free choice mate selection (often with parent's agreement) and other sixteen societies prescribed just marriages by arrangement.[1]

In contemporary Islamic societies which urban life has changed part of traditional norms, we are witnessing the formation of a mate selection pattern which is derived from tradition and modernity. In this pattern, both youth and parents take an active role in mate selection. In many cases, initial familiarity and attachment of the youth to each other take place in social environments such as workplace or school. In next stage, the boy informs his parents and they evaluate the girl intended, if they admire her and her family, they will take a step to ask for the girl's hand in marriage. Otherwise, they will try to discourage the boy by advice or guidance. Given religious values of these societies which require offspring to observe the wills of the parents, being in disagreement with their opinion can bring unfavorable social and psychological consequences for the offspring. Due to the risk of being deprived of this support, they usually prefer not to disagree with the parents' opinion as much as possible. According to some studies, more than 90% of Iranians agreed on the necessity of getting parents' agreement about their marriage as a norm and just 3 out of 100 people disagreed.[2] However, the creation of tensions between the parents and children in this area is not unexpected.

Freedom of youth in mate selection has been emphasized by Islam. It can be clearly perceived from various narrations that Islam recognizes this freedom for the youth- whether boy or girl. Concerning boys, there is no specific ambiguity in the issue. According to a narration, a person said to Imam Jafar Sadiq (AS): "I'm going to marry a certain woman but my parents want to marry me off to another woman." The Imam said: "Marry the woman you like and forget about the other one whom your parents are approved of".[3] Just legal dimension of the issue has been considered in this response, therefore, it's not morally incompatible with preference to obtain parents' approval.

Concerning girls, there are various narrations emphasizing their rights in mate selection; it was said by Imam Ja'far Sadiq (AS) that "the agreement of the woman should be acquired, either virgin or non-virgin, and without her will the marriage should not take place".[4]

Of course, regarding a virgin girl, because of some opposing narrations, marriage is subject to the consent of her father or grandfather. According to many jurists, whether we consider this condition necessary or merely attribute priority to it, undoubtedly, this condition has been assigned to maintain interests of teenage girls; because the ideal social system of Islam sets some boundaries in women and men's social interaction in order to maintain the public health of the society so that it can decrease the possibility of mutual premarital familiarity. Given the mentioned issue and

1. Ingoldsby," Mate Selection and Marriage ", *Families in Global and Multicultural Perspective* , p 138
2. Mohseni , *An Evaluation of Socio-Cultural Awareness , Attitudes and Behaviors in Iran,* p 90.
3. Horr Ameli ,*Wasael al-Shia* ,Vol 14 ,p 22.
4. Ibid ,p214

considering the fact that the youth often miss the ability of prudent and realistic evaluation because of being overcome by their feelings and unthinking craze towards the other party, Islam has tried to compensate these shortcomings partly by involving

fathers in mate selection, especially about girls who are more vulnerable against possible outcomes. According to Master Motahari :

> The fact that a virgin girl must not, or at least should not marry a man without the agreement of her father is not because the girl is considered to be deficient in some respect or is counted as inferior to a man as regards social maturity. If it were so what could be the difference between a widow and a virgin, by which a widow aged sixteen years, is not in need of the agreement of her father, while a virgin aged eighteen years is, according to this opinion. It is related to an aspect of male and female psychology. It relates to the predatory side of man's character, on the one hand, and to woman's credulous in the loyalty and sincerity of man on the other hand. That is why it is necessary for an inexperienced girl to consult with her father and to have the agreement of him, who knows the sentiments of men better, and fathers, except in extraordinary circumstances, wish good and happiness for their daughter.[1]

It is worth saying that this decree, based on religious laws is conditional and it's valid as long as father or grandfather applies it in protecting girl's overall interests and guiding her in the way of true choice; but if the father or grandfather wants to prevent the girl from marrying a man whose homogamy is canonically and conventionally obvious and the girl has a tendency towards him, then their right shall be void and obtaining their consent will not be necessary. [2]

By this explanation, it can be said that the Islamic pattern is compatible with the requirements of modern societies because it is possible to combine youth's freedom in mate selection and parents' expedient supervision in this regard by negating radical individualism.

3-2 Marriage proposal[3]

Why has marriage proposal been made by men in all societies and in different periods? It seems that natural sexual differences have played a considerable role in this matter; because there is no doubt that tendency towards the opposite sex does not appear in men and women in the same way, but there are two different desires – motivational/active desire and accepting/passive desire. Meantime, justifying these differences merely based on social learning factor does not appear very convincing ; because examining the phenomenon of animals' mating which has a considerable similarity with human's mate selection raises doubts regarding the validity of this justification. In an analysis which includes integrating biological and psychological perspectives, Master Motahari says:

---

1. Motahhari ,*The system of Women's Rights in Islam*, p61-63.
2. Imam Khomeini ,*Tahrir al-wasileh* ,Vol 2 ,p393
3. Marriage proposal in this discussion means the initial ask for marriage not its formal and ceremonial request which is performed in matchmaking ceremony.

From time immemorial, the man has approached the woman with his proposal and has requested conjugality from her. This has been the greatest of factors in safe-guarding the prestige and honor of woman.Nature has created man as the symbol of need, love and solicitation and woman as the symbol of desirability and being the beloved. Nature has made the woman the flower, the man the nightingale, the woman the candle, and the man the butterfly. This is one of the creation's wisely plans and masterpiece that has placed need and demand in man's instinct and coyness and parade in woman's. The tenderness of her body thus finds its compensation in comparison with the strength of man. It is contrary to the prestige of a woman to seek a husband for herself and woo him, while for a man it is tolerable to ask a woman's hand in marriage even if he gets a reply in the negative. In that case he will ask one woman after another until he meets a woman who gives him her consent. While for a woman, who aspires to be the object of affection, the beloved and the adored one, to find a way to his heart to govern his whole existence, it is absolutely unacceptable and opposed to her instincts to invite a man to be her spouse, be likely rejected and spurned and go after another man.[1]

So, the role of cultural factors should not be ignored in underlining and emphasizing bio-psychological differences, or inversely in playing down or concealing these differences. In cultures which women's modesty is strongly focused on as a public norm, it is less likely that a marriage proposal be made by women. In some cases, woman indirectly invites a man to herself, not clearly and immediately ask him to marry her. In contemporary Western societies in which the value of modesty has been greatly decreased and, on the other hand, there is increasing focus on an egalitarian character of marriage, many traditional customs of marriage have lost their importance, even though a cursory examination of conventional patterns of mate selection and even dating out of the marital framework indicate that men have preserved their former role regarding taking the lead in marriage proposals and initiating relationships.

In Islamic religious texts, regardless of evidence such as the practical behaviors of Infallible Imams (AS), which may indicate the priority of this tradition, no explicit and strict recommendation has been made in direct reference to it and there is no remonstrative to women proposing marriage;[2] it is even a fact based on narrative and historical resources that the marriage of Prophet Muhammad and Khadijeh was done by Khadijeh's proposition. Some historians have known this offer to be unmediated and some know it to have happened through the medium of another woman.[3]

Therefore, the marriage proposal made by a woman is not regarded as abnormal in the eyes of religion and if this mechanism is combined with mediated means emphasized in Islam,[4] in such a way that the woman informs man about her marriage proposal through the medium of some relatives and near acquaintances, any small

1. Motahhari ,*The System of Women's Right in Islam* , p 47.
2. Horr Ameli ,*Wasael al-shia* , Vol 14, p195 and 202.
3. Majlesi ,*Bahar al-Anvar*, Vol 16 , p16.; Hamiri , *Life of the Holy Prophet*, Vol 1, p 189
4. Horr Ameli ,*Wasael al-shia* , Vol 14, p26-27

possibility or feeling of the woman's dignity and honor being in danger of violation will also be obviated.

3-3 Marriage contract

Religion, tradition and law are three sources of the legitimacy of marital relationships. In almost all societies, religion and tradition are involved in marriage issue through their own specific ceremonies and rituals. In contemporary societies, in addition to religion and tradition, law also engages in marriage by obligating marriage registration in official offices and by issuing a marriage certificate or contract for the wife and the husband. In religious societies, however, this certificate is merely a document of marriage formality not as making it legitimate. That is to say it is considered as only having civil legitimacy not religious one. Thus, sometimes boy and girl marry each other just according to religious laws because of not reaching to legal age and then after a while their marriage is legally registered.

A noteworthy point in this regard is to do with the tradition of creating a space of time between engagement and the wedding. There is no specific recommendation about spacing of time between engagement and wedding in Islamic narrations but it seems some factors have attached more importance to engagement period in present conditions and circumstances. On the one hand, due to the economic problems in Islamic societies which are among undeveloped or developing countries, a high percent of young couples are not ready for arranging wedding ceremony and starting their new life for a while; therefore, they marry by carrying out a marriage contract according to religion, law and custom and this being less costly while easing their concerns about finding a spouse and tormenting sexual tensions and excitements provides the opportunity for them to make preparations for the wedding ceremony and to set up a house and provide the essentials of their future life together.

On the other hand, religious, customary and legal restrictions of premarital relationship between boy and girl which decreases the possibility of mutual familiarity have changed engagement period into a necessary one for increasing two couples' familiarity with their moral and personality characteristics. Although the couples' decision to divorce even in this period brings unpleasant consequences for the parties involved , in comparison with catastrophic consequences of divorce after family formation, especially after having children, most incongruent couples and their families prefer divorce in engagement period and find it more endurable.

3-4 Wedding ceremony

In most cultures, wedding includes a ceremony during which the new couples formally pronounce the beginning of their conjugal life to others. This ceremony is universally celebrated as a happy, joyous and festive occasion and people participate in it wearing their finest clothes.

The importance of wedding ceremony has its root in social functions that the most important of which are relative strengthening of marriage bond, providing an occasion for expressing happiness, reinforcing kinship and friendship bonds and public pronouncement of marriage in order to clear up any doubts regarding its illegitimacy. These functions, especially the last one, have been taken into specific consideration by

Islam and in this regard such customs as public feeding (banquet) has been recommended.[1]

It can be expected that the more controlled and restricted are the premarital sexual relationships in a given society, the more prominent position will be taken up by and the more importance will be attached to the wedding ceremony. However, even in contemporary Western societies which unprecedented sexual freedom has been provided and few boys and girls are found whose first sexual experience take place in the confines of marriage and a large number of girls have children at the time of wedding, wedding ceremony still has particular importance for most of the youth, especially girls.[2]

Based on living and regional conditions, the wedding ceremony may be performed more in specific times and less in other times and it may almost never be performed in some occasions. But the impact of culture on the importance of wedding is more pronounced. For example, beliefs about good omens or ominous days of the week or months of year that can be observed in many cultures including Western cultures have more impact on selecting the wedding date. [3]

In this regard, in a Shiite Islamic country like Iran, most marriages take place in occasions such as mission or birth anniversary of the Holy Prophet (pbuh), birth of Infallible Imams (AS) and Fatimah Zahra (pbuh) as well as other happy religious or national occasions but in times of grief and sorrow, especially in the days of their departure and martyrdom, marriage rates reach to their lowest level.

3-5 Mehriyeh and dowry

In many cultures, marriage bond is accompanied by specific customs regarding the exchange of properties, goods and services. Mahriyeh, which is more prevalent in Eastern cultures such as China , Japan, Islamic societies and many African nations, refers to the amount of money the groom pays to the bride or her family at the time of marriage or undertakes its payment later. Sometimes, mehriyeh can also be anything agreed upon such as doing some services for the bride's family over a certain period. This kind of mehriyeh has been referred to in the Holy Quran in the story about the marriage of Musa (AS) with Shoaib's daughter.[4] Adducing to the findings of Murdock's universal ethnography , some has expressed that in 62% of the world societies a person is charged to pay money or do some services in order to marry a woman.[5]

The main feature of Islam's legal system in comparison with other legal systems is that, accepting the tradition of mehriyeh, it takes the bride to be the unconditional owner of the specified mehriyeh and it allocates no portion of it for the bride's family. Contrary to the mehriyeh to the husband in the case of breaking up the life with him, in

1. Ibid , p65
2. McRae ," Cohabitation or Marriage ? – Cohabitation ", *The Sociology of the* Family ,Allan(ed.),p.181.
3.Ingoldsby," Mate Selection and Marriage " , *Families in Global and Multicultural Perspective* ,pp.140-141
4. Surah Qasas ,27.
5. Ingoldsby," Mate Selection and Marriage " , *Families in Global and Multicultural Perspective* ,p 136

Islam the woman's common tradition in some African societies according to which the bride was obliged to return possession of mehriyeh is considered definitive and divorce or husband's death has no impact on it.

In sociological analyses, it is focused on social functions of mehriyeh such as guaranteeing woman's economic security after divorce or the husband's death as well as increasing security and integrity of marriage in a way that it can be used as leverage the husband when the occasion demands.[1]

Such analyses are not devoid of truth, but it seems that they provide an inadequate explanation concerning the phenomenon of mehriyeh. It can be derived from verses and narrations that Islam, in assigning the tradition of mehriyeh, has not regarded the mentioned social functions as a principal tenet since fulfilling these functions is not possible without specifying considerable amounts of property and riches for the woman, while in some narrations allocating high mehriyeh has been criticized and even in some narrations, teaching one surah of Quran to the woman has been suggested to be worthy, although it doesn't have any economic value.[2] Therefore, other factors should be regarded in explaining custom of mehriyeh and at least mehriyeh in Islam. Master Motahari highlights innate and psychological factors in this discussion. According to him:

> The man is more powerless than the woman in [sexual] instincts. This characteristic has always provided opportunities for the woman not to seek the man out and not give in to him too soon, and, conversely, it has forced the man to express his need to the woman and take a step or two to win her consent.[3]

However, it should be acknowledged that the impact of innate and psychological factors on the formation of mehriyeh custom is surrounded with more ambiguity than matchmaking custom and the absence of mehriyeh custom in many societies implies the pivotal role of cultural factors in the formation and stability of this custom.

As mehriyeh , dowry custom has been and is practiced in many societies. Dowry is usually the amount of money or goods, especially furniture and household appliances which the bride's family provides for the young couples at the beginning of their conjugal life. Here, it can also be seen some cultural differences about the receiver of dowry. While in most cultures, dowry is directly given to the groom and the bride, in some European rural regions, it was given to the father-in-law and he used to give part of his land to his son and daughter –in-law but the dowry itself was used for the marriage of the groom's sister.[4]

In European cultures which mehriyeh custom has not been approved, the groom's family traditionally has offered money as gift to the bride in return for dowry. This amount guaranteed social security of woman after her husband's death; because in

---

1. Goode , *The Family* , pp.42-43.
2. Horr Ameli , *Wasael al-Shia* ,Vol 15 , p 9-12
3. Motahhari , *The System of Women's Rights in Islam* , p 233
4. Goode , *The Family* ,p.41

feudal system woman had no right regarding her husbands' property after his death, meanwhile, she had no portion in the property of her paternal family.[1]

Today, in Western common pattern of marriage, dowry has lost its importance and necessity, although it can pave the way for marriage. But in societies which special importance has been attached to this custom, the bigger and more extravagant the dowry, the more effective it will be in promoting the status of daughter among the bride's family and relatives, because expensive dowry is a manifestation of the bride's honor and respect among paternal family and it signifies their high socio-economic rank and status.

Contrary to mehriyeh on which great importance has been placed by Islam , dowry as a custom receives less emphasis, and it has been just prescribed as a customary tradition in order to bolster the economic basis of the newly established family without any necessity and obligation for the bride's family. According to narrations, simple and modest dowry of Fatimah Zahra (AS) was provided by the money which Ali (AS), the Commander of Believers, had paid as mehriyeh.[2] But unfortunately, this custom and mehriyeh custom have obtained new social meanings in current conditions and it has resulted in some problems. Today, extravagant and enormously costly mehriyeh and dowry and other expenses of marriage in some countries including Iran has turned out to be a hindrance for marriage and a contributing factor in the increase of marriage age.

o **Abstract**

- There have been three main patterns regarding mate selection: the pattern of marriage by capture, the pattern of marriage by arrangement and the pattern of free-choice mate selection.
- In collectivistic societies, the pattern of marriage by arrangement and in individualistic societies free choice mate selection is practiced.
- Islam recognizes the freedom of mate selection for the youth- whether boy or girl.
- Religion, custom and law are three sources of the legitimacy of sexual relations.
- The more controlled and restricted are the premarital sexual relationships in a given society the more prominent position will be taken up by and the more importance will be attached to the wedding ceremony
- In many cultures, marriage bond is accompanied by special customs and rituals regarding exchange of properties, goods and services which have appeared in the form of mehriyeh and dowry.

o **Self-Test**

1. Explain the positive and negative functions of marriage based on romantic love.
2. Why is usually marriage proposal made by men?

---

1. Ibid, p.42.
2. Majlesi ,*Bahar al-Anvar*, Vol 43, p 129

3. State social functions of wedding ceremony.
4. Explain the origin of mehriyeh custom and its social functions.

o **Research topic**

- Research the parents' role in youth's mate selection in a specific region in the country.
- Research the negative and positive functions of engagement period (before marriage contract).
- Research the positive and negative functions of mehriyeh and dowry in contemporary society.

PART II

STRUCTURE OF THE FAMILY

PART II

STRUCTURE OF THE FAMILY

Providing a definition for family poses difficulties as does the definition of marriage. Since the family institution has been realized in different forms in different cultures over history and also due to the fact that a certain family may be exposed to occurrences such as partner's death or divorce and transition to a single-parent situation or an end in sexual relationship, presenting a comprehensive and universal definition for the word 'family' is difficult. That is why the definitions presented are usually faced with the problem of not being either comprehensive or falsifiable. Moreover, presenting a comprehensive definition is based on the presupposition that the family should be regarded as a universal institution, whereas some sociologists, by rejecting this presupposition, have used the word family to refer to the distinctive feature of social life in some cultures and historical periods (particularly, Western culture in recent periods). [1]

Ignoring the problem of not being comprehensive and falsifiable, we make do with quoting some definitions provided by sociologists.

- " Family is a social unit which comes to existence through marriage".[2]
- " Family is a group of people whose relations to one another are based upon consanguinity and who are therefore kin to one another ".[3]
- "Family is a group defined by sexual relationship, sufficiently precise and enduring to provide for the production and upbringing of children." [4]
- "Family is a social group characterized by common residence, economic co-operation and reproduction".[5]
- "The family is a group of people united by ties of marriage, blood, or adoption; constituting a household; interacting and communicating with each other in their respective social roles of husband and wife, mother and father, brother and sister, and creating a common [sub] culture".[6]

The presupposition of some of these definitions that the first definition puts emphasis on and is approved by Islam's point of view is that the concept of family requires the concept of marriage; thus, the terms included in the definition of marriage, such as legitimacy and the bondage between male and female, indirectly limit the concept of family, although the converse of this issue is not generalizable and one can't see marriage as being the prerequisite for establishing a family. According to this point, the units consisting of two people of the same sex or an unmarried man and an unmarried woman cannot be counted as families.

---

[1] Kuper & Kuper (eds.), *The Social Science Encyclopedia* , p.290.

[2] Sarokhani , *The Social Science Encyclopedia* ,p 255.

[3] Mitchell (ed.) , *A dictionary of Sociology* ,p .76

[4] Sarokhani , *The Social Science Encyclopedia* ,p 255.

[5] Lee & Newby ,*The problem of Sociology* ,p.282

[6] Mitchell (ed.) , *A Dictionary of Sociology* ,p.76

In this section, the most important types of family and alternative family patterns in contemporary world as well as two important structural issues, i.e. division of labor and management in the family will be examined.

CHAPTER 4

TYPES OF FAMILY

Chapter 4

Types of family

Learning objectives of chapter 4

Getting familiar with the most important family patterns and alternative family patterns in modern world

Based on stage objective of this chapter, the learner is expected to achieve the following learning objectives and be able to:

1. describe the most important family divisions from the perspective of sociology.
2. recognize the ills of the most important alternative family patterns in modern world.

Introduction

Family has been formed in different types and patterns in human societies. Factors such as closeness and farness of kinship between the members, family structure and residence of wife and husband after marriage have influenced the emergence of these diversities. Sociologists and anthropologists have tried to identify these patterns which are partly common and partly limited to specific societies. In this chapter, first the most important family patterns and then some alternative patterns of family in modern world will be explained.

4-1 Nuclear /extended family

The "Nuclear family" is a family group consisting of the wife and husband and usually their children who live together apart from other relatives. Defining the nuclear family, sociologists usually include the condition "wife and husband" which implies the existence of a man and a woman and realizes marriage between them; but because of considerable changes occurring in the Western family structure in recent decades, they have removed this condition from newer definitions.

Being the predominant family pattern in most societies, the nuclear family was also found in the past but it was not the predominant one. In addition, it lacked some of the features of the contemporary nuclear family such as few children and neolocality (residence of wife and husband in a place other than the father and mother's one).

There can be seen a tendency towards trivializing the pattern of nuclear family in some new approaches of sociology, including feminist and postmodernist approaches. In this regard, sometimes the very low statistics of this type of family in Western societies for example, 12 percent in 1987 and 7 percent in 1989 in the US) is cites as evidence in support of this.[1] The examination of these documents indicates that the term "nuclear family" has been used in a very limited sense in these orientations; in this sense, conditions like the man being employed, the woman being a housewife, and the responsibility of two or more children has been included in the definition of nuclear family. Therefore, there is no incompatibility between these statistics and those about

---

1. Bernards, *An Introduction to Family Studies* , p31.

the US that say by 1998, 53 percent of the families were composed of a wife and a husband and 25 percent of them were composed of a wife and a husband and a child under 25 years old.[1]

The "extended family" is a family in which more than two generations of close relatives reside together in the same household. So, an extended family can include single or married children, fathers and mothers and their grandfather and grandmother.[2]

Removing the condition "living apart from relatives" from the definition of the nuclear family, some sociologists have caused the conceptual opposition of such a definition to the extended family to lose color. For instance, Murdock, in his cross-cultural study demonstrated that the nuclear family pattern in its exact meaning was an accepted norm in 25 percent of the societies studied. In the other 25 percent of societies, polygamy was a predominant pattern, defined as two or more nuclear families united by the diverse marriages of one husband. In the remaining 50 percent of the cases, the extended family pattern was accepted and, according to him, it was where the extended family of a mature married person lived with his parents' nuclear family. Accordingly, Murdock concluded that the nuclear family is a universal social group, either as the sole prevailing form of the family or as the basic unit from which more complex forms are compounded.[3]

Although the pattern of extended family has lost its previous importance and prevalence in many societies because of socio-economic changes, it does not suggest the decline of it. That is because in many other societies, especially in Asia, Africa, Latin America and parts of Eastern and Southern Europe, this pattern is still common[4] and in some countries we are witnessing its revival and adaptation with new circumstances and conditions. According to Giddens:

> In some regions of Poland, the revival of the extended family has been demonstrated in vivid and documented ways. Many industrial workers have farms which they handle part-time. Grandfathers and grandmothers live with their children's family, and help run the affairs of the home and raise children, while the younger generation is employed with different occupations outside the home.[5]

It seems that economic decline of the family as a result of the development of urbanization and the growth of individualistic values, has nearly ruled out the possibility of the formation of traditional extended families. But due to the positive functions of the extended family, especially in the areas of support and care to whose importance even the most individualistic societies attest, and considering the fact that many future grandfathers and grandmothers are these very children and teenagers who grow up with individualistic and democratic norms, it doesn't come at the thin end of the

---

1. http://www.U.S.Bureau of the Census
2. Sarokhani , *The Social Science Encyclopedia* ,p 255
3. Ingoldsby,"Family Origin and University" ,*Families in Global and Multicultural Perspective*,pp.67-68
4. Kendall, *Sociology in Our Times*, p.418
5. Giddens , *Sociology* ,p 422

expectations for them to have more congruity with their children. In other words, since grandfathers and grandmothers of future generations unlike previous generations have less tendency towards exercising domination and authority, it is more likely to be accepted by their children.

As a result, the prevalence of a more limited form of the extended family—consisting of a nuclear family as well as grandfather and grandmother_ can be expected in future decades. This prediction has more strength, particularly in developing Islamic societies; because the abundant emphasis of Islam on treating parents kindly, especially aged ones, can provide a suitable cultural context for the expansion of this type of family.

4-2 Patriarchal / matriarchal family

In most societies and for a considerable portion of human history, men used to have more power than women in the family, although sometimes women have enjoyed considerable power too. Whether power lies in the grasp of men or that of women has huge impact on the structure of the family. Patriarchal family is described as a family in which the father holds primary power.

Patriarchy usually requires other features which the most important ones are as follows:

1. Wife comes to live in the husband's residence after marriage where is usually the residence of husband's parents or it's near to it (patrilocality).
2. Father is the mainstay of lineage, that is, the individuals consider themselves as the child of the father and trace their descent through the father's line (patrilineality).
3. Children get their surnames from father's (patronymic).
4. Chief heritage or whole of it is inherited by the male lineage.
5. After the death of father , his eldest son would be his successor.[1]

The matriarchal family is a family in which the mother holds primary power and it is probably characterized by features such as matrilocality, matrilineality, matronymic and daughter's priority in heritage and succession. Whether such family existed in human's history or it's just a mental assumption, there is disagreement between sociologists. Some believe that the period after sexual chaos was matriarchal period and patriarchy has appeared later in human's history but many researchers regard this theory merely as a hypothesis.

In modern societies, families move towards relative equality of the husband and wife's authority, although no society can be found which men and women have a real equal authority in the family and society. For instance, studies on British middle class family indicated that the men have greater power over the family's economic sources. According to one of these studies, "very important" decisions, financial issues for example, were made by husbands only and "important" decisions, about the education of children for example, were often made by both of them, but, in practice, the woman did not make a decision by herself in none of these two cases; women only undertook

---

1. Sarokhani , *The Social Science Encyclopedia* ,p 525-526

the sole responsibility of those decisions that were considered to be at best of insignificant and marginal importance by both the wife and the husband.[1]

4-3 Family and residence

One the basis of residence, families are classified into three main types. Sometimes, the newly-established family lives with or nearby the husband's family or relatives. This kind of family is called "patrilocal" family. In some cases, the young couples reside nearby the woman's parents or relatives. Such a family is defined as "matrilocal" family. Neolocal family is the family in which the young couples decide on their residence based on occupational and educational conditions or personal preferences and they usually reside away from either the husband's and the wife's relatives.[2]

Neolocality is among the necessary conditions of nuclear family pattern which is becoming increasingly dominant as a result of the development of urban and industrial life. Murdock's cross- cultural study in 1949 indicated following ratios regarding the prevalence of these patterns: patrilocality 58%, matrilocality 15%, neolocality 7% and other secondary and often combined patterns in total 20 percent. Researchers have identified other types of marital or family relationships in some countries such as America and Thailand which, even though it has attracted a small number of couples, is gradually expanding. In this pattern, the husband and wife live in separate dwellings without any incongruity or divorce involved. Some sociologists have called this pattern "living apart together" and some "duel resident marriage". As if people who have turned to this pattern follow two parallel purposes; on the one hand, they seek the continual life of the tradition of marriage, and on the other hand, they do not want marriage to be a barrier in the way of their personal aims.[3]

4 -4 Monogamous/polygamous family

A family pattern in which just a woman lives with a husband is called "monogamous" family and polygamy is defined as a pattern in which a man or a woman lives with two or more partners. Polygamy is of two kinds: the pattern which allows the men to have more than one wife at a time is called "polygyny" and a rare pattern in which the women are permitted to have more than one husband at a time is described as "polyandry". In all societies, most men do not have more than one legal partner and almost all women live with only one husband, because the number of man and woman is almost equal in all societies and, in practice, it's not possible for all men to marry more than one woman or conversely for all women to have more than one husband.

Murdock's cross- cultural survey conducted in 1950s in more than 1100 different societies indicated that just 14/5 percent of cultures, including the Western culture, had officially approved monogamy as the only permissible pattern. In 84/8 percent of the cultures studied, polygyny was permitted and occasionally encouraged and "polyandry" was accepted just in 0/6 percent of cultures.[4] Among Ibrahim's religions, Judaism and

---

1. Giddens, *Sociology* ,p 426
2. Turner, *Sociology : Concepts and Uses* ,p 264-265.
3. Adams , "Families and Family study in International Perspective " , *Journal of Marriage and Family* 66, p.1082
4. Ingoldsby ," Marital Structure " , *Families in Global and Multicultural Perspective* ,p.100.

Islam permit polygyny while Christianity legitimizes just monogamy. Probably, the fact that the woman can be sure that the child she is taking care of is really her own child but that the man often cannot have such confidence, can be one of the most important reasons of societies' tolerance of polygyny and their severity towards polyandry[1] and in a narration by Ali (AS), the Commander of Believers, this difference has also been mentioned.[2] But undoubtedly diverse economic, social and cultural factors have been involved in the development of polygamy, particularly in the form of polygyny. [3]

4-5 Single parent family

The "single parent or incomplete family" refers to a family in which one or two partners are not present because of death, divorce or other reasons and the family is headed by the present partner. As the title implies, the single parent family involves one or more dependent children.

This type of family has existed in all societies and in all historical periods, but the extent and the reasons of its prevalence vary in different societies. In the second half of the twentieth century, along with the rapid increase of the rate of divorce and the increase of illegitimate sexual relationships in Western societies, the number of this family type has always been on the rise in the said societies. For example, in 1976, there were fewer than 4 million American single parent households, but in 1991, this figure reached more than 10 million households. In England, there were about 570 thousand single- parent households in 1971, but it rose to one million and six hundred thousand households in 1996.[4]

The presence of the wife and husband in the family, in order to play their respective maternal and paternal roles, has a significant influence on the growth of children's personality and the two complement each other in terms of the management of home affairs. Hence, the absence of each of them can deal serious damages to the family and its members and, in the meantime, the bulk of the psychological and economic damage is directed at children and women. The families with women as their guardian have more economic problems; because women are faced with occupational problems and low income in most societies. According to some statistics, 90 percent of all poor households are headed by women. According to some statistics, 90 percent of single parent families in the U.S are headed by women and the households with women as their guardian make up all poor households. Likewise, 23 percent of all American households with children are headed by mothers without husbands (divorcee, widow, never married, etc).[5] The rate of Iranian families headed by women reached 8/3 percent in 1996.[6]

---

1. Ibid

2. Majlesi, *Bahar al-Anvar* , Vol 40 ,p226.

3. Refer to: Motahhari ,*The System of Women's rights in Islam* , Section 11 "Polygamy".

4. Allan & Crow , *Families , Households and Society* ,p.26.

5. Lott, *Women's Lives* , p.230.

6. http://www. IranElika.com

4-6 Stepfamily

In recent decades, because of the increase in divorce and remarriage rate in Western countries, we are witnessing the expansion of families in which the father or the mother or both of them are step-parents. According to existing statistics, the families with stepfather in which the woman has the custody of her own children from previous marriage constitute 70% of stepfamilies and the families with stepmother constitute 20% of them. Small percentage of these families have been formed by a father and a mother who have their children from previous marriage. Meantime, in many cases, this new marriage also produces new children.[1] These types of families have their peculiar problems that sociologists and psychologists usually examine them in the discussions about divorce consequences.[2]

4-7 Alternative patterns of family

a) Cohabitation

In recent decades, the expansion of sexual freedoms in Western societies has led to the emergence of other type of more or less stable relations between the man and the woman which is called cohabitation (where two people who are not married live together). According to existing statistics, in 1960, in the US 439000 couples cohabitated while in 1998 this figure rose to 4 million and 236000 people.[3] The figure 4/9 million households in 2000 implies continuing upward trend of this pattern's expansion in the US.[4]

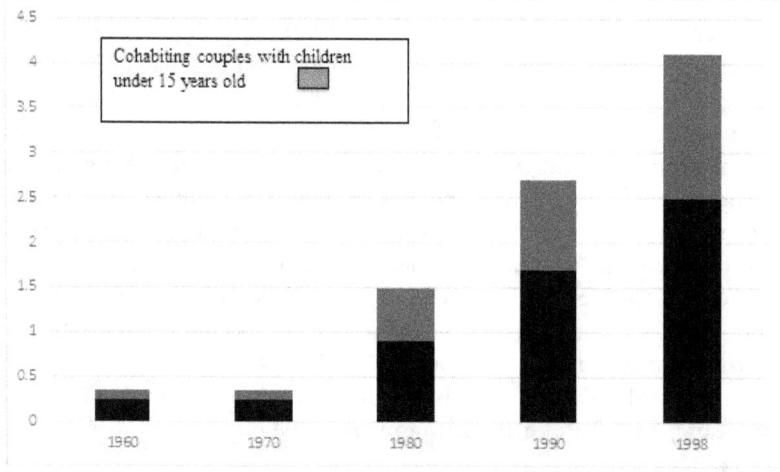

Diagram 3: The rate of cohabitation in the US

(The figures are based on the scale of one million household)

www.u.s.bureau of the census

---

1. Santrocl & Yussen ,*Child Development : An Introduction* , p.343
2. Refer to : Bostan (Najafi) et al, *Islam and Sociology of the Family* ,Chapter 5
3. http:// www.U.S.Bureau of the Census.
4. Ingoldsby, "Mate Selection and Marriage ", *Families in Global and Multicultural* Perspective, p.133

Today, in some Western countries, cohabiting people enjoy rights similar to the rights of married couples and they can refer to the court in the case of having conflicts about property and alimony. [1]

Several factors are involved in the prevalence of this pattern: first, unprecedented freedom of sexual relations which took place in 1960s and its considerable impact on the expansion of cohabitation appeared from the 1980s onwards. In this regard, the decrease of parents' control on sexual behavior of children should be taken into consideration. The youth of today in West are the children of the same generation who launched a movement called sexual revolution in 1960s or were involved in it .Therefore, in comparison with previous generations, they have less tendency and power to supervise and control their own children. Independence and non-commissive ideology has also played a key role in the expansion of cohabitation. Lacking an official and legal aspect, cohabitation has attracted many Western youth, because while offering them the possibility of getting sexual satisfaction without commitment, many young people consider it as a trial marriage which can easily be broken up in the case of the emergence of signs of incongruity between the couples, or their likes and interests turning out to be different. Moreover, factors such as the increasing prevalence of individual residence due to educational or occupational reasons and rental house owners' tolerance of settling cohabiting couples in comparison with the past decades as well as the increase of divorce rate which has forcefully caused the youth's worry about the success of marriage, have contributed to the prevalence of cohabitation.[2]

Cohabitation does not have any legitimacy in Islam's view because of its very non-commissive dimension. This pattern does not provide any appropriate ground for important purposes of marriage, i.e. the emergence of genuine and deep affection between the man and the woman and proper childrearing; because disintegration is the main feature of it. Since cohabitation lasts for a while, it brings intimacy, the conjugal intimacy between the couples, an intimacy that is accompanied by the feeling of monopolizing possessiveness toward the partner; but since the partner can break up partnership any time he/she wishes, both parties live with stress, anxiety and probably suspicion and, thus, emotional satisfaction between them is much less than that of between officially married couples.

Temporary marriage in Islam presents a pattern of marriage which establishes a legitimate religious framework for sexual relationships, while it also carries out the most important functions of cohabitation. Due to the fact that the temporary marriage involves fewer commitments than permanent marriage, if the man and the woman in specific conditions and because of plausible reasons wish to be free of the commitments of permanent marriage, and in the meantime provide themselves with the context and grounds for legitimate sexual relationship, this kind of marriage can be a catalyst and a solution.

---

1. Giddens, *Sociology* , p442
2. Allan & Crow, *Families, Households and Society*, pp.66-68

b) Commune

From the mid nineteenth century and recently since 1960s, communal societies or communes, influenced by some radical views, gradually came to the fore as an alternative for the family and attracted some supporters among Western youth. These communal societies comprised some men and women who had promiscuous and mixed relationship with each other and from ideologue's view were regarded as a return to nature and the revival of prehistoric primitive communes. Negating any domination in the relationship between man and woman and negating the feeling of ownership and competition were the main motivations behind these groups' disapproval of the family institution and their tendency towards this new pattern. Kibbutz in occupied Palestine (Israel) emerged with similar motivations and as an alternative for private and maternal family pattern which was prevailing in traditional Jewish society. The Communes soon lost their social importance and validity; because it failed to achieve much success in purposes intended.[1]

In recent years there is a gradual tendency toward the approval of traditional family norms and structures in these communal societies.

c) Homosexual couples

In almost all societies, establishing sexual relationship with someone of the same sex is considered indecent and reprehensible and in many cases the people who commit such acts face severe physical and even capital punishment. For example, according to Islamic law, if an adult and sane man of his own free will commits such an act and the judge be convinced of this he will be sentenced to death.[2] In many European countries like the UK, until early twentieth century the penalty for such a deed was death and it was considered a criminal act and a felony until recent decades.[3]

However, homosexuality is seen more or less in many societies. According to narrations, the emergence of homosexuality goes back to the tribe of Lot (AS) who lived in the time of Ibrahim (AS).[4] Now, some Western countries experience an unprecedented condition in this regard. In these countries, a considerable number of men and women select same sex partners and establish a fairly long relationship which is similar to that of married couples. Biologically, it is impossible for the same-sex couples to produce children, but many of them bring their children out of previous marriages to homosexual relationships and thus form a family consisting of homosexual couples and children. Some Western governments and American states have officially recognized homosexual marriages and have granted rights fairly similar to those of married couples. However, the homosexual pattern, aversion from innate nature and lacking religious legitimacy, has an uncertain status in terms of legal standing even in the societies like the US.[5]

---

1. Refer to : Segalen , *Historical Sociology of Family* ,p 335, also refer to: Lee & Newby ,*The Problem of Sociology*,p.292
2. Imam Khomeini ,*Tahrir al-Wasileh* ,Vol 2 ,p 469
3. Giddense , *Sociology* ,p 207-208
4. Horr Ameli, *Wasael al-Shia* ,Vol 14,p 260-261
5. Curry et al ., *Sociology for the Twenty-First Century* ,p.260

o **Abstract**

- The "nuclear family" is a family group consisting of the wife and the husband and usually their children who live together apart from other relatives.
- The "extended family" is a family in which more than two generations of close relatives live together in the same household.
- The family in which father holds primary power is called patriarchal family and matriarchal family is a family in which the mother holds greater power.
- In the modern societies, families move toward relative equality of man and woman's authority.
- On the basis of residence, families are classified into three main types: patrilocal, matrilocal and neolocal families.
- A family pattern in which just a woman lives with a husband is called monogamous and a pattern in which a man or a woman lives with two or more partners is defined as polygamous family.
- "Single parent or incomplete family" refers to the family in which one or two partners are not present because of death, divorce or other reasons and the family is headed by the present partner.
- The expansion of sexual freedoms in Western societies has provided a context for the growth of alternative family patterns such as cohabitation, communal society and homosexuality.

o **Self-Test**

1. What is the difference between the contemporary nuclear family and the nuclear family in previous periods?
2. Can one raise the claim that the extended family model is declining in the contemporary times? Why?
3. What features are stated for patriarchal family by sociologists?
4. Analyze the factors contributing to the expansion of cohabitation pattern in Western societies and its damages.

o **Research topic**

- Do a comprehensive research on the family definitions and their critiques.
- Research the prevalence rate of extended family pattern in the country.

CHAPTER 5

DIVISION OF LABOR IN THE FAMILY

Chapter 5

Division of Labor in the Family

Learning objectives of chapter 5

Getting familiar with theories of gender division of labor in the family and Islam's point of view in this regard.

Based on stage objective of this chapter, the learner is expected to achieve the following learning objectives and be able to:

1. describe the situation of gender division of labor in the family;
2. explain the most important biological , psychological and sociological theories about gender division of labor in the family;
3. analyze Islam's point of view regarding gender division of labor in the family.

Introduction

After presenting a brief description about the history and current situation of labor division in the family, different biological, psychological and sociological theories of this subject will be examined and finally Islam's point of view will be stated in two explanatory and normative perspectives of gender division of labor in the family.

5-1 A description of labor division in the family

Labor division in the family has always been formed based on gender. Paleontological studies have demonstrated some forms of gender division of labor in very distant past. For example, it is said that in Paleolithic period, human beings lived in the societies which had been organized based on animal hunting and food gathering. In those societies, men hunted and women gathered fruit, vegetables and corns.[1] Gender division of labor has been continued in the next periods and until contemporary period. Cross culturally, findings of anthropologists have confirmed the universality of gender division of labor. In a cross- cultural survey of 224 , Gorge Peter Murdock found tasks such as lumbering, wood gathering ,digging ,mining , land clearance , house building , hunting , fishing , herding ,trading, boat building and weapon making to be predominantly male roles but vegetable preparing and gathering, water fetching, cooking, sewing , basket making , mat making and pottery making to be largely female roles.[2]

In the previous decade, traditional pattern of gender division of labor in the family partly changed because of profound social and cultural changes in the Western world. Yong and Willmott's studies in 1960s about the increasing employment of women outside the home and men's participation in domestic labors more than ever suggested that the British family moves increasingly toward becoming symmetrical; that is, the roles of husband and wife are going to be similar to each other's and finally they will be

---

1. Sherman Wadud, *Modern Views of Sociology* ,p 142
2. Oakley ,*Woman's work : The Housewife ,Past and Present*,p.166

equal.[1] But other researchers disagree with this conclusion and believe that, except in some new family patterns, in most families gender division of labor is still practiced. Some researchers declare that the change in the reality of gender division of labor in the family is occurring far more slowly than the change in people's attitude towards this subject. For example, although men, more than ever, express more egalitarian attitudes and honor more rights for women to choose a job or keep house, many of them explicitly assert that they wouldn't prefer home roles to their own jobs. According to surveys conducted about teenager's expectations regarding adult's role , many girls expect to work outside the home before and after child-bearing; but at the same time they predict that the responsibilities of child rearing will interrupt their job. In contrast, although boys expect to be involved partly in child rearing, they do not expect it will meddle with their job.[2]

Some believe that people's disagreement with the traditional roles of males and females are limited to public comments and many adults are still bound to traditional views. For example, in the census of 1985 carried out in the US, 50% of men and more than 45% of women agreed that "if the man concerns himself with earning money and the woman with taking care of the home and the family, every party will be much better off." When senior high school students were asked what the most ideal form of adjusting work and responsibility for a man and woman with preschool children would be, their first priority was a full time job for the husband and the woman's completely relinquishing her job. [3]

The statistics of hours spent for domestic labors indicate that in 1975, men and women worked 7 and 21/7 hours at home per week respectively and in 1985, the men worked about 8/8 hours and the women 19/5 hours.[4] Fairly new statistics in England suggest that despite the increase of married women's employment, in 88% of households women shoulder the responsibility of house chores like washing and ironing. In 77% of the households, women routinely prepare dinner and in 72% of the households they clean the house.[5] Of course, compared to housewives, working women with part time or full time jobs are more likely to get regular help from their husbands in some house chores such as washing clothes and dishes. However, a low percentage of men get involved in these chores, cooking in particular which is retained as women's duty and their employment outside the house does not exert any effect on this.[6] Since the birth of the child strongly affects women's employment outside the home, it intensifies the gender division of labor between the wife and the husband; that is, it makes women dependent on men economically and this decreases even further men's already limited participation in house chores – even if it existed before the birth of the child.[7]

1. Abbott And Wallace , *An Introduction to Sociology :Feminist Perspective*, p156-157
2. Burr ,*Gender and Social Psychology* ,p .81
3. Kammeyer et al .,*Sociology :Experiencing Changing Societies*,pp.334-335
4. French, *The War Against Women* , p 303
5. Morris ," The Household and the Labor Market " , *The Sociology of the Family* ,p.217
6. Charles & Kerr , "Women's Work ", *The Sociology of the Family* ,p,201
7. Ibid , p.208

The pattern of the two-job family, i.e. a family consisting of a working wife and a working husband, is a new family pattern which has dramatically prevailed in recent years, particularly in Western countries. According to researchers, even in this type of family, despite the husband's participation in house chores, there is a great deal of pressure on women, because, in addition to working full time outside the home, they are expected to shoulder the responsibility of house chores and care of children and as a result women work about fifteen hours in a week more than their husbands.[1]

5-2 Theories of labor division in the family

Theories with different approaches have been set forth to answer the question "why division of labor in the family has always been formed based on gender"? In this discussion, three classes of theories, including biological, psychological and sociological theories will be examined.

a) Biological theories

Some sociologists argue that gender division of labor between man and woman has its origin in natural sex differences.[2] Proponents of this theory take as a given that the difference of gender roles, as a global fact, must have their origin in a global source and it is on this same basis that they regard biological factors as determining factors in gender division of labor.[3] According to some researchers, greater physical strength of men has been the origin of ascribing specific duties to them.[4] Alice Rossi, focusing on different patterns of man and woman's hormonal growth as an origin of sexual differences, takes women's readiness for taking compassionate care of children in comparison with men to be related to biological differences. According to her, it has been proved that women innately have quicker understanding and greater sensitivity regarding children's needs and the common perception about the clumsy father can have its root in actual reality. [5]

Some psychologists who have studied the relationship between the child's sex and the type of game selected by him/her, state that although parents encourage games suitable with sex, there are some evidences implying that biological factors can influence the children's selection. The likelihood that fathers give dolls to one-year-old boys is outdone by the possibility of giving dolls to one-year-old girls; the boys that receive dolls are less likely to play with it. So, it can be concluded that parents' expectations and encouragements are themselves affected by children's selection and at the same time they create an amplifying effect; therefore, since toys provide good opportunity for the increase of specific abilities and skills of boy and girl, they impact the emergence of gender differences. [6]

---

1. Shepard ,*Sociology* ,p.309
2. Adducing to the research of Gustave Le Bon , Emile Durkheim is inclined to this theory
[3] McConnell & Philipchalk, *Understanding Human Behavior*, p .223
4. Kammeyer et al., *Sociology :Experiencing Changing Societies* ,p .329
5. Lengermann & Brantley ,"Modern Feminist Theory", *Theory of Sociology in Modern World* , p 472. Also refer to :Tong ,*Feminist Thought* ,p .159
6. Carlson , *Psychology :The Science of Behavior*,p.336

Probably, no researcher can be found who assigns definite and determining role for biological factors in the emergence of gender division of labor. Opponents of biological theories argue that if gender was determined through biological factors, rearing the child into the wrong role, i.e. the boy into the role of a girl and vice versa would not have been possible, although previous studies indicate that this is a quite real possibility. Currently, scholars usually accept two points: first, some previous grounds of gender differences may exist at birth, but because these differences are not decisive, they can be eliminated with cultural education. Second, since the differences which have been scientifically proven are rather limited obvious differences of gender roles or sex inequalities which exist in many societies cannot be explained based on them. [1]

b) Psychological theories

Some researchers in a psychological analysis suggested that the difference between the duties and activities of men and women can reflect the tendency of men to create a distinctive masculine identity. Probably, since the women could show their femininity through fertility and the raise of children, the men wanted to have access to a way through which to expose their manhood. Therefore, men in all societies have fulfilled this demand by monopolizing certain activities and precluding women from doing them; war has been one of these peculiarly masculine activities.[2]

Some feminist psychoanalysts have tried to explain gender division of labor within the family according to different personality of girls and boys which is formed during the process of socialization and through identifying children with parents (the boys with their fathers and the girls with their mothers).

Explaining different processes in shaping the personality of boys and girls, Nancy Chodorow concludes:

> The sexual and familial division of labor in which women mother creates a sexual division of psychic organization and orientation. It produces socially gendered women and men who enter into asymmetrical heterosexual relationships; it produces men who put most of their energies into the non-familial work world and do not parent; it produces women who turn their energies toward nurturing and caring for children- in turn reproducing the sexual and familial division of labor in which women mother.[3]

Ignoring social macro structures which influence sex inequalities and role differences and making do with psychic inclinations and structures are features of these kinds of psychological theories which have been criticized by opponents.[4]

c) Sociological theories

Talcott Parsons – a well - known figure of structural functionalism – in his theory, deals with the analysis of labor division between the wife and the husband in American middle class nuclear family. Parsons assumes that assigning different roles to the wife

---

1. Robertson, *An Introduction to Sociology*, p 278-279.
2. Kammeyer et al., *Sociology :Experiencing Changing Societies*, p .329.
3. Chodorow,"The Psychodynamics of the Family ", *The Second Wave*, p.195
4. Tong , *Feminist Thought*, p.157

and the husband, to some extent has a biological aspect; women become pregnant and breastfeed their children and this reality predisposes them to accept the roles associated with the care and raise of the children, but men, because of being free from biological constraints, specialize in the roles that lead them to work outside the home. [1]

He has based his analysis on three research backgrounds: First, Freud's psychoanalytical findings which had emphasized different psycho-sexual development for boys and girls and the formation of their masculinity and femininity as psychological structure.

Second, Bales' empirical studies according to which the groups create two types of leadership role: 1.The role of dominant leader who takes the responsibility of performing the duties of the group, particularly those of adapting to external physical and social conditions which he calls "instrumental role". 2. The role of semi-dominant leader who fulfills the duties related to expressive roles. Parsons and Bales took it for granted that the findings of these studies conducted on test groups are valid about real groups too.[2] Based on these results, they concluded that the women play expressive role in the family: they are kind, attractive, cheerful, pathetic and obedient; but men play instrumental role: they are aggressive, creative and genuine bosses. Man is the breadwinner and the principle role for woman is to be her husband's wife and the mother of his children.[3]

Third, data collected from cross-cultural studies that according to one of them in 46 out of 56 societies studied, as it was expected, there were differences between expressive and instrumental family roles; that is, expressive roles were assigned to the women and instrumental roles to the men.[4]

Depending on these research findings, Parsons stated that an optimal form of gender division of labor between the wife and husband provides the ground for performing basic functions of the family in decisively shaping a solid adult personality and socialization of the children and this issue has a fundamental role in the integration of the family and then in social stability. According to him, women's subordination in capitalist societies, functionally, is required to maintain family unity, and in turn family unity is essential for maintaining the class structure. Maintaining class structure is also essential to ensure the preservation of the established social structure.[5]

In contrast, influenced by Marx and Engels' views, theorists in the traditional school trace the origin of unequal gender division of labor in the class system resulting from private ownership of means of production, a system which has come to take the form of capitalist system in the present era. From this perspective, the continuity of gender division of labor within the family is due to the benefit derived by the capitalist system from women's domestic labor. It has been estimated that 25- 40 percent of wealth generated in industrial countries comes from domestic labors. Domestic labor, by providing free services upon which a large number of working population depend,

---

1. Knuttila , *Introducing Sociology : A Critical Perspective* ,p .267
2. Lee & Newby, *The Problem of Sociology* ,p.288-289
3. Harvey & McDonald , *Doing Sociology* ,p.197
4. Lee & Newby , *The Problem of Sociology* ,p.289
5. Harvey & McDonald ,*Doing Sociology* ,p.197

strengthen the rest of the economy.[1] Women's domestic labor serve the capitalism both as a surplus profit which is finally returned to the capitalist and also by promoting livelihood status or maintaining it in a tolerable level which reduces political pressures that might lead to revolutionary changes (because it keeps the men satisfied with current conditions). It should be mentioned the effects of house chores and emotional support of women to reconstruct and refresh the husbands, older children and fathers to work in other working day.[2]

Patriarchy is identified by the radical feminists as the origin of all sex inequalities. They believe that the cause of the continuity of gender division of labor in the family, as one of the comprehensive manifestations of sex inequality, is the profit that men make of labor division; because in this pattern, all women –including spouses, mothers, sisters and daughters- are subjected to be at the service of men and to satisfy their needs.[3] What is of fundamental importance in this regard is men's greater power which allows them to impose their wills on women. Men possess more power to choose and even when they decide to participate in house chores, they can choose more pleasant works; so, their participation has a "helping" aspect rather than one of "a sense of responsibility".[4]

Ann Oakley – a feminist theorist - regards division of labor in the family as a patriarchal myth which cultural institutions of society have the biggest part in its emergence and strengthening. She assesses ideas and theories of behaviorists, anthropologists, sociologists and child psychologists in this regard which contribute to promoting this myth. According to her, behaviorists posit a biological origin for gender division of labor; sociologists, especially functionalists, remind us its positive social functions and child psychologists always emphasize that the child needs her /his mother not the father. Therefore, the myth that regards the degradation of the position of women to domestic role as a natural, universal and necessary issue has got credit and popularity by adducing to scientific researches. [5]

A number of feminists have tried to present multi factor explanations of unequal division of labor in the family which have usually been done through the combination of previous feminist theories. For instance, Juliet Mitchell uses a combination of psychological, economic, bio-social and cultural theories for explaining this issue. He believes that, apart from unconscious mind which occupies special position in the revival and retrieval of gender roles, some aspects of women's life in the family are economic, i.e. they are the result of changes created in mode of production. Others are of a bio-social character; that is, they are the result of reciprocal effect of feminine biology and social environment, some has ideological nature, i.e. they are the result of ideas that the society has accepted about how women's relationship with men should be. [6]

---

1. Giddens, *Sociology* , p 196.
2. Bilton et al., *Introductory Sociology* , pp.351-352
3. Ibid
4. Burr ,*Gender and Social Psychology* ,p.85
5. Oakely , *Woman's work: The Housewife ,Past and Present* ,p.68,157
6. Tong , *Feminist Thought* ,p.175

5-3 Islam's point of view

Previous theories included two models of explanation: causal explanation and functional explanation. Causal explanations have emphasized three classes of factors (biological, psychic and social) and functional explanations have taken into consideration the positive functions of gender division of labor in order to maintain social integrity or its negative functions to perpetuate the capitalist system. Here, Islam's point of view will be reviewed in this regard.

Regarding causal explanation of gender division of labor in the family, there cannot be found any material at Islamic sources with totally contrast to the triple biological, psychic, social theories. However, brief explanation of Islam's view can be useful. Referring to Islamic sources, we encounter two classes of religious propositions:

1. propositions that regard some inherent and innate differences between man and woman as the cause of the emergence of different occupational and non-occupational interests between them :like narrations which argue that the creation of man from the earth and the creation of the woman from man has an effect on the inclination of men towards the earth (their inclination towards the activities related to the earth and their need to be away from home) and it is also effective in the women's inclination towards men (probably , women's tendency to be attractive for men or their tendency towards the activities which men's presence is required); [1]

2. Propositions that distinguish between desired and undesired patterns of labor division and valuation in this regard; narrations introducing maternal and wifehood roles as superior roles for women,[2] narrations approving men helping women in doing house chores [3]and those narrations which consider enthusiastic cooperation of women with their husbands in business and trade as one of the reproachable signs of the Day of Judgment can be mentioned as examples. [4]

The purport of the last class is that gender division of labor does not have an unchangeable and compulsory characteristic rather it is affected by the individuals' arbitrary and conscious decisions. Therefore, the existence of some innate origin for gender division of labor which, of course, cannot be thought to have a decisive role in the emergence of such division of labor will be necessary for combining these two set of narrations. Gender division of labor has its root in collective decisions, conscious or subconscious, which are based on cultural values. Psychological theories merely explain internalization of these gender roles. Meantime, men's power should be taken into consideration not as an independent factor but as a tool for realizing cultural purposes (in this case, division of labor based on gender).

Regarding functional explanation of gender division of labor we are faced with three main theories: Parsons' theory, Marxist theory and Feminist theory. The common

---

1. Horr Amelli ,*Wasael al-Shia* , Vol 14, p40-42.
2. Ibid ,p115 and 123; Syuti , *al-Dor al-Mansor* , vol 2, p153.
3. Horr Amelli ,*Wasael al-Shia* ,Vol 12 ,p39; Majlesi ,*Bahar al-Anvar* ,Vol 16, p238; Vol 104, p132
4. Majlesi ,Ibid ,Vol 78,p23; Nouri ,*Mustadrak al-Wasael* ,Vol 12, p 237

denominator of these theories is their emphasis on the service and advantage that gender division of labor offers to a comprehensive system, with the difference that while Parsons evaluates this function positively, he regards this functional comprehensive system as a social system in its generality but while Marxist and Feminist theories evaluate this function negatively, they introduce the capitalist and patriarchy systems, respectively, as the functioning systems.

Considering Islamic sources a teleological explanation can be achieved which is somewhat consistent with Parson's functional explanation[1] in the sense that both explanations taking some common values and purposes for granted take a positive view about gender division of labor in family for it realizes those values and goals, but their main difference lies in the values taken for granted by each. While in Parsons' theory, social integrity is the ultimate goal, the Islamic explanation revolves around true prosperity of mankind as the ultimate goal and since spiritual health of the individual and society plays an important role in providing true prosperity of mankind, it finds a special manifestation in not only social but also in gender-oriented relationships as well.

Islam has deprecated the intermixture of non-mahram man and woman and the exchange of feelings and sentiments between them in order to achieve the mentioned goal and to provide the spiritual health of the individual, family and society, and particularly to protect women's human personality and to prevent women from being regarded as only sexual objects to satisfy men's desires. Therefore, gender division of labor, in such a way that for women domestic duties and for men outside labors hold priority, by providing suitable context for women to be less visible through reducing their intermixture with non-mahrams which has an undeniable role in providing society with spiritual heath, is the best option for human's true prosperity among other possible options. According to a narration Ali and Fatima (AS) asked the Messenger of God (pbuh) to pronounce judgment about dividing their duties at home. The Prophet assigned home duties to Fatima (AS) and outside duties to Ali (AS). Fatima (AS) said:" no one but God knows how happy I was when the Messenger of God exempted me from tolerating men's gaze [or engaging with them].[2]

However, the women's less visibility is just one of the facets of this issue and other aspects such as limitations concerning women's production and physical strength compared to men's should not be ignored ; because these affairs have more compatibility with gender division of labor in the family and even in contemporary industrial societies where the decline of production and the development of orphanages and kindergartens have reduced those limitations for women and where physical strength does not play an important role in many jobs, such sex differences still have significant presence and their effect cannot be ignored.

Based on this analysis, the shortcomings of Marxist and Feminist explanations are partly identified. Regarding Marxist explanation, it should be pointed out that there is not a causal functional relationship between family and capitalism; therefore, we cannot

---

1.This explanation should not be considered as merely reflecting Islamic value decree to gender division of labor in the family. In an Islamic society bound to religious values, this explanation can be a basis for analyzing the existing realities.
2. Horr Amelli ,*Wasael al-Shia* ,Vol 14, p123

consider family merely as a production of capitalist system; because if family, as the main unit of a society, is taken as a given in any other alternative system instead of capitalism, it will have a mutual interaction with social institutions of that system and will be conducive to its goals. Therefore, the basis of family life should not be challenged because of disagreeing with capitalism.[1] Moreover, as some feminists have reminded, if we regard women's domestic labors at the service of capitalism, we can make the same evaluation about women's employment outside the home; don't the wheels of capitalist machinery turn faster with the entry of women into the labor market!?

The same criticism can be mounted on the feminist explanation; if any use men make of women's work per se is absurd and condemned, the argument cannot be eliminated by changing the pattern of labor division, because men benefit tremendously from women's paid works as well.

Likewise, the use that women always have and do make of men's paid work is the other side of the issue that the feminist explanation has ignored. Indeed it arises from the direct effect of judgmental ethics in feminist theory. As a result, we should not explain the continuity of gender division of labor in the family merely based on men's use of women's domestic labor, rather we should base our analysis on the mutual advantage and benefit enjoyed by both men and women. As a result, instead of looking at the issue of men's use of women's domestic labor from an anti-male perspective and with an utterly negative attitude, we should study it from another perspective.

It can be said that although Islam has encouraged women to do domestic labors but has not considered them as women's duty and responsibility and, on the other hand, in actual practice, it has placed men at the service of women by obligating them to pay for women's alimony. Undoubtedly, the realities of family life in Islamic societies have been greatly affected by this ethical-legal view; thus, there is vivid and historical evidence before us for rejecting the chivalrously solicitous theory of feminism. Master Motahhari says:

> In Muslim families, the woman is not so much at the service of the man as the man is at the service of the woman by Islamic decree and in Islamic principle, and is the provider of the means for her well-being. It is only in families where the spirit of Islam does not exist or is weak that the woman is subjected to cruel insult and humiliation.[2]

o **Abstract**

- Division of domestic labor in the family has always been formed based on gender.
- Some sociologists argue that gender division of labor between man and woman originates from natural sex differences.

---

1. Tong , *Feminist Thought* ,p.57
2. Motahhari, *A collection of works (vol 19): The Issue of Hijab*, p52

- Some psychologists suggest that the difference between the duties and activities of men and women can reflect the tendency of men to create a distinctive masculine identity.
- Some feminist psychoanalysts have tried to explain gender division of labor within the family according to different personality of girls and boys which is formed during the process of socialization.
- Parsons stated that an optimal form of gender division of labor between the wife and husband provides the ground for performing basic functions of the family in decisively shaping a solid adult personality and socialization of the children and this issue has a fundamental role in the integration of the family and then in social stability.
- Anti- school theorists posit class system as the basis of unequal gender division of labor. As they believe the continuity of this pattern is due to the profit that the capitalist system makes from women's unpaid domestic labor.
- Radical feminists believe that the cause of the continuity of gender division of labor in the family is the profit that men make of labor division. A number of feminists have presented multi factor explanations of unequal division of labor in the family through the combination of existing feminist theories.
- In Islamic explanation, the existence of some innate but non-deterministic origin for division of labor in the family is taken for a given. Gender division of labor plays an undeniable role in safeguarding spiritual health of society by providing suitable ground for women to be less visible in male places which reduces the intermixture of them with non-mahrams.

o **Self –Test**

1. How do you evaluate the impact of biological features of man and woman on gender division of labor in the family?
2. Explain gender division of labor in the family from Islamic perspective.
3. Criticize Marxist and feminist explanations regarding gender division of labor in the family.

o **Research topics**

- Research gender division of labor in the two-job families
- Deduce a theory or some theories from Islamic point of view regarding gender division of labor in the family and do an empirical research about them.

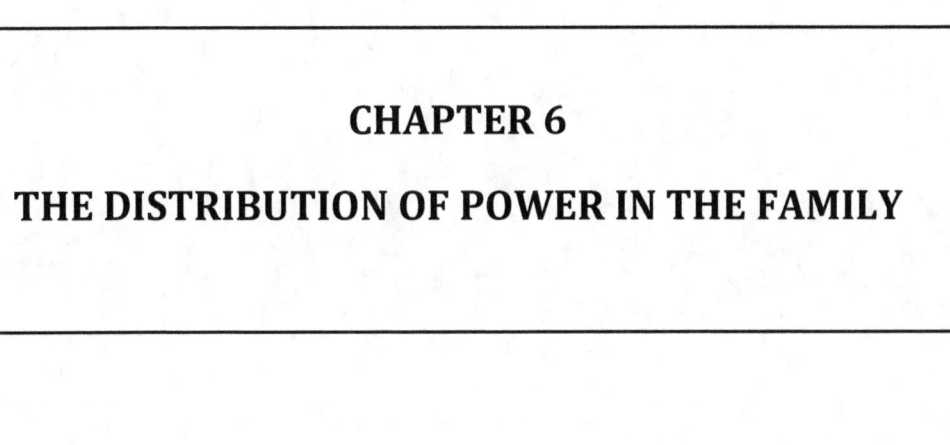

CHAPTER 6

THE DISTRIBUTION OF POWER IN THE FAMILY

Chapter 6

The distribution of power in the family

Learning objectives of chapter 6

Getting familiar with the theories of power distribution in the family and Islam's point of view in this regard.

Based on stage objective of this chapter, the reader is expected to achieve the following learning objectives and be able to:

1. describe the situation of power distribution in the family;
2. explain the most important biological, psychological and sociological theories of power distribution in the family;
3. analyze Islam's point of view regarding the distribution of power in the family.

Introduction

In this chapter after introducing the main concepts and providing a brief description about the patterns of power distribution in the family, different biological, psychological and sociological theories will be reviewed. Then the view point of Islam will be stated based on two explanatory and normative approaches. Finally, a brief evaluation on the democratic pattern of family will be provided.

6-1 Epistemology of the concepts

In the literature of social sciences, the terms such as patriarchy, matriarchy and democratic family are used for analyzing the issue of power distribution in the family, and in Islamic culture the Quranic concept of *'Qavamiyat'* is usually used for this purpose.

Power, Max Weber's states "is the ability of a person to impose his/her will on others despite resistance". This definition and similar definitions merely consider obvious aspects of power which are identified by parameters such as final decision makings in disputed issues.

Modern theorists have also emphasized hidden aspects of power which are associated with powerful and subordinate individuals' conflict of interests. These hidden aspects usually appear when subordinate individuals express their wishes and wills.[1] Considering this point, some have defined power as "the ability to influence, consciously or unconsciously, the feeling, attitude, cognition and behavior of another person".[2]

Since in almost all known societies, power balance, whether in the family or in social environment, has been marked in favor of men, special importance has been attached to the word "patriarchy "in this discussion. Patriarchy is a concept implying men's domination. In Weber's view, this concept refers to a system of power which

---

1.Komter ,"Hidden Power in Marriage " *Self and Society* ,p.360
2.Ibid , p.362

forms common denominator among the traditional societies. In these societies, within a group titled " household "which is organized based on economy and kinship, the authority is exercised by a certain person who is appointed by the definitive principle of inheritance. According to Weber, father, who refers to the master in the Feudal society, exercises his authority to both males and females, and as the head of the household he has complete control over economic activities and the behaviors of other members. It's clear that according to this term, patriarchy will not be a concept confined to the relationship between two sexes.[1] Radcliffe Brown has included features such as patrilineality, patrilocality (the departure of woman to her husband's house after marriage), leaving inheritance to the male linage, succession of son after his father's death and the granting power to father of the family in the definition of patriarchy.[2]

This term was widely used in feminist literature as a concept taking on political importance from the beginning of 1970s.Since common social theories lacked general concepts for explaining men's domination, radical feminists chose the concept of patriarchy to fulfill this purpose which in its new usage it refers to the ideas and practices ranging from the closest sexual encounters to major economic and ideological factors. Patriarchy was gradually used in the meaning that not only implied men's exercise of power over women in general terms , but also it included hierarchical characteristic of man's power and the ideological legitimacy of this power as something natural, normal , right and just.[3]

6-2 A description of power distribution in the family

The superiority of men's power over women, especially in the family environment, has been considered as a universal and common social phenomenon, so that even some limited claims about the existence of matriarchal systems or equality of man and woman's social status in the early periods of human's life and in current uncivilized societies have been questioned by modern anthropologists. As Kleinberg says, societies like Melanesia in which the decent is traced through the female line and the children's authority lies in the grasp of mother's family cannot be regarded as an evidence for matriarchy; since "this authority has been given to the men of the family not women; thus, the child should obey his uncle not his father, and the mother holds less power"[4]. Adducing to some historical evidence regarding the worship of goddesses in idolatry religions in ancient periods has been criticized too. The custom of goddess worship may indicate that the female sex was respected and venerable in old times but it does not prove the women's domination over men or even their equality with them[5]. Therefore, despite the fact that women in different societies and historical periods had different experiences of power and authority in the family and society, they always had less power than men and got inferior status.

But the development of egalitarian or democratic families in contemporary industrial societies indicates the changes occurring in traditional pattern of power

---

1 Bradley ,"Changing Social Structures : Class and Gender " , *Formations of Modernity*, p.181
2 Sarokhani ,*Encyclopedia of Sociology* , p525
3 Ramazanoglu, *Feminism and the Contradictions of Oppression*,pp.33-34
4 Kleinberg, *Social Psychology* , Vol 1 , p319.
5 Huvud, " Four Basic Topics of Feminism " , *Women* , issue 32, p31

distribution in the family. It is supposed that the wife and husband in these families have equal power in different areas of family life, especially in decision makings, the control of family income and sharing resources.

In these families the couples use one of these three methods in order to achieve an equal distribution of power: 1. Equal distribution of responsibilities 2. Full participation in all decision making processes 3. A combination of two previous methods.

Although many couples declare that there is an equal power balance in their marital life, the existing evidence suggests the pattern of full equality has not been widely used. In a research conducted at the beginning of 1980s, more than three thousand American couples were asked about power balance in their family. 64% of them reported equal power balance in their marital life. Most of the remaining couples declared that the husband has greater power and less than 9% reported the woman's domination.[1] According to another research carried out in 1986 in England, the egalitarian pattern was consistent with just one-fifth of the sample households and in other households the system of allocating properties to expenses was practiced in order to decrease or increase inequalities between the wife and husband.[2]

In this regard, it should be mentioned other studies which have dealt with the change of attitudes towards the parameters of marital power in recent decades; for example, according to a research conducted in 1962 on a group of American women, just 33% of the respondents rejected this proposition that " many important decisions in the family life should be made by men", but in 1980, 71% of the same sample rejected the mentioned proposition. [3]

6-3 Theories of power distribution in the family

To answer the question "what are the factors causing men's economic superiority itself?", different theories have been put forward which adopt a different perspective toward explaining the issue. In this discussion, three classes of theories will be reviewed: biological theories, psychological theories and sociological theories.

a) Biological theories

Biological explanations sometimes focus on the involvement of sex hormones in men's domination. According to these explanations, the male hormone (testosterone) strongly increases the men's inclination towards domination and control over others and since men produce higher levels of testosterone than women, they behave in a domineering manner.[4] Sometimes they consider men's greater physical strength as the source of their dominance and power, that is to say, since the man is so powerful to oblige the woman to obey him, it's natural to hold greater power for himself. These kinds of explanations focus on the anatomic sex differences, especially realities pertaining to childbearing and menstruation as factors exerting a debilitating effect on women.[5]

---

1 Taylor et al., *Social Psychology*, p.274
2 Vogler & Pahl, "Money ,Power and Inequality in Marriage" , *The Sociology of the Family*, chap.6
3 Schaefer , *Sociology*,p.324
4 Baron & Byrne ,*Social Psychology* ,p.186
5 Kleinberg , *Social Psychology* ,Vol 1, p319

Some explanations adduce to different evolution of man and woman. Some bio-sociologists argued that men have passed their evolution as hunters and food providers while women have developed as experts in child caring and housekeeping. Adding this fact to the assumption that men's activities are more important, we will conclude that men naturally have gained greater power and prestige and continue to do so.[1]

It is noteworthy that the focus on the biological factors as the source of men's domination and authority over women, can also be seen in some feminist theories. Relying on conducted research in 1970s, radical feminists have declared the role of physical strength in controlling women is more important than what has been previously supposed.[2] In this regard Mary Daly in her book *Gynecology* has dealt with violent methods used by men to dominate women and introduced men's "natural" violence as a determining factor in patriarchy and women's oppression.[3]

b) Psychological theories

Leadership theories in social psychology are among the theories which can present an explanation regarding men's greater authority. Although research on the leaders' unique personality characteristics – despite its rather long history – has not come to a clear and consensus conclusion, some required minimum characteristics have been emphasized by researchers as a distinction between the leaders and the followers. These characteristics include:

1. the superiority of a person in terms of the abilities which help the group achieve their goals ; such as intelligence , physical strength and special skills (for example , the best player of the team automatically undertakes the leadership of the team);
2. Superiority in terms of the skills regarding interpersonal interaction;
3. Higher motivation for being known and exert dominance by possessing characteristics such as ambition and taking responsibility.[4]

Accordingly, the men's authority can be explained based on a natural trend in which men's specific characteristics such as high physical strength, mental and physical skills to achieve the goals of the family group, a sense of adventure, domineering behavior and the like are involved. Furthermore, other theories which focus on the individuals' conscious or unconscious motivations and purposes, have dealt with a teleological explanation of men's domination over women. For instance, according to one of the feminist theories, since mother's body is the first world the child encounters, he experiences it as a symbol of an unreliable and unpredictable world. The mother is either a source of pleasure and a source of suffering for a child who is uncertain whether his physical and mental needs will be fulfilled or not; thus, develops an ambivalent feeling toward mothers (women). Men who do not want to experience absolute dependence on a very powerful authority once again try to control women. Women who are afraid of the mother's power within themselves tend to be controlled by men. These two processes will lead to specific gender arrangements along with some

---

1 Kammeyer et al., *Sociology : Experiencing Changing Societies* ,p.329
2 Jaggar, " Four Interpretations of Feminism(2), *Women*, issue 31, p42
3 Tong , *Feminist Thought* ,p.104
4 Sears et al.,*Social Psychology*,p.403

features which includes men's superiority over women in terms of sexual control and dominance, repressing the women's erotic drive, denying the women's personhood and treating them like an object and the division of labor which associates men to public area and women to private one.[1]

In addition to facing with serious ambiguities and problems regarding testing the hypotheses and generalizing the findings and are more like personal projections than scientific theories, such theories have been criticized because of ignoring physical and external factors of men's domination. Definitely, men could not achieve dominance over women merely by depending on internal motivations and without using levers such as high physical strength, economic dependence of women and legal and cultural supports.

c) Sociological theories

In explaining men's authority, we are faced with a set of sociological theories which form a wide range in terms of an emphasis on the economic and cultural factors or a combination of these factors with biological or psychic factors. Here, some important theories will be mentioned.

According to social exchange theory, three elements including social norms, resources and benefits determine how power should be divided in a relationship. Regarding first element we can set forth the norms such as the necessity of man's top position in the family and his priority in terms of age and money, higher education and a better job compared to women which lead to the men's greater power. The second element, resources, refer to anything which can be used to meet or repress the needs or what helps people get closer to or pushes them away from achieving their goals. Exchange theorists say that each of the couples who possesses greater resources (such as more money or knowledge or more attractive appearance) he/she will hold more power. The third element refers to this general assumption that each of two couples who gains less interests from the relationship, he/she will have more power and who is more dependent on the relationship will have less power.[2]

It is in the critical theories that the analysis of power relations is more frequently seen. Friedrich Engels in the book *The origin of the family, private property and the state*, put forward a view that was used as a basis for many subsequent Marxist and Socialist theories. According to him, at the beginning of human history, in a communal household composed of several couples and their children, women were in charge of managing household affairs but since their work was vital for the survival of the tribe and was regarded as a common essential industry, they enjoyed high social status. But the development of domestication of animals and stock breeding led to the emergence of a new source of wealth for human society, and since the control of the tribe's animals was undertaken by men, the accumulation of wealth by them caused the increase of their power compared to women. In contrast, the value of women's work and production decreased and their social status degraded. As a result, with the emergence of patriarchal families, particularly in monogamy form, the management of

---

1 Tong , *Feminist Thought*, pp.150-152
2 Taylor et al., *Social Psychology*,p.276

home affairs lost its public character and turned into a private service. Woman became the first housemaid and was excluded from engaging in social production.

The essence of Engels' view, i.e. the claim that men's dominance over women have its origin in the control of production means and possession of wealth, has been taken as a given or approved by subsequent researchers. Modern scholars declare that the women had less power in most agricultural societies; because the land was transferred to the son by his father based on inheritance system and consequently, women were not typically the owner of the land. Anthropological findings suggest that with the increase of women's economic participation, especially under the conditions that men are dependent on women's activities, their power increases and even sometimes it equals to men's power; For example, it is said that in some African tribes which women provided 60% to 80% of the tribe's food, their decision making power about the tribe's affairs was equal to that of men. Based on a new cross- cultural study conducted in 111 modern societies, the more the women participate in the work force, the less the men exercise their power over them.[1]

However, merely economic explanations do not provide a clear response to the question "what are the factors causing men's economic superiority itself?" Diverse theories have been put forward by theorists in order to compensate for this shortcoming. Focusing on the biology of reproduction and its necessities such as menstruation, menopause, gynecological diseases ,pregnancy and childbearing suffering, breastfeeding and child caring , some feminists have regarded these affairs as the origin of women's economic dependence on men over the course of history.[2] Others have drawn attention to the role of cultural elements in strengthening the foundations of patriarchy. Simone De Beauvoir has considered the myths made by men as the important factors involved in men's dominance over women and even she has included teachings of religions in these myths. She says:

> Legislators, priests, philosophers, writers and scientists have striven for a long time to show that the subordinate position of woman is willed in heaven and advantageous on earth. The religions invented by men [!] reflect this wish for domination.[3]

6-4 Islam's point of view

Islam's main texts have not directly dealt with the explanation of the factors contributing to men's domination, but by reflecting on religious rules and recommendations regarding family and its assumptions and requirements a multi-factor explanation can be inferred. In explaining this view, first of all, the role of biological factor should be focused on. Some hadiths have emphasized the women's relative inability and weakness and even it is derived from some narrations that this inability has a natural origin.[4] Undoubtedly, man's superior physical strength and woman's relative inability have provided the ground for the man to dominate the woman, whether we

---

1 Kammeyer et al., *Sociology: Experiencing Changing Societies*, p.327.
2 Firestone ,'' The Dialectic of Sex " ,*The Second Wave*,p.23
3 Peach ,*Women in Culture*,p.16
4 Horr Amelli ,*Wasael al-Shia* ,Vol 14, p119,121 and 131; Vol 15, P104-105

attach a deterministic aspect to it or regard other factors such as pregnancy, childbearing and breastfeeding as its origin.

Likewise, the difference between man and woman's psychological characteristics such as the dominance of rationality over emotions in men and the dominance of emotions over rationality in women which have been emphasized by Islamic narrations[1], probably has been the reason in most cases that led men to take over leadership position.

However, accepting the effectiveness of biological and psychological factors does not necessarily have to lead to adopting a deterministic view regarding men's domination , since undoubtedly other variables are also involved in this issue that any change or replacement in them can disrupt power balance between the wife and the husband. Probably economic and cultural factors should be regarded as the most important variables.

Regarding the economic factor, Surah An-Nisa' [verse 34] mentions that " Men are in charge of women by [right of] what Allah has given one over the other and what they spend [for infagh] from their wealth".

Seemingly, this verse is a religious decree which does not rest on objective relations but since the *Infaq* of men has been interpreted as paying alimony and mehriyeh to his wife,[2] this can be considered as a reason to award custody right to men. In addition, this decree has been stated in the form of a declarative sentence '*al-rejalou qawamoun*' which implicitly indicates the popular perception that economic superiority causes greater power. Regarding the role of culture factor, it can be referred to Islam's scientific and cultural combat with superstitious patriarchal beliefs and traditions of Ignorance Period when the women were put in an inferior position.

Therefore, regarding men's authority, we should not attribute a deterministic view to Islam, although by providing an explanation as it was discussed in division of labor, we can achieve a functionalistic explanation according to which man's superficial priority over woman in some areas of conjugal life and in the framework assigned by religious law, is advantageous for individual and social happiness and has positive functions.

So far, Islam's point of view was evaluated from an explanatory perspective. But from normative perspective it will suffice to mention that while Islam rejects many sex discriminations, in some cases it gives superficial superiority to men .On the one hand it has taken place because of considering natural differences between the man and woman and on the other hand given ideal goals of Islam's social system and the difference of man and woman's proper roles in the family system not because of privileging the men. The issue of power and domination does not figure in Islam as it does in secularist views; that is to say no preeminence has been given to these issues, and other issues are not analyzed in the light of them but they are subject to more important affairs such as the interests of the individual, family and society and also religious duties and values which have their root in those interests. Therefore,

---

1 Ibid ,Vol 14, p11; Majlesi ,*Bahar al-Anvar* ,Vol 32, p 73 , 106
2 Tabatabaie, *al-Mizan fi Tafsir al-Quran*, Vol 4, p 346

whenever true individual and collective interests require a specific pattern of roles and relations, that pattern is regarded as an ideal one in Islam .That is why in Islamic law we are sometimes faced with some cases such as the mother's breastfeeding to her infant in which the woman's power in decision making and exercising her opinion is more than that of man.

When it comes to the charge leveled against Islam[1] concerning its having a patriarchal and discriminatory approach, it seems that if we look at this issue from religious pint of view nothing but equality principle will govern the family relations; because any superficial superiority enjoyed by men over woman has been compensated by a kind of superiority or spiritual reward for the woman. In a narration, the Holy prophet (pbuh) says: "The woman's good treatment to the husband and her effort to get his satisfaction and be congruent with him in terms of divine reward equals all the virtues which has been determined to the man".[2]

But if we look at religious rulings and values from merely secularist perspective, we may observe some patriarchal parameters in them, but by reflecting on the extent of the rule of the validity of condition in marriage contract which has been approved in Shia jurisprudence ,it seems that from the Islamic point of view the husband's greater authority in the family to a large extent is a matter of agreement, that is, indeed ,a Muslim woman accepts some aspects of her husband's management despite being able to limit them and just small part of the components of the husbands' authority in the family has a mandatory aspect. Moreover, Islam has predicated the exercise of power, whether in the family or in other social realms upon observing justice, and even permitted the officials in charge to act legally with violators and those men who misuse their power against their wives.[3]

Islam has also tried to intenerate the relationship between the wife and husband and prevent it from turning to a relationship governed by power and dominance by combining power with moral characteristics such as modesty, endearment and forgiveness. In other words, Islam has resorted to moral and nurturing practices to limit the men's authorities; because in the family whose members have been adorned to moral virtues, family management never takes on dictatorial aspect because it is governed by mutual respect, empathy and kindness. It has been proved by experience that an internal control governed by faith and morality are the most effective factors of social control.

We close the discussion by a brief evaluation about the pattern of democratic family. Adducing to some research findings, the proponents of this pattern declare that marital satisfaction is subject to the possibility of equal decision making for the wife and husband, and the gender separation of management roles from the roles pertaining to domestic chores contrasts the wife and husband's harmony and the woman's satisfaction.[4]

---

1 Eferar , Surat al-Marat fi al-Ketabat al-Arabia al-Moaserah" , *Reference bulletin : Feminism*,p 196

2 Syuti, *al-Dorr al-Mansur* ,Vol 2, p153

3 Nouri , *Mostadrek al-Wasael* ,Vol 12, p337

4 Mitchell, *Sociology of Family and Marriage*, p127

One of the informal proponents of this pattern in order to reject the thought of the necessity of a single manager in the family likens the wife and husband to two friends who live together in an uninhabited island , in the sense that difficult condition of life in such an island causes complete co-operation , mutual understanding , affection between them and effaces the egocentric mood in them; similarly, the wife and husband due to strong emotional relationships and mutual need to each another and being aware of their role towards external challenges of life , neither do they develop a sense of officiousness and bossiness nor they find a need to be a nominal boss or subordinate , and in such a condition if they come to conflict with each other , they will resolve it by a peaceful and constructive dialogue which it will definitely lead to mutual understanding and congruity.[1]

Despite its superficial attractiveness, the mentioned pattern suffers from three fundamental shortcomings:

First is its idealistic feature; because none of its assumptions about the couples' strong affection, awareness and mutual feeling of need is compatible with concrete realities of the society. In other words, the democratic pattern or any other pattern is effective when it takes into consideration psychic and social realities such as the fact of many people being afflicted by selfishness, egocentrism and other moral deficiencies and it should not design the family system by ignoring these issues.

Second is the undeniable impact of other factors such as the difference of interests, tastes and the level of cognition and understanding on the emergence of conflict between the wife and husband which renders the expectation that all the marital conflicts will be resolved through dialogue unrealistic.

Third is the dramatic decrease of the family's integrity and the increase of divorce rate in the democratic families, a bitter reality that even the proponents of this pattern acknowledge it and sometimes call it an atonement for the new concept of marriage[2]. It's clear that when marriage institution is degraded to a companionship without commitment between two prospect friends, such consequences will not be surprising.

o **Abstract**

- Radical feminists chose the concept of patriarchy to explain the men's domination over women.
- The superiority of men's power over women has been considered as one of common and universal social phenomena.
- In explaining the men's domination, biological theories emphasize the role of factors such as sex hormones and physical strength.
- According to social psychological theories, in explaining men's greater authority, it can be focused on the factors such as management intelligence,

1 Qobanchi, *al-Marat, Concepts and* Rights ,p 123-124
2 Mitchell, *Sociology of Family and Marriage*, p 176

skills of interpersonal interaction, the motivation for domination, ambition, taking responsibility and a sense of adventure.

- Social exchange theory uses three concepts of social norms, more resources and less interests for explaining the men's greater authority.

- Marxist theory regards men's domination over women due to the control of production means and possession of wealth by men.

- From the Islamic point of view, we can achieve a functionalistic explanation according to which man's superficial superiority over woman in some areas of conjugal life and in the framework assigned by religious law, is advantageous for individual and social happiness and has positive functions.

- The proponents of democratic family pattern believe that marital satisfaction is subject to the possibility of equal decision making for the wife and husband, but this patterns suffers from some fundamental shortcomings.

o **Self-Test**

1. Explain men's greater authority in the family using leadership theories of social psychology.
2. Explain men's greater authority in the family using social exchange theory.
3. Explain men's greater authority in the family from the Islamic point of view.
4. By reflecting on the extent of jurisprudence rule of condition in marriage contract, it can be concluded that from the Islamic point of view the husband's greater authority in the family is greatly a matter of agreement.
5. State the fundamental shortcomings of democratic family pattern.

o **Research Topic**

- Research biological foundation of men's domination over women.
- Research democratic family pattern and its strengths and weaknesses.

PART III

FUNCTIONS OF THE FAMILY

The family in its various patterns has always performed diverse functions. From sociological perspective , the most important functions of the family have been identified as reproduction, protection and care , socialization ,regulation of sexual behavior, affection and companionship , provision of social status , religious education and nurturing , provision of legal father , social control ,meeting economic needs , transfer of material goods, filling leisure times, growth and stability of personality , continuity of gaps in social classes ,continuity of social conflicts and the creation of social changes. In this section, we will examine important aspects of family functions.

CHAPTER 7

BIO- SOCIAL FUNCTIONS OF THE FAMILY

Chapter 7

Bio- Social Functions of the Family

Learning objectives of chapter 7

Getting familiar with biological functions of the family and Islam's point of view in this regard.

Based on stage objective of this chapter, the learner is expected to achieve the following learning objectives and be able to:

1. explain functions of the family as regards regulation of sexual behavior, reproduction and care of the children and elderly from sociological perspective.
2. analyze Islam's point of view about these functions.

Introduction

In this chapter, we are going to examine those classes of family functions which have essentially a biological aspect; although they also carry broad social meanings and effects. These functions entail regulation of sexual behavior, reproduction and care of the children and elderly.

7-1 Regulation of sexual behavior

Human beings like any other animal species possess a strong sexual desire which are naturally drawn towards the opposite sex to satisfy it; but the human has always regulated his sexual relations and prevented from sexual chaos through marriage. Accordingly, sociologists have considered the regulation of sexual behavior as one of the fundamental functions of the family. Even in modern Western societies, despite the fundamental changes occurred in freedom of sexual relations in recent decades, the family still performs the function of regulating sexual behavior, although its exclusive role in satisfying sexual needs has faded into insignificance.

It's clear that performing this function by the family requires conditions beyond the principle of the existence of a legal family. Therefore, it does not come at the thin end of the expectations to see sexual deviations being committed by people suffering from severe family disorders. Phenomena such as incest, child abuse and other illegal sexual relations by married people have their root in the disorders which prevent the family from performing its role in satisfying the sexual desire.

One important point about this function is that unlike the traditional Christianity – which regards sexual desire as a negative issue and asks for repressing sexual desires outside the monogamous family- Islam (from a Shiite perspective) , by offering temporary marriage as a solution, has never identified legitimate satisfaction of sexual desire as an exclusive function of the family institution. The social consequence of these two different religious orientations is that the expansion of sexual freedom in Christian West in recent century has acquired an anti-religious character and a revolt against God while relative flexibility of Islamic rules and values has given Islam the potential to overcome social changes pertaining to sexual relations. Therefore, raising

the issue of temporary marriage in contemporary context of Iranian society has not caused serious tensions because of its religious support, rather it can be regarded as an instance of return to religious traditions which many theorists, regardless their slight disagreements, agree on its principle.

The issue that needs attention is that the capacity of Islamic rules by itself is not sufficient to overcome new emerging problems, and without accurate and scientific expertise in order to apply these rules given specific temporal and local conditions and circumstances, the mentioned potential will not be actualized. That is why despite the legitimacy and legality of temporary marriage in Islamic society of Iran we have been witnessing the expansion of illegal patterns of sexual relations in recent years.

Other point is associated with the difference of men and women's sexual needs. Given physiological differences between the man and woman in terms of sexual activities and desires, woman's sexual pleasure has been considered something of a low value in most societies[1] and it means the function of regulating sexual behavior is not achieved for men and women in the same way. Therefore, feminists have voiced the criticism that the women's sexual desire has usually been held in abeyance or regarded abnormal unless when it is considered as a complement for the men's sexual needs.[2] Even in modern world which women's sexual need has been recognized by virtue of the development of sexual biological studies, satisfying sexual desires is still defined based on masculine criteria and the man's sexual drive is assumed to be stronger than that of woman.[3]

Islam accepts the differences between the man and woman's sexual desire and attaches a biological origin for it. It is derived from Islamic narrations that male's sexual derive is superior and stronger in terms of quantity and female's sexual derive in terms of quality. Female's sexual restraint is more than that of male and the degree of male and female's sexual arousal is also different.[4]

Based on these differences, Islamic jurisprudence has determined different rights and duties for men and women concerning the satisfaction of sexual desire. However, Islam has specifically focused on fulfilling the woman's sexual need within the framework of the family and provided the ground for performing the mentioned function regarding women by making a set of legal regulations as well as obligatory and

1 Goode , *The Family* ,p.15
2 Ramazanoglu ,*Feminism and the Contradictions of Oppression* ,p.64
3 Abbott & Wallace, *An Introduction to Sociology of Feminist Attitudes* , p188
4 Horr Amelli ,*Wasael al-Shia* , Vol 14 , p40-42; Vol 15,p 452; Also refer to : Majlesi ,*Bahar al-Anvar* ,Vol 3, p 62

recommended rules for the husbands.[1] Islam's special attention to the women's sexual need has caused the famous Arab feminist, Naval Al-Sadavi to confess that:

> Mohammad [pbuh] has superiority over most modern men in terms of his understanding of sexuality and also his courage to confess to such affairs like foreplay that most cultivated Arab men never confess or had great difficulty in confessing them. (Eferfar; 1999, P.177).[2]

7-2 Reproduction

The reproduction function which is sometimes called replacement, is one of the essentially biological functions of the family that has always guaranteed the continuity of societies and generally the continuity of human generation. Since reproduction has had a close relationship with satisfying sexual desire, it has followed a relatively steady trend over the course of history but due to profound changes arisen from industrial and scientific revolution in West and along with the development of the means and techniques of birth control which resulted in the separation of these two functions, preproduction function fluctuated over the last two centuries. For example in England, marriages held about the year 1860 produced averagely six children, while this figure decreased to two children in the next two generations.[3] In France, while birth rate stood as 40 per 1000 between 1750 and 1754, it declined to 13/1 per 1000 in 1941 and reached 20/3 per 1000 between the years 1946 and 1953.[4] Coincident with the decrease of birth rate in most Western countries in recent decades the rate of birth decreased in France once again and reached 14 per 1000 in 1987.[5]

Currently, fertility rate in most European countries has reached below replacement level. It means that per two adult persons, less than two children are born. As a result, the number of birth is not enough to keep the population rate stable. For instance, fertility rate in Spain and Italy has reached less than 1/3 children per woman; this rate is 1/8 in Britain and it is 2 children in European Union just in Ireland; fertility rate has decreased to 1/44 children per woman in the whole of Europe.[6]

Now, more than 85% of developing countries have officially approved the policies of family planning or have practically applied methods concordant with these policies which has led to a dramatic decline in population growth. For instance, in Iran, the average number of children per woman has dropped from 6 children in 1961 to 3 children in 1996.[7] In some of these countries, like European countries, the fertility rate has reached below replacement level; for example, the average number of family

1 Refer to : Horr Amelli ,*Wasael al-Shia* ,Vol 14, p82-83 , 100

2 Eferar , Surat al-Marat fi al-Ketabat al-Arabia al-Moaserah" , *Reference bulletin : Feminism*, p177

3 Lenski et al., *Human Societies* ,p.354

4 Segalen, *Historical Sociology of Family* ,p 185

5 Persa," Birth and Fertility ", *Population and Demography*, p66

6 Bernards , *An Introduction to Family Studies* , p41

7 Amani , *Foundations of Demography* , p84

members is 3/51 persons in South Korea, whereas it was 5/29 in 1995 and the rate of fertility in Kuba reached 1/6 in the late 1990s.[1]

Changing the economic activities of traditional families , the process of industrialization has made a major impact on the decrease of birth rate ; but other factors such as the high cost of family formation and managing it and consequently, an increase of marriage age and delay in fertility time, the expansion of contraceptives ,weakening of family bonds, new ideologies regarding women's identity and status and their effort to achieve independence and more freedom and more suitable occupational opportunities were involved in this affair insofar as today in the Western world we are faced with considerable number of the couples who prefer not to have a child at all. According to statistics, in 1995, the families comprising the couples without a child made up 28/9 percent of all American households.[2]

Feminist theorists have articulated different and sometimes conflicting views about reproduction function. Relying on the theory that biological differences between males and females, especially the women's reproduction capacity have been the main factors of sex inequalities over history, Shulamith Firestone recommends the women to resort to the advanced technology of reproduction. He believes that given new technical developments, including reliable ways of pregnancy prevention, the possibility of ectopic pregnancy, the production of in vitro infants and nurturing the children outside the family have made it possible for women to get rid of their biological restrictions.[3] But late feminists have often rejected this theory and warned about the possibility of women being rendered useless and needless by the expansion of the use of reproductive technologies.[4] Many feminists believe that women, instead of taking passive stance toward experiences such as pregnancy and childbirth which makes them alienating experiences, they should treat them actively and revive pleasures of pregnancy.[5]

In an overall evaluation, it seems that although the decrease of reproduction has partly arisen from socio-economic necessities in recent decades, the impact of new emerging ideologies and cultural values cannot be ignored in this regard. If the decrease of reproduction be merely based on the mentioned necessities, it should not be regarded as a social dilemma; but the intervention of radical ideologies which promulgate self-centric and comfort-seeking attitudes can result in a negative growth of population with which most European countries are faced. Although diverse policies have been implemented to increase the birth rate and halt descending trend of fertility in these countries, the efficiency of these actions is vague and limited.[6]

---

1 Adams, " Families and Family study in International Perspective ", *Journal of Marriage and Family 66* ,p. 1083
2 Shepard , *Sociology* ,p.303
3 Jaggar,"Human Biology in Feminist Theory : Sexual Equality Reconsidered", *Knowing Women* ,p.81
4 French ,*War against Women* ,p331-332
5 Tong ,*Feminist Thought* ,p.80
6 Segalen ,*Historical Sociology of Family* ,p323

Given Islam's point of view about reproduction and influenced by experiences of these countries, the necessity of reconsidering some elements of population control policies adopted in the countries like Islamic republic of Iran in recent years, is felt. The main focus of this reconsideration is the distinction which should be made between the two classes of factors, i.e. socio-economic necessities on the one hand and new emerging ideologies and values on the other hand. There is no doubt that religious texts put an utterly positive valuation on reproduction and proliferation of generation; for instance, in a well-known hadith the Holy Prophet (pbuh) has considered a greater number of people in Muslim nations as a source of pride over other nations on the Day of Judgment.[1] However, observing the principle of necessity in Islamic legislation which is one of the definite tenets of Shia dynamic jurisprudence, provides the religious justification required for proper methods of birth control, provided that the evidence of necessity be properly recognized.

Therefore, it would have been more preferable if the policy makers of birth control instead of promulgating values such as the less children ,the more comfort which in addition to be inconsistent with Islamic values it may pose the problem of descending trend of population in the long term for the country, have tried to take advantage of the religious inclination of the majority of Iranian population to internalize the necessity of birth control in public minds as a specific social necessity and in a jurisprudence interpretation as an emergency and alternative order , so that possible changes in the future requires the adoption of policies to increase the birth rate , the rejection of new policies by people among whom the spirit of carefreeness and comfort-seeking have become an established habit would not make trouble for the country.

Reproduction within the family beyond the importance it has in terms of the survival of human generation, possesses other important social effects including legitimizing the children and determining their social status. Legitimizing the children or providing a legal father for them in other words, brings other social effects such as regular transfer of inheritance and the continuity of kinship system. Malinowski has related the legitimacy of the child to the holding of a position inside the network of relatives. In his words it is this kinship system which determines the rights of infant in the area of care, inheritance and education.[2] Malinowski also regards the principle of legitimacy as a universal principal and says:

> In all human societies and in all cases marriage is a pre-requirement for pregnancy. In all human societies, the moral tradition and law do not recognize a group consisting of a woman and her children as a social unit… Law, ethic, customs say: a family without a man is incomplete.[3]

But the dramatic increase of illegal birth in Western societies, especially after World War II, was the issue that caught the attention of many sociologists. In the US, from 1940 to 1969, per 100 Colored new born infants,17 infants were illegal and in 1969 this figure reached 31 and for Whites in the said period it reached from 2 percent

1 Horr Amelli , *Wasael al-Shia*, Vol 14,p3
2 Zanden, *Sociology: The Core*, p.282.
3 Mitchell , *Sociology of Family and Marriage* , p137

to 5/3 percent.[1] In England in 1998, 25/6 percent of the total number of live births took place out of wedlock while ten years before it the mentioned rate was 10/2 percent.[2] Other statistics indicate that in 1994, in England, France, Denmark and Sweden 32, 35, 47 and 50 percent of births took place out of wedlock respectively.[3]

Two solutions have been proposed for this problem: 1. The decrease of sexual behavior out of wedlock 2.The change of cultural attitudes towards sexual relationship without marriage to protect the children born to unmarried mothers.[4] It's clear that the second solution is not a real one rather it's merely coming to terms with the mentioned problem and it can easily be predicted that this solution may cause the expansion of illegitimacy phenomenon. Hence, adopting the policies to decrease non-marital sexual relationships is the only reasonable solution for the problem of illegal births and the only solution which is compatible with Islamic values.

Islam has emphasized the necessity of the child's legitimacy and its effects, particularly taking the responsibility of her/his nurturing by parents, systematic transfer of inheritance and the continuity of kin relationships. We read in a narration:

> A person asked Imam Jafar Sadiq (AS): Why did God forbid adultery? He replied: because of the corruptions which it entails; such as the decline of inheritance system and the breakup of individuals' ancestral lineage. [Probably] the woman committing adultery does not know who from among the men she has had relationship with made her pregnant and the child born does not know her/his father and [as a result] he/she will be deprived of the blessing of kinship ties and familiarity with close relatives.[5]

In some narrations committing homicide (through abortion) and the parents' refusal to nurture their children have been counted as the negative consequences of the child's illegitimacy.[6] Undoubtedly, illegitimacy is among the main factors of the increase of abortion in contemporary world and a large number of nursery children are illegal.

Another effect of reproduction within the family is determining the child's social status. Several ascribed factors (non-acquired factors) such as class, race, ethnicity, sex, age and partly religion have been identified by sociologists as being involved in determining the individuals' social status, i.e. the position they acquire in social hierarchy.

Definitely the family in which a person is born transfers some of these ascribed features through which it determines his/her social status; for example, a person who is born in a poor family will probably be identified as one of the members of the lower class of society.

Similarly, in a society in which racial, ethnic or religious discrimination is practiced, the family depending on which race or ethnicity or religion it belongs to, plays a

---

1 Ibid ,p 157
2 McLoughlin, *The Demographic Revolution*, p.23
3 Giddens , *Sociology* ,p100-101
4 Cotgrove, *The Science of Society : An Introduction to Sociology*,p.61
5 Horr Amelli, *Wasael al-Shia*, Vol 14,p 252
6 Ibid , p 234; Vol 18,p 431

decisive role in acquiring higher or lower social status of its members. Of course, everyone can promote his/her social status by effort and perseverance to obtain its acquired factors such as wealth and education and this is perfectly evident in societies with high social mobility, but acquired factors and opportunities required to acquire them are partly influenced by the individual's ascribed social status.[1]

It seems that Islam takes for granted the difference of individuals in ascribed social status and the role of family in determining this status in most cases. The Holy Quran regards the difference of social status – where it arises from economic factors- as a difference in ranks and hierarchies and places it in the line with social traditions by attributing it to God, the Creator of the Universe.[2] Yet, Islam rejects unfair taking advantage of the mentioned factors.

7-3 Care of the children and elderly

Unlike many animal species, the inability of human baby to protect itself continues until several years after the birth, and it makes the physical care and protection of the child necessary. Moreover, the infirmity of human in old ages which many individuals encounter in their life as well as the disabilities due to a physical defector disease intensify the necessity and importance of caring.

Legal and moral responsibility of performing this important issue has fallen on the family's shoulders over the course of history. Even in contemporary industrial societies where varied welfare programs have been performed to support the infirm individuals, the law asks the parents to protect their children appropriately and the government undertakes this responsibility just when the parents prove their failure to perform this responsibility or when the parents are absent or unavailable.[3] Regarding the care of elderly, the children still shoulder the main responsibility. In 80 percent of cases, any care an elderly person needs is provided by his/her family and this is due to the strong commitment existing between the parents and the child even in the case that their emotional relationship is not strong.[4]

However, many changes have occurred regarding this function: such as the increasing development of nurseries, kindergartens, nursing homes and disabled sanatoriums. It seems that in this case the mothers' employment is also the most important effective factor in the occurrence of these changes. A research conducted in 1976 in France regarding care facilities of 800,000 children under 3 years old with working parents indicates that 143,618 children were supervised by institutions organized and run by government authorities, 70,000 infants were cared for by the individuals employed for this purpose and 85,000 children were cared by grandmothers and 50,000 of the remaining infants were cared for by informal nurses (neighbors or at irregular intervals by different individuals). Also, institutions known as "maternal school" dedicated to older children (above two years old) had about 500,000 infants

---

1 Almquist et al., *Sociology : Women ,Men and Society*, p.346
2 Surah Zokhrof , 32
3 Stokes ,*Introduction to Sociology* ,p.294
4 Zanden ,*Sociology :The Core*, p.298

under their protection at the same time.[1] Also, in the US in 1982, out of the total number of infants below 5 years old with working mothers, 15 percent were cared for in group service centers – nurseries or daily care centers – while in 1965, just 6 percent of infants below 6 years old with working mothers were cared for within a group.[2]

Feminists have viewed childcare function of the family from the perspective of sex inequality. According to them although men in comparison with previous periods have made a greater contribution in taking care of the children and elderly, sex is still considered as an effective factor in the quantity and quality of performing this function. Studies indicate that even in 1980s, the rate of American men's direct and active involvement in nurturing the children was one third of mother's involvement and even in the case of working mothers, the fathers' participation has only increased slightly. In terms of quality, while mothers undertake activities like feeding, bathing and the children's cleanliness, fathers deal with recreational cares and playing with children.[3] Regarding elderly, the girls usually provide practical care and emotional support while the boys often monitor and provide financial assistance and they directly engage in the caring only when there is no daughter available.[4] According to statistics, the girls are likely to care for the parents three times more than boys and in most cases taking care of elderly falls upon the girls and brides' shoulders.[5]

Feminist writers ask: why childcare is considered as a mothers' duty and why fathers do not shoulder the responsibility of caring for the children? According to them, most of the parents' duties towards the children are included within the notion of "motherhood" and the notion of "fatherhood" merely implies a general help and support. Therefore, the women who shirk from the maternal responsibility, finally should apologize or feel sorry, guilty and frustrated.[6]

Giving a mythical image of motherhood in its common cultural meaning and ignoring all biological aspects of motherhood, Ann Oakley declares that the nature of motherhood is nothing but the expression of affection within a warm relationship inclined toward caring. In rejecting the claim of children's need for a mother she cites as evidence what she considers successful experiences such as: adoption systems, social motherhood (in orphanages), contracted motherhood, shared breastfeeding, giving suckling babies to nurses, nurturing by relatives in extended families and collective nurturing in Israeli Kibbutz.[7]

In contrast, many feminist theorists by supporting the pattern of "joint parenting" have adopted a more moderate approach to the child-care issue. A movement known as "family- oriented feminism has taken on the revival of family and maternal role as its principle task. Jean Bethke Elshtain, one of the theorists of this movement says:

---

1 Segalen , *Historical Sociology of Family*, p215
2 Wilkie,"Marriage ,Family Life, and Women's Employment" , *Marriage and Family in Transition* ,p.154
3 Santrock & Yussen ,*Child Development : An Introduction* ,pp.324-325
4 Perlmutter & Hall ,*Adult Development and Aging*,p.375
5 Zanden, *Sociology: The Core* ,p.298
6 Lott ,*Women's Lives*,p.222
7 Oakley, *Woman's work : The Housewife ,Past and Present* ,p.203

Mothering is not a "role" on par with other roles. Mothering is a complicated, rich, ambivalent, vexing, joyous activity which is biological, natural, social, symbolic, and emotional ... A tendency to downplay the differences that pertain between, say, mothering and holding a job, not only drains our private relations of much of their significance, but also over-simplifies what can and should be done to alter things for women.[1]

It is noteworthy that some feminist theorists have even emphasized the role of biological factors in distinguishing the parental and maternal roles. Adducing to the fact that women innately have a keener understanding and more sensitivity to the children's needs, and emphasizing that the mother's bond with her children has a biological aspect and the father's bond with them has a social aspect, Alice Rossi concludes that women unlike men have a closer and natural bond with the children's nurturing and therefore, a more natural environment should be provided for nurturing the children.[2]

Islam has emphasized the necessity of mother's breastfeeding the infant in the cases that his/her life depends on her milk.[3] Furthermore, it can be derived from religious recommendations about breastfeeding that Islam has attached a priority to breastfeeding babies by biological mothers as well as to full breastfeeding that its limit is between 21 to 24 months.[4] In this regard, the mother's milk has been regarded as the the best milk; We read in a narration stated by Imam Jafar Sadiq:" No milk is greater in bounty for the baby than the mother's milk".[5]

Regarding elderly, Islam has emphasized treating the parents kindly and avoiding any treatment resulting in their annoyance. It has been stated in a hadith:

A person said to Imam Jafar Sadiq(AS) :My father is very aged and weak, so, when he has to answer the call of nature we take him on our shoulders .He replied : if you can , you yourself undertake this duty and put the morsel in his mouth with your own hand; because in the Last Day he will be a shield for you against God's torture.[6]

On the other hand , the decrease of family role in this regard and the performance of this role by alternative institutions sometimes bear some requirements or it takes place in such ways that are incompatible with the mentioned values. Negative effects of these methods on the elderlies' personality in the first place and loss of individual motivations for caring and rearing the children in the second place, partly prove the reason for Islam's disagreement with such methods.

It seems that Islam's emphasis on caring by women, especially on maternal role, on the one hand arises from some natural differences between man and woman which

1 Tong, *Feminist Thought*,p.33

2 Ibid,p.159; Hekman ,*Gender and Knowledge* ,p.138

3 Feiz Kashani ,*Tafsir al-Safi* ,Vol 1, p 261; Sistani ,*Menhaj al-Salehin* ,Vol 3, p119-120

4 Refer to Surah Baghareh ,233; Loghman ,14; Ahghaf ,15; Also refer to " Shahid Sani ,*Masalek al-Afham* ,Vol 8, p 416; Sistani ,Ibid, p.120.

5 Horr Amelli, *Wasael al-Shia*,Vol 15,p 175; Also refer to :Ibid, p188

6 Ibid , p 220-221. About treating the parents kindly also refer to : Surah Asra , 23-24

Islam takes for granted and on the other hand it is based on a teleological explanation which revolves around the positive functions of the distinction between the man and woman's duties; as a result, Islam considers this issue as a major priority not a necessity.

The fact that mothers bear enormous difficulties during pregnancy, childbearing, breastfeeding and nurturing the children cannot be ignored and these difficulties naturally impose some restrictions on them; but due to the importance Islam attaches to the mother's unique role in the growth and sublimity of human society, it has tried to strengthen the mothers' psychic health and feeling of satisfaction and hope and encourage them to perform their important role by focusing on the spiritual aspects and otherworldly rewards of motherhood and by strict orders regarding kindness to the parents.[1]

It should be mentioned that negative stance taken up by many feminists about motherhood, partly arises from exaggerated claims made in Western culture about the importance of caring and rearing of children by biological mothers, especially in 19th century and early 20th century. Although Islam has attached a priority to the caring of the children by their biological mothers it has adopted relatively open and reflexible position towards maternal role by accepting the patterns of adoption, contracted motherhood and being cared for in the extended family with relatives' participation.

o **Abstract**

- Regulation of sexual behavior is one of the fundamental functions of the family whose direct effect is preventing from sexual chaos.
- Islam accepts the differences between the man and woman's sexual desire and attaches a biological origin for it.
- Reproduction within the family beyond the importance it has in terms of the survival of human generation, possesses other important social effects including legitimizing the children and determining their social status.
- The decrease of reproduction in recent decades has partly arisen from socio-economic necessities, but the impact of new emerging ideologies and cultural values in this regard should not be ignored.
- Legal and moral responsibility of caring for the children, elderly and sick people has fallen on the family's shoulders over the course of history.
- Feminists have viewed childcare function of the family from the perspective of sex inequality.
- A movement known as family- oriented feminism has taken on the revival of family and maternal role as its principle task.
- Islam attaches a priority to the caring of the children by their biological mothers.

o **Self-Test**

1. Through which mechanisms did the global decrease of birth rate take place?

---

[1] Horr Amelli ,*Wasael al-Shia*, Vol 15,p 204-208,216-218

2. Is the policy of population control compatible with Islamic teachings? Explain.

3. What does the function of determining the social status of the child by the family mean?

4. The function of legitimizing the children has two important social effects; state them.

5. Does the pattern of maternal care have merely social origin or does it have a biological basis? Explain.

o **Research Topic**

- Analyze the realization of the tradition of temporary marriage in Iranian society from a social engineering point of view.
- Research the situation of the care for the elderly in one of the areas of the country.
- Research the family- oriented feminist viewpoints.

CHAPTER 8

SUPPORTIVE FUNCTIONS OF THE FAMILY

Chapter 8

Supportive functions of the family

Learning objectives of chapter 8

Getting familiar with supportive functions of the family and Islam's point of view in this regard

Based on stage objective of this chapter, the reader is expected to achieve the following objectives and be able to:

1. explain functions of the family concerning emotional and livelihood support from the sociological point of view;
2. analyze Islam's point of view regarding these functions.

Introduction

The family institution provides a variety of supports for its members the most important of which are as follows: spiritual support, emotional support and livelihood support. Each of these functions can be subdivided depending on whether it is realized in the relationship between the spouses, the relationship between the parents and children or the relationship between the relatives. In this chapter three kinds of supports in the family will be reviewed in brief.

8-1 Spiritual support

From the Islamic point of view, one of the functions expected from the family is the family members' cooperation and spiritual support for each other. Perhaps in no sociological text this function of the family has been mentioned and that is because the scholars of this branch primarily focus on the actual functions of the family not its expected or potential functions, while even in Islamic societies not so many families can be found to have fulfilled this function, let alone in Western societies which are to some extent materialist and de-spiritualized.

However, religious Saints have paid special attention to this function in order to spread religious culture in the society. It has been mentioned in some narrations that one of the characteristics of a good spouse is helping his/her spouse in worshiping the God and fulfilling religious duties.[1] We observe the same interpretation in words of Imam Ali (AS), the Commander of Believers, who admires Hazrat Zahra (AS) in the first morning after their marriage and says to the Holy Prophet (pbuh) "she [Fatimah] is a good help in worshiping God".[2]

8-2 Emotional support

a) **Emotional support in the relationship between the spouses**

Many sociologists believe that considering the fact that the family institution in contemporary industrial societies has lost many of its former functions, satisfying

---

1 Ibid, Vol 14 and 24
2 Majlesi ,*Bahar al-Anvar*, Vol 43, p117

emotional needs is the most important function that can explain the survival of the family in these societies. It's clear that emotional support can be found, more or less, in other environments such as occupational or educational environments, but a large number of individuals find their most satisfactory personal relationships with their spouses, parents and children or other relatives. Usually individuals look for physical and psychological security within the family and regard family as a refuge against conflicts and struggles which exist in the world outside. Even many people who seek for a divorce because of failing to find the security and happiness they need, form a new family once again to achieve that goal.[1]

In explaining why in industrial societies, emotional support has taken on an outstanding importance among other functions of the family, sociologists mention two classes of structural and cultural factors. The structural factors designate the factors such as life in industrial cities which have caused relative isolation of the conjugal family. Unlike the societies in which the conjugal family is placed within the broad network of kinship and neighborhood relations, in industrial societies the family is almost the only source which provides the most emotional engagement for many adults. Since kinship and neighborhood networks have been weakened, the spouse of a person is inevitably considered as his only friend and companion and the only one with whom he/she can spend most of the time. Cultural factors also designate the change of public attitude towards marriage. In societies like America, the dominant attitude is that marriage should be based on emotional attraction and mutual love between the two couples, and the high rate of divorce in these societies indicates the importance of this function as a basis for marriage; that is, since love is the basis of marriage, with the fading of it we can expect the breakdown of marriage. While in other societies where other functions of the family are considered more important, even if the spouses do not experience a high level of satisfaction, the likelihood of the continuity of marriage bond will be greater.[2]

However, a realistic view to modern family unveils disturbing aspects of family life especially marital conflicts and tensions which have been taken into consideration by critical views. Due to the extensive social changes and the growth of individualistic values, many issues that were agreed upon before, have been turned into a center for disagreements and disputes between the young couples. For example, given high rate of the women's employment, the proportion of the women who expect their husband's participation in house chores has dramatically risen.[3]

Moreover, the women's employment has created new conditions about which there are no established norms; for example, in a conjugal family which both of the couples receive salary, they are likely to come into conflict about how family property should be divided or used.

---

1 Almquist et al .,*Sociology :Women,Men and Society*,p.347

2 Stokes, *Introduction to Sociology*, pp.294-295

3 Wilkie,"Marriage, Family Life, and Women's Employment", *Marriage and Family in Transition*, p.146.

The explanation of some aspects of family tensions which reflect sex inequality has specifically been followed by feminist writers. Ann Oakley says:

> Through the deep separation between lives of men and women, tension is built into the structure of marriage 'it is not an exaggeration to say that the "row" is an institution for the present family .The "row" is the expression of discontent by both of the spouses which has become a regular practice; but the wife's frustrations are more often the activating factor. Her dissatisfactions are greater; while the husband, deprived of emotional satisfaction, protests at his exclusion from the supportive intimacy of close family relationships, the wife, deprived of 'personhood', protests against the completeness of her captivity: 'there's nothing I can do … Where could I go?[1]

In explaining the fact that the family life brings two different levels of emotional support for the man and woman, feminists, in addition to the factors like inequality in division of labor and power distribution between the men and women, adduce to double-standard cultural norms which regard satisfying the partner's emotional needs as the husband's right and the wife's duty.[2]

From the Islamic point of view, peace of mind resulting from the love and affection between the wife and husband are considered as divine signs[3] which may point to the fact that marital relationship unlike other social relationships (occupational, business, educational and etc.) embodies a unifying and binding factor which guarantees the continuity of this relationship despite all contradictions and conflicts of interests and desires between wife and husband. However, there is no doubt that manifestation of this divine sign and actualization of its effects in the family life and then the wife and husband's enjoyment of each other's emotional support depends on the absence of some obstacles which we are going to mention the most important ones.

Of the major obstacles is sexual freedom. In fact, one of the main reasons for the prohibition of extramarital sexual relationships in Islam and also the focus on the women's *hijab* and restriction of the women's association with men is to provide a ground for the formation of families built upon love and intimacy. In this regard Master Motahari says:

> The underlying reason for women's covering and forbiddance of sexual fulfillment by someone other than the lawful wife in terms of family sociology is that the person's lawful wife be regarded as the only means of the man's psychological happiness, whereas in the system of sexual freedom the lawful wife is considered a nuisance and inconvenience and a warden or watchman and therefore the family is come to be based on enmity and hatred.[4]

---

1 Oakley,*Woman's work: The Housewife ,Past and Present*,p.64.
2 Lengerman and Brantley," Contemporary feminist Theory", *Sociological Theory in Modern World* ,p 476.
3 Surah Rome, 21
4 Motahhari , *A Collection of Works* , (Vol 19) : *The Issue of Hijab*, p 437-438

Meaning crisis is the second obstacle for the individuals to achieve love and emotional support within the family, a crisis that West is trapped in because of moving away from religious beliefs and values. The contradiction between personal freedom and emotional security , between independence and responsibility , between egotism and altruism[1] which ultramodern males and females have faced with and in many cases , these contradictions have brought them into conflict and hostility with each other , cannot be removed but by redefining objectives of life based on religious teachings.

Islam on the basis of its world-view regards moral and spiritual values as superior values and tries to instill these values among people; but material and worldly values have been considered not as main and ultimate values but as secondary values and subordinate to spiritual values. Naturally people trained with such an attitude are less likely to feel disappointment and frustration if they cannot completely achieve worldly values such as material comfort, freedom, independence and emotional and sexual satisfaction. Accordingly, affection and mutual emotional support between the wife and husband can be considered as a reflection of this change in attitude within the family.

The weakness of faith and morality is another obstacle which has the potential to problematize the function of emotional support in the family. From the perspective of religious and mystical anthropology, since the human in his nature aspires to absolute perfection and beauty, naturally he loves all perfections and beauties, especially good deeds and moral acts, and inversely hates evil deeds and indecencies. That is why good temper naturally attracts others' affection and the Holy Quran refers to this truth where it quotes:" Indeed, those who believe and do righteous deeds – God the Most Merciful plants the seeds of affection in the hearts of all toward him".[2] Likewise, according to some authentic narrations, faith and good deeds increase the believer and righteous person's affection towards others. In a narration, Imam Sadiq (AS) has specifically mentioned the point that the increase of the husband's faith and religious belief results in the increase of his affection towards his wife.[3]

Furthermore, genuine and lasting affection is subject to fulfilling a set of moral preconditions such as sincerity, trusteeship, faithfulness, respect and benevolence which the lack or deficiency in any of them from any party, can bring emotional instability of other party involved. Thus, the weakness of faith and morality, due to its negative effects on the individual's behavior, has a direct relationship with the decline of emotional function of the family. Scientific findings and even daily experiences of the individuals strongly confirm this correlation.

Apart from the mentioned obstacles, the lack of skill in establishing an intimate relationship with others plays a significant role in failing to fulfill emotional needs of the family members which strengthening communication skills through public education using facilities of mass media, schools, consultation centers and the like can be very effective in removing this obstacle.

---

1 Heller, "Women, Civil Society and the State," *The Second Sex*, p 60.
2 Surah Maryam, 96.
3 Horr Amelli, *Wasael al-Shia*, Vol 14, p 9.

It is noteworthy that Islam's specific attention to satisfying emotional needs of the wives by their husbands, suggests non-discriminatory approach as well as a favoring and supporting attitude to woman in the area of emotional support. Among abundant evidence of this issue we can refer to recommending the men to maintain an appropriate association with their wives,[1] introducing the husband's forgiveness of the spouse's fault as a rights of woman over man,[2] recommending to verbal expression of affection to the wife,[3] recommending the husband to keeping an elegant and attractive physical appearance for his wife[4] and dressing nicely for the sake of her.[5]

b) Emotional support in the relationship between the parents and children

Parents and children play a significant role in satisfying their mutual emotional needs. Given the parents' more outstanding role in this regard, psychological and sociological studies often have dealt with the parents' emotional support for the children , whereas the impact of children on meeting the parents' emotional needs occupies a position of great importance as well , an impact which is made unconsciously and consciously during the children's childhood or after their maturity respectively. For example, the parents can go back to their childhood through playing with their young children and thus reduce psychological pressures and tensions of daily life.[6]

Regarding the parents' emotional support for the children, one of the issues which has caught the attention of many social specialists is evaluating the impact of mother's employment on children. According to a radical view, the importance of the relationship between mother and child is to the extent that even temporary separation of the child from his mother, for example when the mother goes to work, leaves unpleasant and irrecoverable effects on the child's life. Ignoring exaggerated aspect of this view, the idea of the children's emotional needs to mothers in itself, in addition to cultural support, has proponents among theorists among whom we can mention John Bowlby. He believed that long term separation of child from his mother in childhood could cause anxiety in the child and produces an effect that can be compared to grief experienced when a loved one is lost. Such an experience can have an effect on forming the emotional structure of the child in the future and impair his ability in establishing a stable emotional relationship.[7]

In contrast, adducing to new studies, another view denies the negative effects of the mothers' employment on children. The proponents of this view claim that there was not a major difference between the children with working mothers and other children and in specific cases where there were some differences, they must be rooted in other factors such as the quality of alternative care (like the proportion of the teachers to children in an orphanage) not in mothers' employment. Moreover, children with working mothers did not have any difference with other children in terms of most

---

1 Surah Nisa ,19.
2 Horr Amelli, *Wasael al-Shia*, Vol 14, p118 and 121.
3 Ibid, p10.
4 Ibid, p183; Vol 1, p399.
5 Ibid, Vol 3, p 336 and 358.
6 Harvey & McDonald, *Doing Sociology*, p.196.
7 Bilton et al., *Introductory Sociology*, p.307.

of the developmental measurements and they had a better state in terms of social adjustment compared to other children; meantime they have more positive attitude towards the women's employment and are less bound to traditional views consistent with gender roles.[1]

The third view claims that there is a difference between full-time employment and part-time employment. According to this view, long hours of the mother's employment and spending less time with children, particularly in elementary school period, lead to unpleasant psychological and social consequences; but having part-time job seems to be advantageous for children of all ages, probably on the grounds that it enables the mother to meet their needs.[2]

There is a great deal of evidence for Islam's effort and concern to meet emotional needs of the parents and children. On the other hand numerous recommendations about expressing affection to the children by parents[3] and being playmate with young children[4] implicitly indicate the key role of the parents' emotional support of children in the growth of their personality. In this connection, it has been narrated from the Holy Prophet (pbuh) who said: "One who kisses his child, God will record this as a virtuous act for him and one who makes his child happy God will make him happy in the Day of Judgment.[5] According to another narration, Fatima (AS) used to play with her young children, Hasan and Hussein (AS), by murmuring some verses.[6]

However, such religious recommendations are too general to be of any use in approving or rejecting the aforementioned views. So, there is a need to refer to other evidence regarding the issues such as the impact of mothers' employment on children. On the other hand, abundant recommendations have been made by Islam about treating the parents kindly.[7] For instance, the Holy Quran describes the ideal form of the relationship with elderly parents with an incomparable subtlety:

> And your Lord has decreed that you worship none but Him, and that you be kind to parents. If one or both of them reach old age with you, say not "Fie" unto them nor repulse them, but speak unto them a gracious word. And lower to them the wing of humility out of mercy and say, "My Lord, have mercy upon them as they brought me up in childhood." [8]

In some narrations the expression "*Sukun*" has been used about children and they have been described as a means of the parents' mental peace and their companionship and establishing a strong emotional bond between them by easing their loneliness.[9]

---

1 Wilkie ,"Marriage, Family Life ,and Women's Employment", Edwards and Demo (eds.) ,*Marriage and Family in Transition*,p.156.
2 Berk, *Child Development* ,p.585.
3 Horr Amelli ,*Wasael al-Shia* ,Vol 15, p201-203.
4 Ibid, p203;Majlesi ,*Bahar al-Anvar*,Vol 43, p285-286.
5 Horr Amelli, Ibid, p194.
6 Bohrani Esfahani, *Avalem al-Olum va al-Maaref va al-Ahval* ,Vol 2, p898.
7 Horr Amelli, *Wasael al-Shia*,Vol 15, p204-207.
8 Surah Asra ,23-24.
9 Horr Amelli, *Wasael al-Shia*,Vol 15, p106.

It is worth mentioning that Islam by putting greater emphasis on treating mothers kindly in comparison with fathers, has removed the doubt of gender discrimination in favor of men with regard to emotional support. We read in a narration:

> A man came to the Holy Prophet (pbuh) and asked him: O, the Prophet of God, whom should I treat kindly? The Prophet replied, "Your mother". The man then asked, "Who after that?" To which the Prophet replied again, "Your mother". Asked who is next, the Prophet again replied, "Your mother". When the man asked who after that, the Prophet said, "Your father".[1]

8-3 Livelihood support

During the history, family has been an economic unit whose members have always cooperated with each other to provide their common livelihood needs. In traditional societies, the man and woman's marriage with each other not only has guaranteed a long-term economic cooperation relationship but also production tended to be an economic investment and it was expected that the children of this marriage should contribute to the economic condition of the family in the future. The transfer of goods and properties from one generation to the next one, whether in the form of the parent's financial support for the children during their life time or in the form of inheritance, was another supportive function which has always been performed by the families. Another aspect of livelihood support performed by the family has been the cooperation of family members to overcome the problems and supporting each other against different dangers and threats. These kinds of supports are more consistent with the traditional pattern of family life and kinship, particularly with its common practices in rural and tribal societies.

In contemporary industrial societies, the family has almost lost its economic function as regards production and has turned into a consumption unit for goods and services. In these societies, many people neither feel the necessity to cooperate with other members of the family to meet their economic needs nor do they see any necessity to live within a family.[2] Although many needs which made the help of the family members and relatives necessary in the past have partially or completely been effaced, sometimes the support of relatives is still very helpful. Despite the weakness of kinship ties compared to previous periods," relatives are still the first ones we turn to for help - whether financially or non -financially.[3]

In critical views, economic functions of the family become prominent in two aspects: the use that women make of family in order to supply their own livelihood and the advantages that the system of family and the women's domestic works give to capital owners. The first aspect has been emphasized by Marxist feminists who believe that in capitalism, since the women are deprived of sufficient access to the labor market, they are obliged to depend on the men financially to continue their life. In criticizing women's domestic labor they go so far as to consider the difference between a prostitute and a wife as merely a difference of degree, not of kind; because both sell

---

1 Ibid, p 207.

2 Kammeyer et al., *Sociology: Experiencing Changing Societies*, p.376.

3 Gordon, "Industrial Life and Family", *Modern Sociology*, p 241.

themselves to make a living, i.e. their sexual service and, in the case of the housewives, their domestic services. As a result, as long as many women do not get enough salary, their economic dependence causes them to sell their bodies to protect themselves and in some cases their children.[1]

Concerning the second aspect, Engels considers the advent of monogamous family a result of the tendency towards leaving the wealth for the children and the continuity of men's property ownership among their children. Modern Marxists declare that the contemporary nuclear family serves capitalism in several ways: production and re-production of workforce, providing a place to keep reserve army of labor (women who are hired in the market when it's necessary and are laid off when no longer needed) and facilitating the consumption of vast quantities of consumer goods.[2]

Apart from the functions like reproduction, socialization and childrearing which have partly an economic facet and apart from their direct services to capitalism via domestic labor and the consumption of goods and services, critics even explain private aspects of the family such as satisfying sexual and emotional needs as directed toward fulfilling capitalist goals.[3] The issue of transferring the properties from one generation to the next one and its impact on the continuity of social inequality and the gap between the rich and the poor have also been taken into consideration by critics.[4]

In an overall evaluation, it should be said that the family as the smallest social unit in all societies performs certain functions for society, but this cannot solely explain the existence of causal relationship between the type of the social structure and functions of the family. To put it more plainly, it cannot be ignored that the nuclear family in industrial societies serves capitalism but we should not conclude that capitalism has imposed these functions on the family to achieve its own goals; since the family has performed and continues to perform the same functions in non-capitalist systems too. According to Elshtain , one of the family- oriented feminists :

> The family is not simply and finally the Frankensteinian creature of capitalism, manufactured to reproduce labor power at women's expense. Rather, the family is the only place where human beings can still find some love, security, and comfort- indeed, the only place where human beings can still make decisions based on something other than a monetary bottom line.[5]

Similarly, the benefit women enjoy from family in terms of providing livelihood should be merely regarded as the secondary and subordinate result of family life .Thus, identifying the wifehood with the prostitution would be nothing more than a baseless value judgment. Meanwhile, Engels' historical evaluation about the origin of the genesis of family has faced with the disagreement of anthropologists and archaeologists due to lacking the required evidence. [6]

---

1 Tong, *Feminist Thought*,pp.64-65.
2 Knuttila, *Introducing Sociology: A Critical Perspective*, p.271.
3 Bilton et al., *Introductory Sociology* ,p.352.
4 Segalen ,*Historical Sociology of Family*, p304-306.
5 Tong, *Feminist Thought*, pp.61-62.
6 Lengermann & Brantley ," Modern Feminist Theory", *Sociological Theory in Modern World* ,p481.

The impact of inheritance system and parents' financial supports of children on the continuity of social inequality seems to be undeniable, but a deeper consideration will make us understand the main origin of social inequality is not located in the system itself but in the structural bases of unequal distribution of the wealth, because the issues such as inheritance or giving a gift to the children are merely the nominal means for the transfer of wealth possessed by one generation to the next one. It's clear that by reforming economic structure and introducing an equal distribution of the wealth this issue will not automatically influence the social inequality.

Furthermore, criticizing the economic functions of the family has arisen out of certain ideological foundations such as the denial of private property, emphasis on communal property and absolute disagreement with the capital which are not compatible with Islamic value system. Of course it does not mean that Islam confirms the capitalist system, but the rejection of some elements of capitalism does not involve a negative evaluation of family life and domestic work because of their mutual interaction with capitalist system, since interaction between the family and the other social institutions exists in any alternative system. Hence, as Islam suggests modification or elimination of the capitalist system should focus on the basic strategies other than adopting an antagonistic approach to family.

From the Islamic point of view, the mutual support of wife and husband for each other with regard to livelihood is considered as one of the functions of the family. In Islam, a virtuous woman is the one who helps her husband to obviate livelihood needs of the family, particularly by doing domestic labors,[1] and it has encouraged the women in this regard by assigning spiritual rewards such as regarding as equal the reward of domestic services with *jihad*[2] in the way of God.

However, Islam has legally exempted women from doing domestic labors[3] and obliged the husband to pay alimony even when the wife is financially needless.[4] Thus, it has defined the livelihood support of couples for each other as a reciprocal relationship. But Islam's emphasis on the importance of woman's domestic roles should not lead to a radical interpretation. In Islam the women enjoys complete freedom and will in determining her destiny and as Islamic jurists emphasize, she can set terms to fulfill many of her wishes including education and working outside the home in the marriage contract and her condition is also valid.[5]

Islam has helped the development and the stabilization of livelihood support function performed by family by presenting a set of obligatory and recommended guidelines. Irrespective of the extensive rules of inheritance, the parents and children have been considered as having a religious duty toward each other concerning paying alimony, meaning that providing the expenditures of children's life is undertaken by the father (or grandfather), and in the case of his absence is fallen on the mother's shoulders, and providing the expenditures of the parents' life is undertaken by the

---

1 Horr Amelli, *Wasael al-Shia*, Vol 14, p14 & 24.
2 Syuti ,*al-Dor al-Mansour* , Vol 2,p153.
3 Bani Hashemi Khomeini,*Tozih al-Masael Maraje*,Vol2,p 407.
4 Imam Khomeini ,*Tahrir al-Wasileh* ,Vol 2,p319; Khuyi , *Menhaj al-Salehin*,Vol 2, p291.
5 Khuyi, *Serat al-Nejat fi Ojubah al-Esteftaat*,Vol 2, p361.

children and even legal compulsion and necessity have been predicted in this regard.[1] Great emphasis on the values such as kindness to the parents and relatives, cooperation in good deeds and kin relation in its broad meaning which also embodies all kinds of help, demonstrates other aspects of Islam's concern for this function. It has also been focused on the importance of supportive role of relatives in some narrations.[2]

o **Abstract**

- From the Islamic point of view, one of the functions expected from the family is the family members' cooperation and spiritual support for each other.

- Satisfying emotional needs is the most important function that can explain the survival of the family contemporary industrial societies.

- The expansion of sexual freedom, meaning crisis and the weakness of faith and morality are three important obstacles for the wife and husband's enjoyment of each other's emotional support.

- Parents and children play a significant role in satisfying their mutual emotional needs.

- Three different views have been put forward regarding the negative impact of women's employment on children.

- Family has been an economic unit whose members have always cooperated with each other to provide their common livelihood needs but in contemporary industrial societies, the family has almost lost its economic function as regards production and has turned into a consumption unit for goods and services.

- In critical views, economic functions of the family become prominent in two aspects: the use that women make of family in order to supply their own livelihood and the advantages that the system of family and the women's domestic labors give to capital owners.

- Criticizing the economic functions of the family has arisen out of certain ideological foundations such as the denial of private property, emphasis on communal property and absolute disagreement with the capital which are not compatible with Islamic value system.

o **Self-Test**

1. Why emotional support function in contemporary industrial societies has gained unique importance among the family functions?
2. How does the expansion of sexual freedoms make a negative impact on the supportive function of the family?
3. How does the weakness of faith and morality damage the family in terms of its function of emotional support?
4. State the most important views about the negative impact of women's employment on children.

1 Horr Ameli ,*Wasael al-Shia*,Vol 15, p237; Khuyi ,*Menhaj al-Salehin* ,Vol 2,p288.
2 *Nahj al-Balagheh* ,Vol 1,p 62: Vol 3, p57.

5. According to Marxist theory, the contemporary nuclear family serves the capitalism in different ways. Explain this theory and then criticize it.

o   **Research Topic**

-   Research the spiritual support function of the family members.
-   Research the children's emotional support of their parents in Iranian families.
-   Research the impact of women's employment on children in Iranian families.
-   Research the economic functions of the family in Iran.

CHAPTER 9

UPBRINGING AND CONTROL FUNCTIONS OF THE FAMILY

Chapter 9

Upbringing and control functions of the family

Learning objectives of chapter 9

Getting familiar with upbringing and control functions of the family and Islam's point of view in this regard

Based on stage objective of this chapter, the learner is expected to achieve the following learning objectives and be able to:

1. explain functions of the family concerning socialization and controlling the members' behavior from sociological perspective;
2. analyze Islam's point of view regarding these functions.

Introduction

In this chapter, upbringing and control functions of the family will be reviewed. Sociologists usually discuss the issue of upbringing function under the title of socialization or acculturation. Although many sociologists have not explicitly included supervision and control among functions of the family, they have caught much attention in other fields such as social pathology and criminology.

9-1 Socialization

Socialization is a process through which people learn the appropriate attitudes, values and actions of any individual as a member of a specific culture.[1] Some sociologists have regarded religious education, the process of transferring knowledge and values of a certain religion to a person, as one of the family functions which can be included under the title of socialization[2] by allowing some indulgence. Children acquire the necessary capacity to shape their mentality about fundamental questions of life by learning religious stories, beliefs and religious practices of the family. According to a research carried out in 2003, 85 percent of American parents recognized it their responsibility to teach their children spiritual and religious affairs.[3]

There is no doubt that the family plays an important role in this regard, but considering that in addition to family, other agents are also involved in the children's socialization, depending on the extent of the involvement of each of these agents, the role of family changes in different cultures and over different historical periods. In many societies, socialization by the family encompasses all the things that a child should learn to become an adult; but at the lowest level, the family provides the ground for the child's familiarity with the language, learning main values and practices of society and the formation of his identity. It is certain that the family has precedence over other socialization agents; the child's socialization begins at birth and even the program of the child's breastfeeding – regular and scheduled breastfeeding or

---

1 Schaefer ,*Sociology*, p.90.
2 Ibid ,p.324; Winch ,*The Modern Family*.
3 Despres & Griffin,*The Truth about Family Life* ,p.139.

breastfeeding whenever the baby desires it - influences the way his character will be formed, either he develops a secure or insecure personality.[1]

Three points should be mentioned regarding socialization: the first point is that given that society is made up of different groups and sometimes heterogeneous groups , and in other words , given every culture embodies a set of sub-cultures which may be in conflict concerning some of their values , the direct function of socialization lead to two indirect functions , one at the micro-level (norm conflict) and another one at the macro-level (the continuity of heterogeneity and cultural pluralism in the society).

At the micro-level, the socialization of individuals within the family can bring about a conflict in norms for them. This appears sometimes due to the conflict which exists between the values approved by the parents and the values that other agents of socialization such as school, television or peer groups instill in the individual and sometimes because of the conflict that is created between parents of different cultural backgrounds.

But, the fact that at the macro level, socialization leads to heterogeneity and cultural pluralism does not need to be proved. If in an imaginary society the government and affiliated institutions be the only agents of the humans' socialization, a single set of values will be instilled in the minds of all individuals, but in real conditions since the families belong to different social classes or strata or different religious, ethnic, racial and political groups, they pass on different values, attitudes and actions to their children. Of course, we should avoid extremes, because the other side of the coin is the impact of socialization on maintaining social integrity. Parson says:

> The most important function of the family is providing the ground for "emotional cathexes" and "identification" to integrate the child in the set of social systems within which he will act as an adult in the future. Specifically, the family is likely to be the first agent in the development of the child's abilities to show integration with others, to trust and to be trusted upon, to exercise authority and accept it.[2]

The second point is the transference of the function of children's socialization from the family to other social institutions. Today, socialization function of the family has strongly been influenced by the development of communication technologies along with the emergence of visual and electronic media as well as the development of alternative institutions of the family such as orphanages, kindergartens and schools. However, the family has greatly preserved its importance and role in the socialization of the children. Parsons declared that the modern nuclear family – which he regarded as a feature of industrial societies and its emergence concurrent with the decrease of the functions of traditional family- will maintain the function of socialization of children and providing an environment for the development of adult's personality.[3] He has gone further than just describing and explaining the realities of nuclear family's status and functions and adopted a normative approach by focusing on the point that socialization

---

1 Cotgrove , *The Science of Society : An Introduction to Sociology* ,p.62.
2 Parsons ,*Man and Civilization*,p.44.
3 Knuttila , *Introducing Sociology : A Critical Perspective*, p.266.

of children by the family is the best and the most complete form of children's socialization.

But socialist theorists have criticized this view and declared that it will bear unpleasant consequences such as the limitation of women's activities to housekeeping and upbringing the children and consequently ,impeding the equality of man and woman, failing to provide suitable conditions for humane upbringing in the small families , the expansion of existing sex conflicts in the family upbringing, limited trainings of enlightening and spiritual powers of the infant and methods of upbringing based on submission.[1] Ignoring the biological basis of the family, they have posited a socio-historical character to it and thus, provoked controversies on structural and functional integrity of the family. They believe that "between early upbringing of the children which exclusively takes place in the family and public centers ... there are many other types of upbringing which neither anyone has thought of it nor it has been implemented by organizers up to now".[2]

The third point refers to the issue of learning gender roles. Different methods of upbringing for male and female children cause to form distinctive personalities displaying different feelings and behaviors during their life. Learning gender roles by children takes place through two main ways: first, direct training through which "significant others", especially parents, reward the child for his/her behaviors suitable with gender roles and second, modeling by which the children observe significant others behaving in a certain way and then they imitate it.[3]

Socialization of gender roles in the family has been one of the main concerns of feminists; that is because they consider it as one of the main causes of sex inequalities in the family and society. Simone de Beauvoir in her book *The Second Sex* declared that if the baby girl was nurtured with the same expectations and rewards and the same restrictions and freedoms that her brothers were nurtured, and she had the same education and games and was promised for the same future of that of her brothers and was surrounded by the man and woman who were equal in her eyes, definitely the personality of girls and women could be formed very different than that of current situation.[4]

Accordingly, in order to achieve a society free of sex inequalities , many feminists have asked for converting traditional pattern of the girls and boys' socialization into another pattern which focuses on nurturing androgynous humans, the humans who , according to the most common interpretation, the best masculine and feminine attributes are embodied in their personalities.[5] Identifying the upbringing patterns for girls and boys and purging films, books and journals from the stereotypes promulgating sex distinction can be regarded as the serious demands of feminists in this regard.[6]

---

1 Rozen Bowm, *Structural Family against Society*, p 164.
2 Ibid ,p 183.
3 Kammeyer et al., *Sociology :Experiencing Changing Societies* ,pp.335-336.
4 De Beauvoir ,*The Second Sex*,p.726.
5 Sterba , " Is Feminism Good for Men and Are Men Good For Feminism ?" , *Men Doing Feminism* ,p.291.
6 Mitchell , *Combat with Sex Discrimination*,p130.

However, androgynous ideal has met with two criticisms from feminists themselves. The first criticism doubts the practical possibility of attaining this ideal. Focusing on the existence of biological differences between the man and woman, Alice Rossie regards this issue as an effective factor in the process of identification of the children with parents. She believes that psychology and biology of women embodying menstruation and pregnancy can entail that girls always identify with their mothers more than boys do. The biological difference between son and mother results in his maintaining a bigger gap with his mother.[1]

The second criticism concerns the consequences of attaining the mentioned ideal. Some feminists have raised the question "If the existing gender differences be removed what may really be replaced with them? Removing the differences carries the risk of enabling men to define the single or multiple gender patterns which appear in the future. Therefore, while some feminist theorists respect at least part of feminine aspects, they have opposed to the idea of a world free of gender differences.[2]

From the Islamic perspective, we note three points regarding the function of socialization: the first point concerns the conflict between the functionalists and socialists. It seems that this issue is strongly influenced by value and ideological elements and it cannot be analyzed without considering common values in the industrial societies. In other words, determining "the best form of the children's socialization "without considering a specific value system is meaningless and the difference of value systems makes us talk about various methods each of which suits best one of the value systems instead of focusing on the best method of socialization. Accordingly, accepting the values such as absolute negation of domination in the process of children's upbringing, complete sex likeness and equality, absolute sexual freedom, maximum individual well-being and comfort opens the door to criticize the prevalent style of socialization by the family. In contrast, accepting conservative attitudes concordant with the capitalist system which we observe in Parsons' view can lead to advocating socialization within the nuclear family.

As a result, for determining the best method of children's socialization in Islam, the value system of Islam in general, and specifically the goals Islam follows in marriage and family formation should be taken into consideration. It can be generally derived from verses and narrations that given the parents' natural and mental capacities and their commitment towards the children and also in terms of other positive individual and social functions of the family which Islam takes into consideration, upbringing in the family environment has a priority upon other methods of the children's socialization.

The second point is the socialization of gender roles which is conceivable only in the framework of Islamic values. Although Islam has not involved sex in all family and social activities and has also set common domains of activity for the man and woman, in its ideal social system it has determined some distinctions between the man and woman's roles, often as a priority and sometimes as a necessity. Sex equality in Islam, on the one hand is based on the principles of understanding human nature (specifically,

---

1 Tong, *Feminist Thought*, p.159.
2 Ramazanoglu , *Feminism and the Contradictions of Oppression* ,p.185.

natural sex differences) and on the other hand, it is in line with fulfilling the ultimate goals (particularly inner peace of the spouses, upbringing healthy children, spiritual growth of the family members and moral health of the society and finally, human's eternal prosperity). As a result, Islam does not approve of full sex likeness where it is incompatible with Islam's ideal and general interests. For example, the likeness of women to men and the likeness of men to women (similarity in the kind of dressing and appearance in public view are the evidence of it) has been heavily criticized by the Islamic narrations.[1] It is due to the fact that these kinds of similarities in addition to be incongruent with the necessities of natural sex differences, they seriously damage religious development and society's spiritual life. Also, it can be said that preventing the women from judgment or direct participation in the war is because of their specific natural characteristics (physical and mental) and consequently, because these rules are more suitable with Islam's goals.[2]

Accordingly, rejecting the principles such as absolute sexual freedom and absolute sex likeness by Islam cannot be consistent with the boy and girl's socialization in the same way. In contrast, Islam does not negatively evaluate the kind of socialization of gender roles which is consistent with natural sex differences and in parallel with achieving the goals of Islam's social system; for example, preparing the girls for accepting maternal and spousal role and preparing the boys for undertaking the role of breadwinner, not only necessarily is not forbidden by Islam , but also it is regarded as an ideal and common affair in terms of its positive functions to fulfil the intended goals of Islam. Definitely Islam does not approve of the radical patterns of gender role socialization which are inconsistent with religious values, the patterns which socialize females as powerless slaves for males and socialize the males as lords and despots to women.

By this explanation, Islam's point of view regarding androgynous ideal becomes clear. Undoubtedly, in some cases, social and cultural factors can even change public values of the society and also influence the individual's morality. For example, norms such as indecency of crying and admirability of aggression for men are originated from illusory and invalid cultural and religious roots. Therefore, if androgynous upbringing does cause the actualization and raising common moral virtues such as awareness, wisdom, kindness and being soft-natured in both sexes, it will be acceptable, but if such upbringing requires different capacities of both sexes and negatively affects the values of social system such as modesty and moral health of the society, it will be rejected in Islam.

The third point is noting the great importance that Islam attaches to religious teaching and upbringing. The emphasis on teaching children and teenagers the Holy Quran,[3] religious beliefs and rules, particularly prayer which is seen in Islamic narrations, indicates Islam's concern over this crucial issue. Of course, given functional interference of family, religious and educational institutions in contemporary societies, the role of the family in religious education has partly been reduced. In Iran, for

---

1 Horr Amelli, *Wasael al-Shia*,Vol 12, p211.
2 Tabatabaiee, *al-Mizan fi Tafsir al-Quran*, Vol 2, p272-275.
3 Horr Amelli ,*Wasael al-Shia*, Vol 15, p 182 ,194-196.

instance, we are witnessing increasing investment of religious and educational institutions in this regard and the rapid development of religious institutions and journals after the Islamic revolution.

9-2 Social control

Social control is one of the important functions of the family which is either fulfilled through direct supervision of family on the behavior of the members or indirectly as the consequence of functions such as satisfying sexual and emotional needs, protection, care and socialization. Of course, given the prevalence of individualistic and liberalistic attitudes in Western societies, the role of the family has strongly been decreased in direct controlling of the spouses and children's behavior. Also, due to the increasing dysfunction in families and the development of phenomena such as free sexual relations, divorce and single-parent families which have weakened other functions of the family, the role of family in indirect controlling of the members has been decreased. Nonetheless, some sociologists believe the family, even in modern societies, is also the first agent of social control, particularly sexual control of adults and children.[1] With this introduction, the discussion will be centered on the spouses and children.

a) Controlling the spouses

Direct control of either of the spouses over the behaviors of the other party, particularly extra-marital sexual relationships, is something that is seen in many past and present cultures, although due to the factors such as men's greater power and different gender roles of the wife and husband, this control has been exercised more by men compared to women. Women's sexual control by their husbands has existed from very distant past and enjoyed strong cultural, religious and philosophical backings. Generally, philosophers and social thinkers have agreed on Rousseau's view that "the husband should supervise the behavior of his wife; because it is important for him to know the children he is obliged to identify and nurture, belong to nobody other than himself".[2]

Contrary to this view is the idea of free choice that a group of feminists has advocated to wipe out any domination of men over women. The proponents of this idea believe that sex equality is achieved only when men are prevented from any attempt to impose their will on the women. Accordingly, even abnormal behaviors such as the women's prostitution should be approved.[3]

Regarding indirect control, we can mention the findings of the research pertaining to suicide according to which marriage prevents the individuals from suicide, and the individuals with children are less likely to commit suicide compared to married individuals without children. For instance, the statistics of suicide among the individuals from 20-70 years of age in France between the years 1889 and 1891 suggested that on average per 100 suicides of married men, 280 single men and 218 widowers committed suicide. Also, per 100 suicides of married women, 167 single

---

1 Goode ," The Sociology of the Family ", *Sociology Today* ,p.189.
2 Oliver ,*Family Values* ,p.163.
3 Siegel ,*Criminology* ,p.385.

women and 178 widows committed suicide.[1] Relying on the similar data, Durkheim, in the theory of social solidarity, has considered the weakness of individuals' social and family ties as the cause of their suicide. It's clear that mental tranquility arising out of marriage prepares the human to accept the responsibilities and makes him patient against the problems of life and increases his enthusiasm in whatever he does; because he feels that both he himself and his loved ones, his wife and children, enjoy the result of his work and effort. In contrast, feeling lonely decreases the individual's hope and enthusiasm and produces an irresponsible person who easily gives up when he encounters difficulties and because of lacking a reliable emotional haven commits suicide or turns to crime in order to compensate his failures and frustrations.

Beyond asexual deviations, there is a close relationship between dysfunction in family and sexual offences. Undoubtedly, deviations like sexual assault and rape of women and children, prostitution and homosexuality are strongly associated with the individuals' deprivation of a close and loving family, and if the weakness of the family institution is not considered as the only factor of unprecedented prevalence of such deviations, it is definitely one of the most important factors contributing to it.

b) Controlling the children

Controlling the children's behavior by older members of the family, particularly the parents, has two direct and indirect aspects. Among different factors influencing the children's deviation, sociologists have identified some familial factors. Apart from the weakness of direct supervision over the children's behavior which is more likely in the single-parent families, other factors such as the parents' conflict and incongruity, the lack of warm, loving and supportive relationships between the parents and children, the parents' deviation and their mistreatment of children have been identified as effective factors in the tendency of the children towards deviation and crime. [2]

For instance, studies carried out regarding the causes of prostitution indicate that the prostitutes often belong to the problematic families suffering from poverty, pugnacity and sever hostility, divorce, the death of one of the parents, the absence of father or sexual abuse of the individual by family members in childhood.[3] In a research about the impact of being deprived of the parents' presence on teenagers' delinquency, three groups of teenagers aged 11-17 years were compared to each other: one group of 33 dangerous criminals, a group of 33 accidental criminals and a group of 33 non-criminals. According to the results of this research shown in the following table, 96 percent of dangerous criminals were influenced by the problems arising from different forms of separation of parents in their families; that is, only 4 percent of them had a healthy family environment, while 53 percent of non-criminals lived in the healthy families. Moreover, 34 percent of dangerous criminals and 28 percent of accidental criminals were those who have permanently or alternately been deprived of their parents, while among non-criminals, the rate of the parents' deprivation was less than 10 percent in this age group.[4]

---

1 Halbwachs ,*The Causes of Suicide* ,p.130.
2 Siegel , *Criminology*,p.197.
3 Ibid ,p.384.
4 Mosavati Azar , *Social Pathology of Iran* ,p337.

Table 2: the impact of the teenagers' deprivation of the parents on their delinquency

Family situation considering the child's age	Dangerous criminals	Prisoners of correctional facilities	Non-criminals
Before age 5			
Deprivation of permanently mother	12/4 %	2/1 %	0 %
Alternatively	3/1 %	6/2 %	0 %
Deprivation of permanently father	12/4 %	12/4 %	6/2 %
Alternatively	6/2 %	6/2 %	3/1 %
From 5 to 11 years			
Deprivation of mother	9/3 %	6/2 %	6/2 %
Deprivation of father	15/5 %	18/6 %	6/2 %
Chaotic families	12/4 %	6/2 %	0 %
	15/5 %	6/2 %	2/4 %
Disturbances of the environment	4 %	17 %	53 %
The individuals who has not experienced such disturbances			

Some of the points to be considered about control function of the family concerning the spouses and children's sexual and asexual deviations which have been emphasized in religious texts are as follows:

- **The role of satisfying sexual and emotional needs in the family**: in some Quranic verses and narrations the word "ehsan" has been used to express marriage derived from the word *"hesn"* meaning fortress and it implicitly alludes to the fact that each of two spouses is considered as a fortress for the other party involved which keeps her/him from the risk of committing sexual deviations.[1] Other narrations imply that preventing a person from being driven by uncontrollable lust and sexual deviations is another valuable consequences of the marriage.[2] Surah Bagharah [verse 187] which has considered the women as clothing for men and the men as clothing for women, seems to be pointing to the fact that as clothing covers indecencies and the private parts of human body and becomes an ornament to him and keeps him from falling into disgrace, similarly, the wife and the husband by satisfying their mutual sexual need and preventing deviations and indecencies, cover each other and are regarded as embellishment for each other.[3]

- **Strengthening spirit of sexual zeal**: sexual zeal is considered to be a sexual morality whose emergence and development can be seen in the family environment more than anywhere else. Contrary to the view that regards zeal as a category of jealousy and merely the product of cultural factors and due to the tendency of men to possess the women,[4] Islamic narrations have declared positive valuations about the moderate state of this character as an effective factor in decreasing sexual deviations and have classified zeal and jealousy into two distinct areas: faith and infidelity. [5]

---

1 Surah Nisa ,24-25 ; Horr Amelli , *Wasael al-Shia* ,vol 14 ,p 21 , 323.
2 Horr Amelli ,Ibid , p 19 , 179 & 265.
3 Qotb , *Fi Zalal al-Quran* ,p174.
4 Kleinberg , *Social Psychology* , vol 1 ,p 165
5 Horr Amelli, *Wasael al-Shia* , vol 14, p 107-111.

- **Religious and moral upbringing of the children**: religious and moral upbringing of the children which involves familiarizing them with religious and moral beliefs, rules and values is among the duties which has been fallen on the parents' shoulders more than others.[1] It's clear that the children internalize a strong factor of control and restraint against social deviations within themselves during the process of moral and religious education, and piety and moral conduct of the parents themselves make a profound impact on it.

- **Parental supervision over children**: proper control of the children's behavior by the parents, in addition to its common aspect,[2] has also been taken into consideration from a specific aspect, i.e. sexual control According to the narrations, parents should prevent children from witnessing sexual intercourse being performed; because it leaves a profound impact on the children's tendency towards sexual deviations.[3] The focus on training the etiquette of entering to the adult's bedroom to the children and teenagers reveals even more the seriousness of Islam's concern about this issue.[4] Besides, the parents are obliged to separate their children's bedroom, especially the boy and girl's bedroom before puberty which some narrations have set 10 years old for it.[5] Also, the necessity of helping the children to form a family,[6] the emphatic recommendation on facilitating the marriage,[7] obligating the fathers to support the children financially in cases they need it,[8] focus on expressing affection to the children and mildness in upbringing and avoiding insulting treatment with them[9] are other religious recommendations which observing them can lead to the decrease of the rate of children's deviation.

o **Abstract**

  - Socialization is a process through which people learn the appropriate attitudes, values and actions of any individual as a member of a specific culture.
  - Given that the society is made up of heterogeneous groups, the function of socialization in the family lead to two indirect functions, norm conflict in the family and cultural pluralism in the society.
  - Today, institutions such as orphanages, kindergartens and schools have undertaken part of the function of children's socialization.
  - In order to achieve a society free of sex inequalities, many feminists have asked for converting traditional pattern of the girls and boys' socialization into the pattern of upbringing androgynous humans.
  - Children learn gender roles by two methods: direct training through reward and punishment and indirect training through modelling.

---

1 Ibid ,vol 15, p 193-195.
2 Surah Tahrim ,6.
3 Horr Amelli , *Wasael al-Shia*, vol 14, p 94-95.
4 Surah Nour , 58-59; Horr Amelli , *Wasael al-Shia* , vol 14, p158-160.
5 Ibid , vol 15, p 182-183.
6 Ibid, p200.
7 Ibid, vol 14, p 51-52.
8 Ibid, vol 15, p 237.
9 Ibid ,p 194-195, 199-203.

- From the Islamic point of view, upbringing in the family environment precedes other methods of children's socialization.
- While Islam has determined domains of activities for man and woman, in its ideal social system it has established some distinctions between the man and woman's roles, often as a priority and sometimes as a necessity.
- Social control is one of the important functions of the family which is either fulfilled through direct supervision of family on the behavior of the members or indirectly as the consequence of functions such as satisfying sexual and emotional needs, protection, care and socialization.

o **Self-Test**

1. Explain the role of the family in achieving consensus and conflict at two micro and macro levels.
2. What is the substance of androgynous ideal? What criticisms have been mounted against it?
3. Explain Islam's point of view regarding socialization of gender roles.
4. Explain the relationship between the family and suicide based on Durkheim's theory.

o **Research topic**

- Research the role of Iranian families in the children's religious training and upbringing.
- Do a pathology research regarding how the parents supervise the children's behavior in Iranian families.
- Research the situation of zeal, as one of the sexual ethics in some of Iran's urban and rural regions.

PART IV

PATHOLOGY OF THE FAMILY & THE STRATEGIES FOR STRENGTHENING IT

Pivotal status of the family institution in social system requires specialists, individuals and organizations involved in the family affairs to be always sensitive to its issues and consider its actual and potential damages to provide the ground for adopting scholarly approaches to remove the damages of the family and strengthen it. In this section, after examining two main damages of the family institution, domestic violence and divorce, we will have a reflection on the strategies of strengthening the family.

CHAPTER 10

DOMESTIC VIOLENCE

Chapter 10

Domestic violence

Learning objectives of chapter 10

Getting familiar with sociological explanations and Islam's point of view regarding domestic violence

Based on stage objective of this chapter, the learner is expected to achieve the following objectives and be able to:

1. present a description of the situation of domestic violence;
2. explain micro and macro factors of domestic violence from the sociological perspective;
3. explain Islam's point of view regarding domestic violence.

Introduction

After a brief description of the situation of domestic violence in different societies, we will state diverse views about the factors and causes of the emergence of this phenomenon by separating three approaches: micro causal explanation, macro causal explanation and teleological explanation and finally we will mention Islam's point of view in this regard.

10-1 A description of domestic violence

Domestic violence is considered as a dark side of family life. Domestic violence which can be defined as a physical, verbal or emotional abuse used by one of the family members against another one, is not a new phenomenon and it has also existed in the past. Even in industrial countries despite the change of public attitudes and the promotion of legal supports, this problem still exists in many families.

Reports suggest that domestic violence is a multilateral phenomenon which affects children, spouses, sisters, brothers and elderlies. According to some statistics in the US, nearly one- fourth of adults reported that they have been physically abused in childhood. The evidence indicates that child abuse including burning the children with cigarette, imprisoning them in a place, fastening them for hours or days and breaking their bones, has been terrifyingly prevalent and it is likely to be the cause of more than 2 million children getting away from home .The research conducted in this country indicates that annually about 7 million wives and husbands involve in violent conflicts in which one of two parties hurts the other one. While women use violence as much as men do, there is a difference between the men and women's violence in terms of quality. Violence between the sisters and brothers is up to high rates too which can take place because of competition, jealously, conflict on personal belongings or sexual relation with each other. The rate of elderly abuse has been estimated 2/5 million cases annually which is usually appeared in the forms of psychological or physical abuse, exercising economic pressure or to stop providing care for the elderly.[1]

---

1 Robertson, *An Introduction to Society*, p316-317, also refer to: Shepard , *Sociology* ,pp.305-306.

The extent of this phenomenon in many societies including industrial societies has placed a considerable proportion of the families in a situation that not only do not provide the expected function in the area of emotional support, but also they have been turned into a breeding ground for anxiety, insecurity and even crime. As Anthony Giddens says:

> Home is, in fact, the most dangerous place in modern society. In statistical terms, a person of any age or of either sex is far more likely to be subject to physical attack at home than in the street at night. In England, of four murders, one is perpetrated by a family member against other.[1]

Among different kinds of above mentioned domestic violence, marital violence, particularly men's violence against their wives, is one to which a great portion of studies conducted on domestic violence has been dedicated. Marital violence, in its broad sense, implies abuse by one of the couples against the other one which has the potential to bring physical and mental damages to the other party involved.

Although this phenomenon which beating and murder are of its common examples, historically has a long background, paying serious attention to it, as one of the important research topics in social sciences goes back to 1970s when radical feminists revealed the hidden aspects of marital violence and analyzed it as one of the striking aspects of sex inequality.

Historically, men in ancient Rome were permitted to beat their wives because of doing actions such as attending public sporting contests without getting their permission, drinking alcohol or going outside the home without face covering. In the early Middle Ages women were under intensive supervision and their violation of the duties could lead to severe punishments inflicted by their husbands. It was expected that the man should beat his wife because of her improper behavior and if he was not able to do this he himself might be punished by the neighbors. From the Late Middle Ages to modern world (1400-1900) the man who used force against his wife was not faced with public disapproval, unless when his violence reached to a certain level and this level was usually the woman's death or losing her beauty. In the mid-19th century, there was disagreement over sever beating of the women and the husbands accused of such an act were derided by public. Finally, in the late 19th century in England and America laws were passed which forbade the husband from beating his wife but the husbands' violence against their wives continued because of its long historical background. Documents obtained from British courts indicates that even after World War II, beating the wife by her husband due to her disobedience was regarded as a permissible punishment.[2]

Irrespective of historical considerations, varied reports suggest the pervasiveness of this phenomenon in modern world and in different societies, although despite universal efforts made in recent years to collect the reliable information in this regard, the information pertaining to this issue is not reliable enough which the most important causes of that are considered to be the difficulty of defining violence, the problems of

---

1 Giddens, *Sociology*, p 438.
2 Siegel, *Criminology*, pp.300-301.

sampling and the lack of individuals' tendency towards reporting violence.[1] However, we refer to some statistics as samples:

According to some reports, half of married men in Bangkok and Thailand regularly beat their wives. In Quito and Ecuador, 80 percent of women have reported that they have been beaten by their husbands and according to some estimations more than 1/8 million husbands in the US brutally beat their wives.[2] Other estimations imply that at least 4 million women in the US are beaten by their husbands and more than 4 thousand women are killed as a result of being beaten.[3] In Iran, irrespective of some survey researches conducted in recent years,[4] case studies and the individuals' daily observations confirm the relative prevalence of violent actions against the wives.

Regardless of quantity aspects, paying attention to quality aspects of violence against the spouses is of great importance which in this regard it will suffice to mention what Giddens says:

> Violence against the women in the house is thought to be very unimportant; but the evidence of battered women's havens indicates the contrary. It has been reported in a survey that: some women have tragically been hurt; they suffer broken bones, knife wounds and sever injuries. Some have been hit on the head by a chair; some have been pushed down the stairs and a nail has been driven by a hammer in one's foot.[5]

Given the fact that marital violence is reciprocal and the women also resort to violence against their husbands, can marital violence be related to the individuals' sex? According to the new research conducted in Western countries, there is a significant relationship between sex and marital violence, it should be made clear that although women use violence as much as men do, and sometimes more than them they do not usually trigger violence and turn to violence for defending themselves or taking revenge. It should be said that the injuries suffered by women are more than that of men.[6]

The results of a research conducted on 96 British cohabiting couples indicate that if merely the quantity of violent actions be considered and context and underlying meaning of violence be ignored, women use violence even more than men (in this research, 38 percent of men and 55 percent of women perpetrated violence in the relationship with their partner).Considering the quality, we find out that men are far more likely to trigger the violence or use dangerous violence. Moreover, in terms of consequences of violence, especially physical damages and mental effects such as anxiety, male violence is more likely to bring serious consequences (in the mentioned research 18 men and in contrast 12 women used traumatic violence; 19 percent of men and in contrast 4 percent of women triggered the violence .Of 96 men, just one person

---

1 Adams ," Families and Family study in International Perspective", *Journal of Marriage and Family 66*, p.1080.

2 French, *War against Women*, p308.

3 Shepard, *Sociology*, p.306.

4 Refer to : Qazi Tabatabaiee et al, *A National Plan for reviewing Domestic Violence against Women*.

5 Giddens, *Sociology*, p201.

6 Shepard, *Sociology*, p.306.

experienced serious trauma by his partner, whereas of 96 women, 9 people experienced serious trauma by their partner).[1]

10-2 An explanation of domestic violence

In this discussion, we will have a brief review of factors involved in domestic violence. Since a detailed examination is not intended, there has not been made a distinction between specific factors and the common factors of violence committed by husband, woman, parental violence and child violence.

In explaining the factors of perpetrating domestic violence we are faced with three different approaches: micro causal explanation, macro causal explanation and teleological explanation. In each of these approaches, it has been focused on the aspect or aspects of domestic violence as the factors or causes of the emergence and continuity of this phenomenon which we will examine briefly.

a) A micro causal explanation

The theorists who examine domestic violence based on this approach, focus on a set of factors among which biological factors should be mentioned as the primary factor. Physiologists have considered high levels of male hormone- testosterone- as the effective factor in their aggressive behaviors,[2] while in some radical feminist theories, the role of biological factors, particularly the important role of men's physical strength in sexual violence have been emphasized.[3] But clearly it is not possible for us to imagine a greater importance for biological factors beyond the fact that men in comparison with women possess a greater capability and potential for committing violence. Therefore, we need a further explanation to demonstrate how this capacity is actualized.

Other important factor in this approach is learning. The theory of social learning considers crime and deviance as the result of learning norms, values and behaviors pertaining to these phenomena. According to this theory, children learn behavioral patterns and methods of using domestic violence from their parents and follow these patterns and methods in the future.[4] Confirmed by diverse studies, this theory partly explains the fact that why women who are faced with their husband's violence, continue to live with them; this to some extent relates to the background of women who received physical violence: the women abused by their parents have been socialized to play the role of a victim. As a result, the repetition of this situation in marital life does not lead to their escape. [5]

But weakness in self-control can be considered as the most important factor of perpetrating domestic violence at the micro level. Based on the psychological approach of social control theory, the lack or weakness of individual control through internal and external forces is the cause of deviant behavior. Religious beliefs, moral conscience, the individual's commitments towards others and his social ties play the role of preventive

1 Nazroo,"Uncovering Gender Differences in the Use of Marital Violence: The Effect of Methodology ", *The Sociology of the Family*, Chap.7.
2 Baron & Byrne ,*Social Psychology* ,p.186.
3 Jaggar," Four Interpretations of Feminism (2) " ,*Women* , n 31, p42.
4 Siegel, *Criminology* ,pp.200,301.
5 Curry et al., *Sociology for the Twenty-First Century*,p.269.

internal and external forces against the individual's tendency towards deviance and violation - specifically domestic violence.[1]

Furthermore , other factors at the micro level have been identified as affecting domestic violence, e.g. alcohol consumption , hostility due to the man' dependence on his wife, the man's obsession and excessive worry about the behavior of his wife and , burst of anger, particularly after verbal argument and the man's military service in the past or present.[2]

b) A macro causal explanation

At the macro level some factors have been identified as affecting domestic violence. Some of these factors have their root in cultural and legal acceptance of this kind of violence. Some believe that the origin of inattention or being slow to react and attend to the issue of domestic violence is the cultural and legal background of not interfering in the affairs of others and considering family conflicts as a private issue.[3] In explaining the factor of cultural acceptance, Giddens says:

> In the workplace and other public places, the general rule is that nobody has the right to beat the other, although his behavior is objectionable or provocative. It's not the same within the family. Many research studies have indicated that a considerable proportion of wives and husbands believe that in some conditions one of them has the right to beat the other. Of four American wives and husbands, one believes that the husband can have a justified reason for beating his wife. Lower percentage of them believe that the opposite is also true.[4]

In this regard, feminist sociologists have regarded obvious and hidden patriarchy in marital relations which is strengthened by men's greater power and women's economic and emotional dependence on their husband, as the cause of domestic violence.[5]As they say, since in patriarchal cultures the women are identified to be irrational creatures and close to the nature, the men are taught and perhaps encouraged to resort to violence inevitably whenever they cannot convince these irrational creatures with a rational argument.[6] Some evidence implies that violence is more prevalent in the patriarchal families and the lowest rate of violence can be found in egalitarian families.[7]

Discriminatory laws, unwillingness of the police to interfere in the family conflicts and inadequacy of punishments which the court metes out for offending husbands show the aspects of legal acceptance and leniency about men's violence against their wives. Hence, as a woman marries a man, she loses part of her rights in terms of

---

1 Siegel, *Criminology*, p.207.

2 Ibid,p.301.

3 Kendall, *Sociology in Our Times*, p.436.

4 Giddens, *Sociology*, p 439-440.

5Nazroo, "Uncovering Differences in the Use of Marital Violence: The Effect of Methodology", *The Sociology of the Family*,p.151.

6 Seidler,"Masculinity ,Violence and Emotional Life", *Emotions in Social Life*,pp.202-203.

7 Lindsey & Smith," Women in the Two-Thirds World", *Families in Global and Multicultural Perspective*,p.339.

protection by law against physical damage or intimidation. Minimum penalties enforced for transgressing men which often do not go beyond a warning, suggests that wife beating is sometimes considered less important than simple driving offences.[1] It is noteworthy that despite the seriousness of the issue of domestic violence against women around the world, only 44 countries have enacted laws for it.[2]

Aside from the legal and cultural factors, sociologists have also emphasized the role of economic factors. Men as breadwinners of the family who feel helpless in providing for living costs due to the economic pressures, become frustrated and this may lead them to use violence against wives.[3]For example, transitional economic conditions in Eastern Europe which were accompanied by insufficient support of the governments, along with the change of gender roles have placed families under sever and constant pressure.The entrance of women to the labor market, on the one hand has added occupational responsibilities to their domestic responsibilities and on the other hand, has enabled them to earn part of family income and sometimes whole of it. In contrast, the inability of a large number of men to come to terms with the role of providing livelihood, as expected role in the society, has created a sense of powerlessness as well as physical diseases and depression in them. In such circumstances, marital incongruity and men's violent reaction in the form of abusing their wives and children are more likely to increase. In many other countries of the world in which the men have become displaced or unemployed due to the economic instability, we are witnessing a similar situation.[4] Observing a certain degree of correlation between economic poverty and domestic violence has led some to consider men's violence at home as a phenomenon specific to the lower class of society, especially the working class and thus support the popular assumption in this regard. According to them:

> Family can be an important place for venting frustrations arising from an inappropriate occupational situation, particularly for unskilled workers who receive little rewards from their work and who have little autonomy. The family is a refuge from these frustrations and this can explain more aggressive relationships with the wives and more violent upbringing methods which working class fathers adopt.[5]

But according to recent research, male violence is a trans-class phenomenon and probably the origin of this misconception has been the difference of social classes in terms of modes of violence and specific class values. Based on the research, men from lower class of society usually use violence by hitting on the face which leaves visible evident marks, while men from middle or upper class of society usually hit other parts of the body which their effects are less visible in public view. Additionally, women from middle or upper class of society are less likely to report violence to the police compared to women from lower class of society.

---

1 Bilton et al., *Introductory Sociology*,p.310.
2 Russo & Smith," Women in the Two-Thirds World", *Families in Global and Multicultural Perspective*, p.340.
3 Siegel,*Criminology*, p.301.
4 Cotgrove, *The Science of Society: An Introduction to Sociology*, pp.64-65.
5 Curry et al., *Sociology for the Twenty-First Century*, p.269.

c) A teleological explanation

Considering the motivations of men to commit domestic violence as well as the reasons and motivations of women to put up with violent husbands is the third approach of domestic violence issue. In feminist analyses men's violence is usually explained based on their tendency towards domination over women.Contrary to the notion that men's violent assaults at home are out of control and accidental, feminists believe men's violence is not a sign of the lack of control but a means to control. Some social psychologists have argued that aggression and violence are coercive processes which reflect the aggressive individual's conscious decision to use force against the victim and punish her because of some inappropriate acts she has committed. So, according to both feminists and these psychologists the use of force is optional and under the individual's control. Moreover, the aggressive person interprets domestic events in a certain way that supports and justifies the use of force.[1]

Furthermore, according to the studies carried out, the most important reasons for a woman to continue to live with her abusive and violent husband are as follows:

1. Fear of her husband's vengeance on her relatives or children;
2. The hope to change her husband's behavior eventually;
3. To protect herself against blame and social stigma;
4. Fear of admitting failure in life;
5. Lack of a safe haven;
6. Lack of child care facilities;
7. Fear of dealing with social problems of divorced women. [2]

10-3 Islam's point of view

Islam's approach to the issue of domestic violence, like in most other issues, is mainly a normative approach. Yet, by scrutinizing the necessities of religious recommendations, a theoretical framework can be achieved in which different micro and macro factors have been taken into consideration.In this theoretical framework, the impact of factors such as biology, learning, alcohol consumption, poverty, sexual frustrations, etc are assumed in domestic violence. Although Islam has adopted a specific position in dealing with each of these factors which are beyond the scope of this book, its special emphasis on some factors affecting domestic violence requires to provide an explanation regarding them though briefly.

The first and perhaps the most important factor from the Islamic point of view is the individual's lack of adherence to the ethical standards, and Islam's specific attention to this factor can be perceived from its abundant recommendations regarding morality in general and associating with women in a proper manner specifically. At the general level, the famous narration "Worldliness is the origin of all faults"[3] contains a general religious explanation which can be used in many social occasions. By breaking down the concept of worldliness to parameters or more detailed concepts such as arrogance,

---

1 Klein, *Multidisciplinary Perspective on Family Violence*, p.8.
2 Curry et al., Sociology for the Twenty – First Century,p.269; Bilton et al .,*Introductory Sociology*,p.310.
3 Horr Amelli, *Wasael al-Shia*, vol 11, p308.

prejudice, avarice, jealousy, stinginess, etc, we come up with diverse propositions that can be used for explanatory purposes and in particular, for explaining domestic violence.Moreover, ample recommendations about associating with women in a proper manner,[1]observing piety and avoiding beating them,[2] tolerance against women's moodiness and forgiving their faults[3] and focusing on piety as a criterion for selecting the husband[4] are just a fraction of Islam's moral recommendations which implicitly introduce bad temper as the cause of much marital violence.

Islam has recommended the women to associating with their husbands in a proper manner[5] that is because abusive women and those who lack internal control have a significant role in creating domestic tensions and finally male violence. In some narrations, the woman who use her tongue to utter word in ingratitude and cursing and insults to her husband is considered "pagan" and deserving divine retribution. [6]It's clear that by obliging women to moral values in practice, the cause of many marital conflicts is removed and in this case, the possibility of men's violence against their wives reaches to its lowest level.

The second factor involved in domestic violence which has received Islam's special concern, is the weakness in social control. The unique and progressive principle of ordering for good deeds and forbidding from evil deeds, in its wide range, includes different strategies of controlling the individual by the society and the government.Concerning the social control aspect, it can be clearly deduced from many verses and narrations related to this issue that what a high position Islam has attached for public supervision and public responsibility towards others and their deviant behaviors.Undoubtedly, the institutionalization of this significant principle in its correct and complete form will have a considerable impact on reducing or even eliminating many social deviations, including domestic violence. For example, if it comes to the point that committing domestic violence is faced with sever social punishments like "public shunning"(breaking off public relationship with the violent person which is one of the methods of forbidding from evil deeds) [7]it is very unlikely that such deviations will persist in the society.

---

1 Surah Nisa,19; Horr Amelli ,*Wasael al-Shia*, vol 14, p122.

2 Horr Amelli ,Ibid, p18,119; Nouri , *Mostadrek al-Wasael* , vol 14,p250.

3 Horr Amelli, Ibid, p 121,124.

4 A man consulted with Imam Hasan(AS) about the marriage of his daughter. The Imam said:" Marry your daughter to a religious and pious man; for such a person if he loves your daughter he will treat her honorably and respectfully and in case he does not love her, he will not oppress her.

5 Horr Amelli,*Wasael al-Shia*, vol14 ,p14-15, 113-116.

6 Ibid, p125,vol 18,p199; Also refer to : Nouri ,*Mostadrek al-Wasael*, Vol 14,p 240,248.

7 Imam Sadiq (AS) while making complaining comments said thus to his companions: " Am I not entitled to reprimand the innocent among you because of the sins of the sinners, while if you learn about the indecent act of one of you, you do not oppose or reject him and do not shun him and do not persecute him until he gives up his indecent act". Also, in another narration it has been quoted from him that: "I wish that whenever you get informed about someone's indecent act, all of you would go to him and declared that you must either keep away from us or quit this behavior, if he accepts that would be all right, and if not you would shun him. (Horr Amelli, *Wasael al- Shia*).

Concerning the governmental control the following narration is evident enough to show the crucial role and duty of the government in controlling domestic violence. It has been narrated by Imam Baqir (AS) that:

> One day Imam Ali (AS), the Commander of the believers, returning home in a very hot day found a woman standing next to her house. The woman said: "My husband has oppressed me and swore to beat me". Imam said:" Wait until it gets cooler, then I shall come with you". The woman said:" in this case, his anger will intensify". For a moment he bowed his head and then raised it up saying: "By Allah! The right of the oppressed should certainly be taken from the oppressor without hurting him/her". The Imam further asked where her house was and she told him. He accompanied her to her house and stood at the door and called loudly, "O master of the house! Peace be upon you." A young man came out. Imam Ali (AS) said:" O servant of God, fear God; you have frightened this woman and turned her out of the house". The young man [who did not recognize the Imam] said:" In what way does it concern you? By God, I shall throw her into fire because of your word". The Commander of the believers replied: "I'm ordering you to good deeds but you are doing evil deeds and turning away from good? [At the same time, he drew out his sword in a threatening way] at that time a crowd gathered there and saluted Ali (AS) addressing him the Commander of believers. When the rude young man recognized Ali (AS), he fell to his feet trembling and said: "O Commander of believers; forgive me; By God, I will treat her nicely and respectfully. Then Ali (AS) sheathed his sword turned to the woman and told her: "go to the house and do not behave in such a manner that your husband be forced to behave you in this manner".[1]

It cannot be denied that proper interference of the government has a significant impact on controlling domestic violence and it is remarkable that in Western countries in recent years, more attention has been paid to strengthen the role of police and the legal system in this connection.[2]

In short, given Islam's special concern for maintaining and strengthening the family institution, it has focused primarily on educational strategies centered on morality as well as cultural and governmental strategies centered on fulfilling the duty of ordering for good deeds and forbidding evil deeds for solving the problem of domestic violence.

o **Abstract**

- Domestic violence defined as physical, verbal or emotional abuse used by one of the family members against another member is a phenomenon which is seen more or less in all societies.
- The theorists who examine domestic violence based on the micro causal approach, focus on a set of factors such as biology, learning , weakness in self-control, alcohol consumption, hostility due to man' dependence on his wife

---

1 Nouri, *Mostadrek al-Wasael*, vol 12, p337.
2 Curry et al., *Sociology for the Twenty-First Century*, p.269.

,the man's obsession and excessive worry about the behavior his wife, burst of anger and the man's military service in the past or present.

- In macro causal explanations, the factors such as cultural and legal acceptance of domestic violence and economic factors have been identified as affecting the emergence of this phenomenon.

- In feminist teleological explanations, men's violence is explained according to their tendency towards domination over women.

- The most important factors of domestic violence from the Islamic point of view are the lack of adherence to ethical standards and weakness in social control. Hence, Islam has primarily emphasized the educational strategies centered on morality as well as cultural and government strategies centered on fulfilling the duty of ordering for good deeds and forbidding evil deeds more than other things to remove this phenomenon.

o **Self-Test**

1. Explain domestic violence based on social learning theory.
2. Explain domestic violence based on social control theory (psychological approach).
3. Does the men's violence against their wives is a specific phenomenon of lower class of society or a trans-class phenomenon? Explain.
4. What are the most important causes of women to live with abusive husbands?
5. Explain domestic violence from the Islamic point of view.

o **Research topic**

- Do a meta-analysis of research studies that have examined domestic violence in Iran.
- Research the factors of domestic violence in one of the country's cities or provinces.

CHAPTER 11

DIVORCE

Chapter11

Divorce

Learning objectives of chapter 11

Getting familiar with social factors involved in the increase of divorce rate and Islam's point of view in this regard

Based on stage objective of this chapter, the reader is expected to achieve the following objectives and be able to:

1. explain the growth of divorce rate in recent decades from the sociological perspective;
2. explain Islam's value and legal point of view regarding divorce.

Introduction

After presenting the definition of divorce and some of its statistics, we will review the most important factors involved in the increase of divorce in recent decades including the change of attitudes towards marriage, de-stigmatization of divorce, the change of family structure , the change of gender roles , the women's economic independence , economic welfare , sexual freedom , the change of divorce rules and demographic changes .In the following , value and legal view of Islam about divorce and its strategies to decrease the rate of divorce will be explained.

11-1 Definition of divorce

In Western legal systems, "divorce" implies the dissolution of a formal and legal marital relationship when both parties are still alive and after it they can marry once again.[1] "Marital dissolution "is a broad concept which divorce is one of its causes. Death of one of the spouses, separation and annulment of marriage are other forms of marital dissolution. "Separation" defined as social dissolution of marriage, occurs when one of the spouses leaves the other for a long time or prefers to stay away from him/her. What comes close to this concept, is the concept of "desertion" which is described as physical separation of wife and husband which often does not have formal and legal aspect, but in some Western countries we are faced with a form of legal separation which usually occurs before getting divorced and it is in such a way that two spouses agree upon to live in two distinct dwellings.

Islam's legal system has given special consideration to the legislation of divorce which also influences the definition of divorce. For example, since Islam distinguishes divorce and annulment, it considers the condition of "pronouncing the formula of divorce" valid in the definition of divorce and therefore, it excludes the dissolution due to marriage annulment which takes place without any certain formula from the definition. Also, unlike the aforementioned definition which has predicated remarriage upon being divorced, in the Islamic and other legal systems which permit polygyny,

---

1 Abercrombie et al, *A Dictionary of Sociology*, p125.

there is not such a condition for the man's remarriage. Moreover, such a condition is also void about the women's remarriage; because in the Islamic legal system a concept termed *"iddah"* has been included in the legislation and it refers to a certain period after divorce or the husband's death during which the divorced or widow woman is not permitted to marry once again. Accordingly, in "revocable divorce", a kind of divorce in the Islamic jurisprudence, the husband has the right to take the wife back before her iddah ends, without a new marriage contract and likewise, remove the validity of divorce. It should be mentioned that during this period the husband should pay the woman's alimony and provide her with a house. Considering these considerations, it can be said that from the Islamic point of view, divorce is "the dissolution of a legal marital relationship when the two parties involved are still alive, by pronouncing a certain formula which according to the rule is done by the husband, and after it and when *Iddah* ends, the woman can marry again".

11-2 A description of divorce phenomenon

Divorce, whether formal and legal or informal, such as separation and desertion, is a well-known phenomenon in all societies .Sometimes, a high rate of divorce has been reported in the primitive societies and also some known nations in previous periods (such as in Japan between the years 1887-1919, Algeria between the years 1887-1940 and Egypt between 1935-1954).[1] But as a result of value and legal changes in most of the Western countries in recent decades, divorce faced with an unprecedented growth, so that it is discussed as one of the parameters of "sexual revolution" in West.

Statistical data shows that the US has the highest divorce rate among other countries of the world. About 2/1 million divorces have been taken place in this country in 1997 which it shows a double increase compared to 1960.[2] The proportion of divorces granted during a year in the US to the marriages registered in the same year is 50 percent; that is every year per two marriages one divorce is granted. Calculating the frequency of divorce in proportion to total population indicates that per 1000 people, 4/1 people divorce.[3]

Rate of divorce in Canada which was less than 38 people per 1000 in 1951, reached more than 270 people per 1000 in 1991[4] and in some European countries like Sweden, Denmark, Hungary, Finland, West Germany and France, every year per one thousand marriages more than three hundred divorces are granted, although in the countries like Spain, Italy, Greece and Holland the rate of divorce is still relatively low and per one thousand marriages about 135 divorces are granted.[5]

Countries like Iran have experienced an increase in the divorce rate in recent years and this increase, especially in big cities, has been very remarkable. In 1992 the number of divorces for the whole country was 33,983 cases, while the figure reached 53,797 cases by 2000. The rate of divorce in the whole country increased from 0/63 per 1000

---

1 Goode, *The Family*, pp.92-93.
2 Allan & Crow , *Families ,Households and Society*,p.26.
3 Ward & Stone, *Sociology for the 21st Century*, p.296.
4 Allan & Crow , *Families ,Households and Society* ,p.26.
5 Grusec & Lytton, *Social Development: History ,Theory and Research*,pp.411-412.

to 0/85 per 1000 between the years 1996 and 2000 and this means that the rate of divorce has increased 35 percent during these four years.[1]

Likewise, the proportion of marriages to divorces in the whole country was twelve times as much in 2000, meaning that per 120 marriages 10 divorces were recorded, while this proportion was about 6/1 in Tehran; that is per 10 divorces, 61 marriages have been registered.[2]According to these statistics, the proportion of divorce to marriage in the whole country in 2000 was 8/33 percent which it dramatically rose to 12/09 percent (14/16 percent in urban areas and 6/88 percent in rural areas) by 2006.[3]

11-3 The factors affecting the growth of divorce rate in recent decades

Sociologists have emphasized several fundamental factors for explaining unprecedented growth of divorce in recent decades which will be reviewed in the following discussion.

a) The change of attitudes towards marriage

New concept of marriage in contemporary Western societies is considered as the most important factor affecting the increase of divorce rate. According to some sociologists, family and marriage have been changed from an "institution" into "companionship" from modern Western point of view.[4] From the view of Western couples, marriage is a contract taking place by utterly free choice and is based on romantic love. Such a concept of marriage in itself includes the concept of divorce and marital dissolution; because due to the instability and transience of romantic feelings, people may get out of romantic relationships as quickly as they get involved in them. With the fading of initial love, young couples not only don't see any reason to continue the relationship, but also have a justifiable reason to get out of it. A survey suggests that keeping romantic feelings alive is considered as an important thing for a successful marriage from the view of 78 percent of American women, while just 29 percent of Japanese women have such an insight.[5] On the basis of these considerations, some believe that high rate of divorce is not a short-term phenomenon, rather an atonement for the new concept of marriage.[6]

b) De-stigmatization of divorce

One of the factors playing a role in the integrity of the family is the sensitivity of public culture towards divorce.Sociologists have considered cultural restrictions of divorce, particularly stigmatization of divorce in public opinion and the frustration arising from it, the decline of divorced individual's social status and in some cases her/his social isolation as the factors contributing to family integration in many traditional societies; because these restrictions lead to the instilling of the family status in public opinion and the decrease of the likelihood of its dissolution. In contrast, the less the extent of

---

1 Amir Khosravi,: A Preliminarily Review of Divorce Statistics in the Last 10 Years in Iran", *Population*, n 35,36,39,40.
2 Ibid, p48.
3 Kord Zanghaneh, Jafar, "A Survey of Dynamics of Marriage and Divorce in Iran Relying on the nation-wide census of 2006", *Cultural Engineering Monthly*, n 21,22, p22.
4 Kuper & Kuper ,*The Social Science Encyclopedia* ,p.208.
5 Myers, *Exploring Social Psychology* ,p.284.
6 Mitchell, *Sociology of Family and Marriage* , p176.

divorce stigmatization and feeling of disgrace because of it, the more the possibility of the increase of divorce. This is a situation which is clearly seen in contemporary industrial societies.[1]

c) The change of family structure

The transfer from the extended family system to the nuclear family has played a significant role in the increase of divorce rate. In the first pattern, divorce is deplorable and maybe prohibited; because considering that marriage displays a unit of kinship relationship, political integration and economic benefits, divorce will require the dissolution of several complex and valuable social relationships. But divorce in the nuclear family merely ends the relationship between two people and does not have a direct impact on kinship relationships. As a result, the dissolution of marriage is faced with less restriction and particularly kinship groups do not put high pressure on the individual who asks for a divorce. Furthermore, the nuclear family is also more vulnerable in other respects; Independence and isolation of the nuclear family make it have less supportive sources outside of itself and this can lead to emotional and financial pressures.[2]

d) The change of gender roles

The change of spouses' family and social roles due to the change of social structures and the norms related to the pattern of traditional family (man as the breadwinner and woman as the housekeeper), is another fundamental factor affecting the increase of divorce rate. In a situation which gender equality is prevailed and approved as a public value, the feeling of injustice regarding domestic division of labor decreases the women's personal satisfaction of marital life and makes them to contemplate divorce more than men do. [3]Also, the women of today in comparison with their mothers and grandmothers are more likely to ask for a divorce. Whenever women want to have common decision making power and the husbands' participation in house chores and conversely, the husbands prefer traditional style of marital life, marital dissatisfaction will increase and the likelihood of divorce between such couples will rise.[4]

e) Women's economic independence

In the past, one of the most important reasons that kept women in the marital relationship was providing financial security; but unprecedented increase of the women's entrance to the labor market in recent decades has led to their economic independence and this has partly made the prospect of divorce bright and promising for the women who are dissatisfied with the marital condition. For this reason, studies show that working women are more likely to seek divorce than non-working women.[5] On the other hand, sometimes the woman's economic independence strengthens the husband's motivation for divorce; because the man who divorces his working wife can

---

1 Goode ,*The Family* ,p.94.
2 Curry et al., *Sociology for the Twenty-First Century*, p.267.
3 Huber & Spitz, "Trends in Family Sociology", *Handbook of Sociology*,p.432.
4 Lindsey & Beach , *Sociology : Social Issues*,p.384.
5 Segalen , *Historical Sociology of Family*, p181.

easily evade the responsibility of paying the expenses of the child care.[1]

However, the possibility of reciprocal causal effect in these kinds of variables should not be ignored. While the women's entrance to the labor market can be considered as one of the causes increasing divorce, it can also be one of its consequences and effects. Some researchers have gone so far as to regard the increase of women's employment as their reaction against the increasing possibility of divorce. They believe that married women, after observing the fact that increasing divorce is just around the corner, join to the work force to secure their future.[2]

f) Economic welfare

Economic welfare allows the individuals to focus their minds on the subjects beyond getting through daily life and consider the right of choosing personal happiness out of the marriage framework. Based on some comparative studies, very poor and very rich societies have the highest divorce rates and the societies whose position is at the intermediate level of economic development hold lower rates of divorce. [3]The intended hypothesis, i.e. the impact of high economic welfare on the increase of divorce rate, has specifically been emphasized about the society of America by some sociologists. Adducing to available statistics, they have indicated that the lowest rate of divorce in the US over the last 60 years belongs to the years of economic depression in this country, while the highest rate of divorce in the history of the US was in 1981(the period of economic flourish and public welfare).[4]

g) Sexual Freedom

Confining the function of sexual satisfaction to the family institution, has always been the main supports of the integrity of this social institution, and by escaping this confinement it should be naturally expected that a decrease of the individuals' commitment towards maintaining the family and consequently the increase of divorce rate will be experienced. Some sociologists believe that the traditional public attitude towards sexual activity as an act confined to reproduction has superseded by a new attitude which regards it as a recreation act and this is one of the factors which has led to the increase of promiscuity in the form of extra-marital relationships and then the increase of divorce rate.[5]

h) The change of divorce laws

There were numerous legal restrictions on divorce in Western countries in the past. One of these restrictions was the high cost of divorce which restricted divorce to rich and high-income individuals.For example, the average cost of a divorce was seven to eight hundred pounds in England during the Victorian era and most of the individuals who were not able to pay these costs were compelled to resort to the ways such as turning to prostitutes or servants, the separation from the spouse or abuse and violence

---

1 Curry et al., *Sociology for the Twenty-First Century*, p.268.
2 Huber & Spitz, "Trends in Family Sociology", *Handbook of Sociology*,p.432.
3 Sabini, *Social Psychology*, p.519.
4 Ward & Stone, *Sociology for the 21st Century*, p.296.
5 Ibid,p.297.

toward him/her. Currently, the decrease of financial costs of divorce has made it easy to obtain it whether for the rich or low income individuals.[1]

Another restriction placed by divorce laws was related to divorce causes; for example, the courts of America before 1970s followed the system of fault proof to issue a divorce decree according to which the causes of divorce such as adultery or alcohol consumption should be proved by the spouse and the proof of these causes required to distinguish a guilty from an innocent. The person who was found guilty, rarely could undertake the custody of the children and was faced with financial restrictions placed by the court but today the system of "no-fault divorce" has been approved in most states of the US and the incongruity of the couples can solely be the cause of legal dissolution of marriage.[2]

i) Demographic changes

In explaining the causes of the increase of divorce, the likelihood of the interference of demographic changes should not be ignored. In societies like Iran which after a period of rapid increase in population, the rate of population growth has been controlled and consequently the most population density has been placed at young ages, the rate of divorce increases naturally; because principally the highest percent of divorces belongs to young ages. It's clear that this increase is temporary and by passing through of the dense generation from young period to middle-age period, the rate of divorce-supposing the lack of other factors- declines and returns to the previous conditions.

Some have tried to explain the increase of divorce in American Society based on this point. They believe that the increase of divorce rate, especially in 1970s, due to the fact that the baby boom generation have passed the age of marriage in the period of the increase of birth rates (after World War II).This generation which was extraordinary dense and populous figured the highest rate of divorce in the US from the late 1960s to early 1980s.[3] But it seems the demographic factor dose not play a significant role in American society; because the rate of divorce in this country has gone through a relatively steady trend and one without dramatic increase during the last two decades and it means other factors have influenced the rate of divorce.

11-4 Islam's point of view

a) Divorce valuation

In explaining Islam's valuation about divorce, some set of religious prepositions should be noted. One set has introduced divorce as a very hated and absurd phenomenon; for instance, it has been narrated that "Nothing is more detestable by God than the family which is torn apart by divorce" and "God has not permitted anything more detestable to Him than divorce and God considers as His enemy whom divorces his wife capriciously.[4] Second set of prepositions including the recommendations of Islam to patience and the spouses forgiving each other and enduring economic failures and

---

1 Bilton et al., *Introductory Sociology*, p.300.
2 Ward & Stone , *Sociology for the 21st Century* ,p.296.
3 Shepard, *Sociology*,pp.304-305.
4 Horr Amelli ,*Wasael al-Shia* ,vol 15, p 267.

other marital problems implies that Islam hates divorce even in the case of the existence of endurable problems, and tries to prevent the sacred institution of family from being collapsed as far as possible.

But the third set includes the narrations which have considered divorce permissible and sometimes necessary in specific circumstances; for example, divorce in the cases of the spouse being irreligious and, having ideological or moral deviation has specifically been prescribed.We read in a narration that Imam Kazim (As) in his answer to a man who was going to ask his daughter's divorce said:" If you feel any dislike for your son-in-law because of religious causes and intend to release your daughter from him, do it, otherwise don not take a step to divorce".[1] Moreover, it has been narrated that some infallible Imams (AS) divorced their wives because of religious deviations.[2] Also, "judicial divorce" (obliging the husband to divorce by the court or granting divorce by the judge) has been established[3] in the case of avoiding the husband to supply his wife's alimony as it has been established after four years of the husband's missing.[4] Islam approves divorce regarding prostitution committed by the spouse.[5]

Consequently, irrespective of the mentioned exceptions, it can be said that Islam considers divorce as an extremely detestable thing and tries to keep the couples away from doing it. Of course, the reprehensibility attached to divorce has different levels and the highest level is related to capricious divorces as the following narration from Imam Baghir (AS) partly confirms this point:

> The Prophet went to a man and asked him: "What did you do about your wife?" He said: "I divorced her." The Prophet asked, "Did you find her doing anything wrong?" He answered "No, I didn't". The matter stopped here, and the man married again. After some time the Prophet again went to that man and asked him "Did you marry another woman?" He said, "Yes."; "What did you do about your wife?" He said: "I divorced her." The Prophet asked him, "Did you find her doing anything wrong?" He answered "No, I didn't". The Prophet said "Allah considers as His enemy and damns the man and woman who marry one after the other because of lust.[6]

b) The rights of wife and husband in divorce

In Islamic legal system unlike marriage which is of a contractual nature (mutual agreement), divorce has a unilateral obligation aspect; that is, the composition of it is done by one person who is according to the rule, the husband. In this regard, there is no disagreement between Shia and Sunni jurists and they generally agree that the right of divorce as a prior decree belongs to the husband and the wife cannot independently seeks for a divorce. Moreover, it can be inferred from some narrations,[7]practical

1 Ibid ,p 42-43.
2 Ibid , vol 14, p425.
3 Ibid ,Vol 15,p223.
4 Ibid, p389-390.
5 Ibid, Vol 14, p333.
6 bid, vol 15, p267.
7 Ibid, p 340; Nouri, *Mostadrek al-Wasael* ,vol 14, p 285; vol 15, p306.

behaviors of the Muslims and the fact that in the Quran and hadiths , divorce has always been attributed to men.

However, Islam has given the right of divorce to the woman through certain procedures. Firstly, the possibility of agreement divorce without financial cost by the woman and also the possibility of *khula* divorce (in the case of woman's aversion to her husband) and *mubarat* divorce (in the case of the couples' mutual aversion to each other) are provided which in these two last cases the woman pays an amount of money to the husband or forgives mehrieh or portion of it to him so that he may divorce her. Secondly, judicial divorce has been appointed in cases such as the avoidance of the husband to pay alimony;[1] according to some jurists in all of the cases which the woman will have to bear loss or severe hardship to continue her conjugal life, the legitimacy of judicial divorce can be proved by adducing to the rules preventing loss and distress.[2] Thirdly, the rule of condition attached to the contract as a clause added to the rules and initial orders which many Shia jurists approve it and civil code of Islamic republic of Iran has been drawn up on its basis has provided the possibility of decision making in divorce for the women, for example in such a way that the woman stipulate as a condition either absolutely or conditionally to the marriage contract to represent her husband in executing the divorce contract.[3]

Despite the mentioned strategies, the question remains why has Islam given the right of divorce to the husband as a prior decree and has not set forth other patterns in its legal system such as confining the right of divorce to the courts or the equality of wife and husband in this right,[4]although at first glance these two patterns may seem to be serving justice more? It seems that the first pattern requires ignoring marital emotional aspects as a relationship belonging to a private area and reducing it to a mere legal relationship belonging to the public area. Therefore, it is more compatible with the contexts in which the family has lost its holiness and turned into a partnership unit such as trading companies. Aiming at maintaining and strengthening emotional bonds between the wife and husband, Islam has taken a step to decrease the interference of law in the family conflicts and divorce and does approve it just in the cases that the couples themselves do not have the required competence to protect rights and to carry out justice.

Regarding the disagreement of Islam with the second pattern, no clear-cut reason has been mentioned in the religious texts, although we cannot consider none of these differences as an independent cause or sufficient condition, it seems that some biological and social differences have been taken into consideration in this regard. Regarding natural differences, we can mention some cases like the dominance of the spirit of hunting in male sex and the spirit of submission in female sex, the intensity of man's sexual need to woman in comparison with woman's, and generally the difference

---

1 Horr Amelli, Ibid ,p 223-226.
2 Tabatabaee Yazdi, *Takmelah al-Orvat -ol-Vosgha*, vol 1.p 75; Motahari , *The System of Women's Rights in Islam*, p347-359.
3 Horr Amelli, Wasael al-Shia,Vol 15,p30; Imam Khomeini, The Book al-Bie , Vol 5, p 170-173; 173; Safayi & Emami , *The Rights of Family* ,p 287-289.

between man and woman in the kind of their feeling to each other. Master Motahhari in his book *The System of Woman's Right in Islam* has explained some of these differences by adducing to the research conducted by psychologists and in justifying the granting of divorce right to the men says:

> Woman's attachment to man is the result of man's attachment to her and depends upon it. Nature has placed the key of their mutual love within the control of man. If the man loves his wife and is faithful to her, woman also loves him and remains faithful to him... Nature has put the key of the dissolution of marriage in the hands of man. In other words, it is man who by his own apathy and unfaithfulness towards his wife makes her cold and uninterested. Conversely, if the apathy begins on the side of the wife, it does not affect the man's affection, rather occasionally makes the affection more acute. Hence, man's apathy to woman leads to mutual apathy but woman's apathy does not. [1]

The difference between economic roles of man and woman should also be noted in social differences; because the possibility of the continuity of family life greatly depends on the man's ability to meet the livelihood needs of the family, but the woman's inability to support the family economically does not usually expose the family life to a fundamental crisis, therefore, deciding on the continuity of marriage has given to the man. In this regard, the issue of financial costs of marriage , particularly mehriyeh of previous marriage and possible remarriage, which have been fallen on the man's shoulders and the woman are exempted from those, has probably been involved in granting the right of divorce to men; because these costs are more likely to deter men from getting a divorce.

c) Strategies of decreasing the rate of divorce

Islam has proposed different strategies for decreasing the rate of divorce which will be examined in the following chapters. Here, it can be said in brief that Islam has greatly emphasized moral, upbringing and educational strategies and has resorted less to setting legal obstacles. That is because setting legal restrictions against divorce does not help strengthen marital relationships so much, because supposing the disturbance of these relationships, by setting a legal obstacle against divorce, other unfavorable alternatives such as emotional divorce due to extreme coldness of relationships, domestic violence or informal separation will be expected. A legal obstacle on divorce can decrease the individuals' motivation for getting married and this is contrary to the goal which Islam follows in its social system.

Nonetheless, Islam has determined specific criteria and rituals for pronouncing the formula of divorce which can be effective in deceasing the motivation for divorce if the conflicts are not serious; including that the woman should not be in menstrual period at the time of divorce and after the end of period the divorce is valid only in the case that no sexual relationship is has taken place and additionally, the presence of two just witnesses is necessary for the authenticity of divorce.[2] The existence of these criteria

---

1 Motahhari, *The System of Women's Rights in Islam*, p316-317.
2 Horr Amelli, *Wasael al-Shia*, vol 15, p277-284.

which commonly delay divorce, provides a suitable ground for the couples to review and then to subside their anger and fleeting excitements and more reflection on its outcome.

o **Abstract**

- Divorce, death of the spouse, separation and the annulment of marriage are different causes of marital dissolution.
- As a result of value and legal changes in recent decades in most Western countries, the rate of divorce has faced with an unprecedented growth.
- In explaining unprecedented growth of divorce in recent decades, sociologists have emphasized the factors such as the change of attitudes towards marriage, de-stigmatization of divorce, the change of family structure from extended system to nuclear one, the change of the spouses' family and social roles, the women's economic independence, economic welfare, sexual freedom, the change of divorce laws and demographic changes.
- Irrespective of the exceptions like the spouse being irreligious or moral deviation of the spouse, the husband's avoidance of supplying alimony for the spouse and committing prostitution by the spouse, Islam regards divorce as an absurd affair and tries to prevent the individuals from it.
- The right of divorce as a prior decree granted to the husband; however, Islam has given the woman the right to choose in the matter of divorce through certain procedures.
- In order to decrease divorce rate, Islam has greatly emphasized the moral, upbringing and educational strategies and resorted less to setting legal obstacles.

o **Self- Test**

1. Define divorce from the Islamic point of view.
2. How has the change of family structure from extended to nuclear form helped the increase of divorce rate?
3. What is the relationship between economic conditions of society and the growth of divorce rate? Explain.
4. Why has Islam granted the right of divorce as a prior decree to the husband?
5. Why has Islam resorted less to setting legal obstacles to decrease divorce?

o **Research topic**

- Research the change of attitudes towards marriage and divorce in one of the regions of the country.
- Research the relationship between divorce and the women's socio—economic status and role in Iran.
- Research social consequences of divorce.

CHAPTER 12

STRATEGIES OF STRENGTHENING THE FAMILY

Chapter 12

Strategies of strengthening the family

Learning objectives of chapter 12

Getting familiar with the Islamic strategies of strengthening the family

Based on stage objective of this chapter, the learner is expected to achieve the following learning objective and be able to:

- state the most important strategies of strengthening the family from the Islamic point of view.

Introduction

In this chapter, the most important internal[1] and external[2] strategies of strengthening the family will be introduced on the basis of religious teachings and sociological findings. These strategies will be discussed in the following eightfold topics: Improving the process of mate selection, training the spouses, improving the attitudes, regulating sexual issues, reproduction, social support, social monitoring and moral-religious upbringing.

12-1 Improving the process of mate selection

Since a proper and rational choice in the process of mate selection can greatly guarantee the integrity of family life, a significance portion of scientific discussions and religious themes tends towards presenting the strategies which help the individuals and families to choose the best options from among the available ones. In the following, we will mention the most important strategies.

a) **Conscious choice**

Many family conflicts arise from hastiness and failing to do a detailed research in mate selection and sometimes from deliberate deception and delusion. A large number of people who seek for a divorce consider their wrong choice in the process of mate selection as the reason for their decision.

On the other hand, sometimes we are witnessing the expansion of inefficient ways to acquire the necessary information for this purpose in the society. For example, today many individuals in West turn to cohabitation and regard it as a trial period to acquire sufficient knowledge of the attitudes, behaviors and mood of each other before marriage , while according to diverse studies, cohabitation does not have any impact on marital congruity and satisfaction and the couples who have previously experienced cohabitation have a slight chance to achieve the marital success in comparison with

---

1 Internal strategies designate the methods which should be implemented by the members of the family.
2 External strategies rest upon the methods whose responsibility of implementation is fallen on the shoulders of the agents outside the family, educational and legislative institutions and social control.

others and are less satisfied with their marriage and have less commitment to it.[1] A survey in America and Sweden indicated that the divorce rate among the individuals who have previously spent a period of cohabitation is 80 percent more than the divorce rate among those who have not had such an experience.[2] Perhaps the reason is that trial aspect is usually overshadowed by other aspects. The results of some research indicate that unlike many women who consider cohabitation as a trial marriage, a large number of men look at it as an alternative for marriage and as a way for satisfying the sexual need.[3]

In the Islamic texts, many methods have been prescribed or encouraged by observing specific limits and standards in order to guarantee a better understanding of the two marrying parties of each other. Among these methods we can mention the "consultation" which has been emphasized in the Quran and hadiths either in general and in particular (marriage counseling), and we encounter abundant instances in this regard in the practical behaviors of the Holy Prophet (pbuh) and Infallible Imams (AS).

Islam has prescribed and encouraged the girl and boy's meeting before marriage in order to get familiar with each other's outward characteristics and even has removed some of canonical restrictions of looking at non-mahram in this special case.[4] Meantime, any false claim about possessing special advantages or resorting to any deceptive means in order to conceal his/her defects has been prohibited under the rubric of "guile' and in this case, the other party involved has the right to dissolve the marriage.[5]

Moreover, given relative restriction of the girls in obtaining the required information, Islam, aiming at increasing the confidence of the girl in mate selection, has predicated her marriage, in addition to her own consent, upon the consent of her guardian (father or grandfather) who is usually a competent and reliable reference for this work. Although some jurists have come to conflict with each other regarding the necessity of this legal policy due to the difference existed in the themes of narrations related, it can make possible a conscious choice; because it provides the possibility of taking advantage of the father's valuable knowledge and experiences as a reliable asset for the girl.

a) Respect for the boy and girl's opinion

One of the things which has had relative prevalence in traditional cultures was forcing the girl and sometimes the boy to marry. Specific structures of traditional societies were consistent with these kinds of forced marriages and sometimes even as a norm it has been encouraged. But in current conditions we are witnessing the emergence of tensions in this regard arising from the tendency of past generation towards maintaining old beliefs and the tendency of new generation towards possessing an

---

1 Kendall, *Sociology in Our Times*, pp.428-429.
2 Turner, *Concepts and Applications of Sociology*, pp.428-429.
3 Lindsey & Beach, *Sociology: Social Life and Social Issues*, p.387.
4 Horr Amelli, *Wasael al-Shia*, vol 14, p59-61.
5 Refer to : Safayi & Imami, *Family Rights in Brief*, p190.

independent identity. Consequently, if a girl or a boy is forced to marry against her/his will, most likely there will be incongruity and conflict in such a family.

Based on this and given the emphasis of Islam on the right of boy and girl in mate selection, [1]we can regard the necessity of considering and respect for their choice as one of the strategies of strengthening the family.

b) Establishing the boy and girl's maturity

The maturity of boy and girl is one of the effective factors in fulfilling marital congruity and guaranteeing the integrity of the family. The research conducted on the factors of family disturbance in Western countries, has placed early marriage in line with the most important factors.[2] It's clear that the correlation between lower age at marriage and the increase of marital disturbance greatly results from the lack of the spouses' maturity in different age, sexual, mental, intellectual, emotional and social dimensions.

While Islam has placed its orientation towards reasonable decreasing of marriage age, it has also emphasized the necessity of the girl and boy's achieving the minimum of growth in the afore-mentioned dimensions.[3] Therefore, irrespective of different interpretations about the concept of the boy and girl's maturity, establishing their maturity can be regarded as another strategy for strengthening the family in the stage of mate selection.

c) Observing homogamy

Family experts regard cultural and personality similarity of the spouses as a determining factor in the integrity of the family life as they have considered other kinds of homogamy such as homogamy in education, family status and age effective in marital congruity .It seems the importance of such similarities is because of their close relationship with personal or cultural similarity.

The wife and husband's cultural similarity which includes common language, religion, nationality, values, insights and beliefs, provides a basis for common interests and understandings and plays an important role in decreasing the misunderstandings and in providing an easier solution for the possible problems, while the difference between the wife and husband in the areas of religion , ethic, class or even geography causes them to build varied expectations regarding the issues such as nature and content of marital roles which provides the ground for the emergence of tension and incongruity and consequently the disintegration of the family.[4]

Similarity in personality traits also increases the likelihood of the individuals being attracted to each other and establishing more stable relationship between them. Conversely, the couples who have completely opposite temperament are more likely to be incongruent and in conflict with each other. Of course, as some psychologists have

---

1 Refer to : This book , chapter 3, " Patterns of Mate Selection".
2 Sabini, *Social Psychology*,p.519.
3 Regarding age and sexual puberty, refer to Horr Ameli, *Wasaiel Al-Shia*,Vol 14 , p 72; Regarding mental and intellectual maturity, refer to :Ibid , p 56-57 , Regarding emotional maturity, refer to Ibid 15-21,54; Regarding social maturity, refer to : Ibid , p 14 , 13,18.
4 Winch, *The Modern Family*,p.554.

noted, there must be a distinction drawn between different personality traits. While contrasts such as hot temperament in sex –sexual frigidity, introversion- extroversion, being organized- disorganized and cleanliness- dirtiness are more likely to lead to the incongruity between the couples, contrasts like the tendency towards guardianship – attachment, domineering-submission, masculinity - femininity and other reciprocal traits which complement each other, play a significant role in strengthening the marital bond.[1]

Islam has focused on the homogamy in mate selection under the rubric of "being well-matched"; although, in the definition presented by Islam regarding the wife and husband's being well-matched, religious and moral homogamy have taken on special importance.[2] Abundant historical evidence from the advent of Islam and next periods and even many evidence of contemporary periods indicates the fact that the Islamic homogamy pattern has been a successful pattern in terms of providing the family's integrity, and pious spouses and those who adhere to religious values are less likely to be trapped in the family conflicts due to the secondary incongruities.

d) Training the spouses

The integrity of family relationships greatly depends on the spouses' possession of certain knowledge and skills related to marital and parenting roles including which we can point to sexual knowledge and skills, getting familiar with sex differences, having an awareness of the needs of parenthood and having proper understanding of the requirements of different periods of family life. Accordingly, training marital and parenting roles becomes necessary, whether formally (holding educational courses and classes for the couples before and after marriage) or informally (socialization by the agents such as family, peers, mass media and religious centers).

Informal training has always played a role in the process of preparing the youth for marriage and it has an undeniable importance even in modern world, whether in industrial societies or non-industrial societies, with the difference that some changes have occurred in the agents of socialization and the extent of their effectiveness. One of the obvious aspects of these changes is the decrease of the teenagers' relationship with adults in modern societies which the factors such as geographical separation of workplace and residence, the disappearance of neighborhood phenomenon, the impact of television and the mothers' employment have been involved in the emergence and expansion of it.[3] However, the family is still one of the main agents of socialization and has profound effects on the people's individual and social life.

Despite the importance of informal methods, it seems that formal training has also been turned out to be an inevitable necessity for most contemporary societies. The increase of cultural and class heterogeneities, the rise of the rate of social mobility, the complexity of roles and extended value changes in these societies can expose the solidarity and integrity of the families to serious perils and damages. Therefore, the rapid expansion of counseling centers and the inclusion of educational courses in high

---

1 Aronson, *The Social Animal*, pp.375-376.
2 Refer to this book, Chapter 2," Homogamy".
3 Segalen , *Historical Sociology of Family*, p224.

schools and universities which have also been welcomed by the public, should be taken as a good and auspicious sign as an effective action to increase the family's integrity, provided that these programs are not designed and performed against religious standards and in a traumatic way.

12-3 Improving the attitudes

One of the things which seriously damages the family's integrity is the spouses' utterly idealistic and irrational expectations of the family life. The more rational and realistic are the couples' expectations, the less likely it is that predictable or unpredictable effects will harm the unity and integrity of the family. In fact, one of the distinctions between the Western marriages and traditional marriages lies behind this point. The dominance of romantic attitude toward marriage in West imposes very high and unreasonable expectations on the families which often are not met and this causes disintegration in the marital relationships. According to William, J. Good:

> A young Western youth who looks at marriage from a romantic love perspective, has very high expectations and is dissatisfied with his /her steady and boring life though accompanied by comfort, while in many societies the youth are taught to expect respect from their partner in the best of conditions but they should not expect happiness.[1]

That is why according to some estimates in the US, of 100 love marriages 93 cases ended in an agonizing and abject failure and in France the average length of every love marriage was three and a half months[2].

In the Islamic insight, it has been focused on the rationality of expectations, i.e. realism and avoiding being dominated by imaginations and illusions in different ways, such as reminding material and spiritual functions of the family and encouraging to acquire otherworldly rewards. Also, focusing on hidden and ignored advantages of marital relationship can prevent the hasty decisions which may be made due to failing to meet some irrational expectations. In this regard, the Holy Quran says:" treat them [your wives] kindly and if you dislike them [for any reason] [immediately do not seek for a divorce and remember that] perhaps you dislike a thing and Allah makes therein much good".[3] In order to reduce idealistic expectations, some hadiths have focused on the point that the husband's insistence on changing his wife's bad mood – the converse is also true - can bring negative effects on their relationship. [4]

In the light of this rational view, the position of love in marriage finds a distinctive interpretation. As one of the scholars interprets:

> A love deserves to be praised which grows gradually and naturally, its life source is intimacy and closeness and the compatibility of temperaments and its fruits and products are gentleness and sweet and calm constancy. On the basis of such love we can establish a stable, happy and healthy life. An intense love is

---

1 Goode ,*The Family*, p.93.
2 Keyniya, *The Underlying Tenets of Criminology*, Vol 2, p 808.
3 Surah Nisa, 19.
4 Horr Amelli, *Wasael al-Shia*, vol 14, p123-124.

like a hot fever which soon brings sweat and cools itself down.[1]

12-4 Regulation of sexual issues

a) Satisfying sexual need

Since satisfying sexual need is one of the important goals of forming a family, the fulfillment of this goal should be regarded as an effective factor in strengthening the family and in contrast, by occurring any disturbance in its fulfilment we should expect the disturbance in the marital relationship.

In this regard, the difference between the man and woman's sexual need should be taken into consideration. Diverse researches imply that the men in their overall evaluation of marriage value sexual relationships more than women do. That is why in marital conflicts and even in divorce cases, complaint about unsatisfactory sexual relationships is usually expressed by men.[2] Other studies have shown that rejecting man's request to have sex by his wife leads to his great agitation, while the woman's agitation appears when she feels that her husband does not love her anymore.[3] Therefore, in discussing the impact of sexual satisfaction on the family's integrity it's necessary to pay enough attention to the role of sex, as verses and hadiths have paid special attention to both mentioned points, i.e. the importance of satisfying sexual needs of men and women and the role of sex differences.[4]

b) The restriction of sexual relationships

One of the important social factors which has a determining role in propelling the individuals to form a family and then maintain its integrity is the restriction of satisfying sexual instinct to the marital relationship. Understanding the causal relationship between these two categories is not difficult, particularly for those who have experienced contemporary Western societies and observed devastating effects of sexual freedoms and the expansion of diverse, low cost and more attractive alternatives for marriage every day. Western scholars acknowledge that when the individuals do not look at the family as an exclusive place for satisfying the sexual need, the extent of public commitment to maintaining this social institution strongly decreases.[5]

Islam has taken a step to strength the family by setting boundaries between the legal and illegal ways of satisfying sexual desire and trying to institutionalize legal ways and removing illegal ones. Homosexuality, masturbation and "adultery" in the form of the ways such as friendly relationships between boys and girls, rape, prostitution have been identified as the most obvious illegal ways which have been rejected by Islam and heavy penalties have been issued for those who commit them.

It is noteworthy that we are faced with the legitimization of temporary marriage in Islam as one of the legal ways of satisfying sexual desire which some people might

---

[1] Keyniya, *The Underlying Foundation of Criminology*, Vol 2, p 809.

[2] Goode, *The Family*, p.97

[3] Baron & Byrne, *Social Psychology*, p.308.

[4] Refer to: This book, chapter7, "Regulation of sexual behavior".

[5] Heler, " Women, Civil Society and Government", *The Second Sex*, p58.

wrongly consider as a way of promoting sexual immoralism and in opposition to the ideal of the family's integrity, but by a reflection on the narrations of Infallible Imams (AS), incorrectness of this impression and Islam's realistic view will become clear; because according to these narrations, the primary reason behind the legitimization of temporary marriage is to provide the possibility of satisfying sexual desire for single men or men who are away from their wives,[1] but there is no encouragement to temporary marriage for married men those who do not have any problem in satisfying their sexual desire but it has been used to revive the Prophet's (AS) *sunnah* and to combat heresy and in fact it has assumed a political-cultural feature. Therefore, in some narrations, stubborn insistence on temporary marriage and neglecting the permanent spouse have been criticized.[2]

Furthermore, historical and cross –cultural examination of illegal sexual relationship imply the universality of this phenomenon and this indicates the existence of natural needs which the family institution has not had the capacity to meet them by itself. It seems that Islam, by legitimizing temporary marriage, has tried to fill the gap of a regulated and legal way for meeting this class of needs, the needs that in any case – even if the family institution occupies the highest social status –lead at least a part of the society's population to adulterous relationships. In a narration, Imam Ali (AS), the Commander of the Believers, says:" If second Caliph had not opposed to me and outdone my decree and not prohibited temporary marriage, nobody but ill-fated individuals would have committed adultery".[3]

c) The restriction of man and woman's mixing

The restriction of man and woman's relationships in public social interactions is one of the effective factors in strengthening the family. Given the attractions and provocations that naturally governs the interaction of the two sexes, their mixing in public environments provides a breeding ground for the growth of lustful desires and impermissible pleasures and consequently the weakness of their motivation for forming a family and maintaining it, and the emergence of consequences such as tension, conflict, problematic relationships, infidelity, divorce and frequent remarriages. According to a comparative study conducted in 66 countries, the more the men and women intermingle in a society, the higher the rate of divorce will be. [4]

Various recommendations have been made in the Quran and narrations in order to decrease the man and woman's mixing including which we can point to the necessity of hijab , prohibition of showing ornaments and wearing make up by woman in front of a non-mahram man, the necessity of preserving coyness, modesty and sobriety in walking and talking, prohibition of being alone with a non-mahram, prohibition of lustful gaze at a non-mahram, abomination of inviting a non-mahram to join for a meal and prohibition of physical touch with a non-mahram.[5] In addition to decreasing

---

1 Hor Amelli, *Wasael al-Shia*, Vol 14, p 440-449.
2 Ibid, p 450.
3 Ibid, p 436,440.
4 Sabini, *Social Psychology* ,p.519.
5 Refer to: Surah Nour,30-31; Surah Qasas,25 ; Surah Ahzab ,32; Horr Amelli, *Wasael al-Shia*, vol 14, p133-174.

adulterous relationships in society, these recommendations aim at minimizing the natural sensitivity towards sex subject in public places in such a way that it reduces the preoccupation that this subject might create for men and women who get engaged in social interactions. Undoubtedly, the resolution of such preoccupations is the main precondition for God's remembrance and the tendency towards spirituality which has been given a high status in Islamic teachings and without a doubt play a significant role in strengthening the family.

12-5 Childbearing

Many studies and objective experiences have shown that birth of the child plays a prominent role in strengthening the family and in contrast, infertility imposes a natural dissatisfaction on the couples, particularly if the spouses have an abundant enthusiasm to have a child and also it exposes the family to disintegration despite the various attractions that family life offers. Will Durant says:

> Marriage before having a child is a contract to provide mutual physical comfort, but after the birth of the child it obtains its actual meaning .The child… is like the water which is absorbed by a plant to make it fresh and full-blown. [1]

However, in Western societies along with the development of individualistic attitudes, the tendency towards having a child has decreased; because the children naturally impose different mental and economic restrictions and pressures on the family and significantly reduce individual freedoms to perform favorite occupational , educational and similar activities; as a result, the children have been turned into a factor responsible for decreasing the couples' marital satisfaction and this has led to the increase of the families without children in industrial societies. For example, in America, in 1998, of total 53 percent of the households in which the wife and husband lived together, just 25 percent had children and 28 percent of them were childless. [2]

It is supposed in Islam that the child imposes different physical and mental problems on the parents during different stages of her/his life.[3] Nevertheless, religious recommendations embody the strategies through which Islam has tried to make children the cause of increasing the parents' satisfaction and as a result strengthening the marital bond instead of being the cause of their frustration and dissatisfaction. Of these strategies it can be referred to a great encouragement to childbearing and upbringing the children by reminding material and spiritual interests that children bring for parents,[4] the institutionalization of treating the parents kindly in order to bolster the motivations of childbearing and upbringing the children in them[5] and finally trying to bolster kinship ties.

---

1 Duran, *Pleasures of Philosophy*, p177.
2 http:// www.U.S.Bureau of the Census.
3 Surah Ahghaf, 15; Horr Amelli, *Wasael al-Shia*, Vol 15, p 99,100,198.
4 Ibid, p95-100, 106, 211.
5 Surah Bagharah ,83 ; Nisa ,36 ; Anam, 151; Asra, 23-14; Ankabut, 8; Loghman,14-15; Ahghaf, 15.

12-6 Social support

Since the continuity of family life as a social unit depends on fulfilling its different financial and non-financial needs and considering the fact that family cannot fulfil all of its needs by itself, providing social support for it as one of the main strategies of strengthening the family becomes necessary. Of the most important types of social support, it can be referred to support of relatives, friends, neighbors and the government.

The supportive role of relatives is more pronounced in traditional societies. Due to the dominance of extended family pattern in these societies, relatives are usually available to help small family groups and consequently, family tensions are less likely to harm the individuals. In addition to relatives, friends and neighbors can also bond the couples by their supports and it seems that their effectiveness is also compatible with the conditions of modern societies.[1]However, negative impact of the aforementioned groups on strengthening the family should not be forgotten, particularly in the cases that there is an opposition to marriage or there is dissatisfaction and disapproval for either one of the spouses. In societies like Iran, conflicts arising from the interference of relatives makes up high percentage of marital disputes.[2]

The government has also a duty to support the family in different economic, educational, legal and similar aspects. These supports are as follows: economic aspect which includes facilitating and providing support in marriage and solving the youth's unemployment problem; educational aspect, taking advantage of educational, counselling and media facilities in order to promote the couples' awareness and skills, and legal aspect, eliminating the shortcomings of legislation and enacting more effective laws to strengthen the family foundation.

It is worth noting that the government's active support to strengthen the family should not be confused with passive support which maintains the current situation and which sometimes leads to the dissolution of the family. Supporting the family in West by welfare states was dependent on a pattern which made the family redundant by degrees. In addition to educating the youth and offering health services to the public, the welfare state shouldered the responsibility of caring for the children and elderly by expanding nurseries, kindergarten and nursing homes and therefore, replaced the family, a trend which played a significant role in the dissolution of a warm and intimate family.[3] Accordingly, there is a need to observe prudence and foresight in the policies of family support and avoid taking a shallow and on the surface attitude and unjustified imitation of Western patterns.

12-7 Social monitoring

Social monitoring can be found in different aspects of mutual family monitoring as well as monitoring by relatives, friends, neighbors, public and government. It is considered to be one of the most effective strategies to strengthen the family. For instance, we can point to the spouses' mutual monitoring on each other's behaviors and the parents'

---

1 Goode,*The Family*,p.96.
2 Behnam & Rasekh , *An Introduction to Sociology of Iran*, p181.
3 Heller," Women, Civil Society and the State", *The Second Sex*, p59.

monitoring on their children's behavior including sexual issues, monitoring by neighbors and friends through positive interference in the family tensions, public monitoring as a strong support for normative system of the society which makes the violation of accepted values difficult, and the monitoring by the government on legislation and law enforcement.

Islam has made various recommendations which represent some aspects of Islamic monitoring system e.g. encouraging zealotry among men as a protective shield, the necessity of relatives' intervention in severe marital conflicts by determining an arbitrator of man's relatives and an arbitrator of woman's relatives, the necessity of ordering good deeds and forbidding evil deeds for all the people in the society especially authorities, the necessity to deal with domestic violence by the government and forbidding the negligence of the officials in implementing divine punishment.

12-8 Reinforcing the religiosity

Reinforcing the religiosity or religious and moral upbringing is one of the main strategies of strengthening the family which not much attention has been paid to it. For example, some views tend to focus on the couples' cultural, educational and age incompatibility or economic problems as the factors involved in family disruption more than the couples' weakness in religiosity and morality. However, there are some evidences indicating that even in the case of the homogeneity of the couples in different dimensions, weakness of religious and moral upbringing by itself can breakdown the family. On the other hand, there are some cases in which, in spite of the couples' heterogeneity in different ways, their commitment to religious and moral principles has brought the family's integrity. Hence, a greater share should be assigned for the element of faith and morality than other factors in maintaining the integrity of the family. Religious faith makes life meaningful, creates a sense of satisfaction and hope for the future in the people and therefore, causes them to tolerate the vicissitudes of life. The religious people while reasonably strive to provide material needs and create an ideal family do not get disappointed dealing with problems such as poverty, family conflicts but believe on the promises of God and by the sweetness of faith and remembrance of God turn the life's bitterness to sweetness. Also having valuable moral characteristics such as honesty, loyalty, respect, kindness, compassion, humility, patience, forgiveness, gentleness, fairness and being free from arrogance, superiority complex, feelings of inferiority, envy, avarice, greed, malice and duplicity and hypocrisy can eliminate conflicts and mistreatments in the families .Therefore, of multiple criteria for mate selection, Islam has put an extraordinary emphasis on the individual's religious-moral upbringing.[1]

o **Abstract**

From the Islamic point of view, the most important strategies of strengthening the family are as follows:

1. Modifying the process of mate selection through providing a suitable ground which makes a conscious choice possible, respect for the boy and girl's

---

1 Horr Amelli, *Wasael al-Shia* , vol 14, p 14, 51,54.

opinion , establishing the boy and girl's maturity in different age, sexual, mental ,intellectual , emotional and social aspects and establishing homogamy;

2. Training marital and parenting roles, formally and informally;
3. Modifying the attitudes to develop realism and rationality of expectations in marriage;
4. Regulating sexual issues in three pivotal bases: satisfying sexual needs , confining the satisfaction of sexual instinct to marital relationship and restricting the men and women's mixing in public environments;
5. Reinforcing the parent's motivations for childbearing and upbringing the children;
6. Social support of the family in the form of the supports by relatives , friends, neighbors and the government;
7. Social monitoring of the family in different aspects of mutual family monitoring , the monitoring by relatives, friends and neighbors, public monitoring and government monitoring;
8. Reinforcing religiosity or religious-moral upbringing of the individuals.

o **Self-Test**

1. What ways has Islam set forth for increasing the boy and girl's mutual familiarity before marriage?
2. Do opposite personality characteristics of the wife and husband cause the integrity or disintegration of the marital bond? Explain.
3. Why has formal training of marital and parental roles have become a necessity in modern societies?
4. Does the legitimization of temporary marriage in Islam contrast with the ideal of the family's integrity? Explain.
5. How does the individuals' religious and moral upbringing affect the integrity of the family?

o **Research topic**

- Research to what extent the parents' agreement with the boy and girl's marriage affects the success of their marriage.
- Research the situation of early marriages in Iran.
- Research the extent of the success of Islamic pattern of homogamy in fulfilling the family integrity.
- Research the extent of Iranian young couples' awareness of and skills at marital and parental roles.
- Research the impact of sex mixing on the disintegration of the family in Iranian society.
- Research the impact of the children on the integrity of the family in Iranian society.
- Research the role of the individuals' religious –moral upbringing in the integrity of the family in Iran.

PART V

THEORETICAL PERSPECTIVEOF SOCIOLOGY

OF THE FAMILY

Today, theory occupies a significant position in the research of different fields including humanities and that is because of its important functions, particularly regulating and consolidating diverse and scattered data, providing the likelihood of explaining and predicting the phenomena and human behaviors and helping adopt more accurate methods of policymaking and social planning.

Theorizing on the family has mainly developed in sociology and social psychology but other fields of social sciences have not generally paid enough attention to this issue or have considered it as secondary and subordinate. Even social psychologists until recently when dealing with the issue of family, usually did not consider it as one of the main topics but as one of the grounds of as a basis for the development of main interests of this field such as socialization, intimacy, love and violence, but from the early 1980s, by founding the field of family knowledge and professional branch of family sociology, we have been witnessing the development of theoretical thinking in this field.[1]

Although family theories have had significant improvements in terms of providing explanations for the processes and interactions in the family, given the weakness of philosophical foundations and the dominance of empiricist insight over Western scientific circles which have led to their inability in presenting comprehensive explanations regarding the causes of family formation, continuity and dissolution, they cannot be taken as a given in Islamic studies of the family.

In this section, after examining some important and famous theories of family sociology, we will examine the philosophical and ideological basics of family sociology and finally, we will present a theoretical framework of family based on Islamic teachings and relying on the ideas of Muslim thinkers.

---

1 Bengtson et al.(eds.),*Sourcebook of Family Theory & Research*,p.36.

CHAPTER 13

SOCIOLOGICAL THEORIES OF THE FAMILY

Chapter 13

Sociological theories of the family

Learning objectives of chapter 13

Getting familiar with main sociological theories of the family

Based on stage objective of this chapter, the learner is expected to achieve the following learning objective and be able to:

- state the main sociological theories of the family given its most important concepts and assumptions.

Introduction

The field of family sociology suffered the lack of an independent theory until the 1960s.The theories used for analyzing family issues either have borrowed their concepts from other fields of humanities or were macro theories with diverse functions such as Talcott Parsons' functionalism, George Homans' exchange theory and George Herbert Mead's symbolic interactionism which the field of family was merely considered as one of their functions.By the late 1960s, a movement emerged in sociology of the family to construct specific theories of the family.After a hiatus which occurred in the mentioned movement in 1980s due to the dominance of inductivism and pure empiricism in the research of family sociology, from early 1990s, there appeared a tendency towards theoretical studies among family sociologists.[1]

In this chapter, we will briefly examine some important theories in sociology of the family such as social exchange theory, functionalism, symbolic interactionism, social and feminist conflict.

13-1 Social exchange theory

Social exchange theory emerged within social sciences in the latter part of the twentieth century. It arose out of the philosophical traditions of utilitarianism, behaviorism, and neoclassical economics. Early applications of this theory in family sciences arose out of the work of sociologists like Thibault, Kelley, Homans and Blau.Generally, social exchange theory provides an economic metaphor to social relationships. The theory's fundamental principle is that humans in social situations choose behaviors that maximize their likelihood of meeting self- interests in those situations.[2]

Social exchange theory includes a number of key assumptions:

- Individuals are generally rational actors and reactors and engage in calculations of costs and benefits in social exchanges.
- The individuals engaged in interactions are rationally seeking to maximize the profits or benefits to be gained from those situations, especially in terms of meeting basic individual needs.

---

1 White, *Advancing Family Theories*,Chap.2.
2 Chibucos & Leite , *Readings in Family Theory*,p.137.

Exchange processes that produce pay- offs or rewards for individuals lead to patterning of social interactions. These patterns in addition to serve the individuals' need, put a good deal of pressure on how these needs should be met. These patterns of social interaction not only serve individuals' needs but also constrain individuals in how they may ultimately seek to meet those needs.[1]

Social exchange theory also includes other key concepts:

- **Reward** is described as any benefits exchanged in personal relationships. They may be concrete or symbolic and particular to one individual or more universal.[2] In close relationships, the individuals exchange different kinds of rewards: affection , emotional support, satisfying sexual desire, property , social status, physical attraction and so forth.[3]

- **Costs** are either punishments or forfeited rewards that result from social exchanges. Generally speaking, social exchanges carry three potential costs: 1) Investment costs represent the energy and personal cognitive or emotional investment put into an exchange by the actors involved. 2) Direct costs include time, financial resources, or other structural resources that are dedicated to the exchange. 3) Opportunity costs represent possible rewards that may be lost as a result of the relationship or social exchange.[4]

- **Resources** : resources refer to anything which can be used to meet or repress the needs or what makes the persons nearer or farer of their goals; such as money, more knowledge , more attractive appearance ;[5]

- **The value of alternative relationships**: Individuals assess the outcomes of their social exchanges in relation to other possible relationships or exchanges. When the outcome of the current relationships fall short of the outcomes of the alternative relationships people will probably choose to abandon the current relationship;[6]

- **The amount of the person's cathexis in current relationship:** theorists of exchange school by using two latter concepts explain why problematic marital relationships do not always dissolve but may continue. As they say, a spouse may feel little gratification due to the fact that his received rewards are much less than costs, but because the value of alternative relationships is also low in his opinion (for example, he has not any opportunity for remarriage) or because he has invested more in his current relationships (for example, he has reared several children), continue the marital relationship.[7]

- **Comparison level:** comparison level is the person's judgment criterion about the benefits and costs of the relationship. A person who has high expectations

---

1 Ibid, p.137
2 Ibid, p.138.
3 Bedar et al, *Social Psychology*, p203.
4 Chibucos & Leite , *Readings in Family Theory* ,pp.138-139.
5 Taylor et al., *Social Psychology*,p.276.
6 Chibucos & Leite ,*Readings in Family Theory* ,p 139.
7 Forsyth, *Our Social World*,p.435.

and had a very satisfactory relationship before, will tend to have a very high level of comparison. For being satisfied, he needs a relationship in which the benefit level is higher than cost level. Also, a person who has a less expectation from the relationship and he has not been involved in any intense love, will have a very low comparison level; he will be satisfied with his relationship, even if the cost and benefit he gets are at the same level.[1]

Relying on the mentioned assumptions and concepts, social exchange theory explains different perspectives of social relationships like family relationships. According to this theory, at first glance the individuals try to maximize their benefit, but if we look deeply we will understand that the groups typically want to maintain the integrity of social relationships with the development of fairness and justice systems for their members and to encourage the members who inspire others to follow it. When people see they have been threatened unfairly feel it necessary to try to establish fairness and injustice once again.[2]

So, it can be said that individuals understand justice in the form of equality and they will be more satisfied if they come to the understanding that the advantages of the relationship almost equal its costs. But if a person contributes more and gains less benefit, he will feel exploited and consequently will be outraged. The other party involved may sometimes feel guilty as a result of being an agent of other's exploitation, but this is not always the case; because the individuals despite the agreement on the definition of justice as equality, may come to conflict with each other about the equality or inequality of their relationship due to the cultural backgrounds and different expectations. That is why the spouses feel high level of marital gratification during honeymoon and empty nest (the parents' loneliness after the marriage of their children); because they feel equality more than any other time but during the child-caring period the women often feel they get less benefit and so, the marital gratification usually decreases.[3]

13-2 Functionalism

Functionalism is considered to be one of the most common theoretical approaches in the family studies. What is assumed in this approach is that the society tends to be like an organism which tries to resist against the changes and keep itself in balance and equilibrium. The concept of function refers to essential activities to maintain species, societies or social group such as reproduction, economic production, education and so forth.[4]

Despite abundant diversity in the family patterns, functionalist theorists have tried to identify some relatively common functions of the families. Six fundamental functions of the family were identified by Ogburn and Tibbitts in 1934 including: reproduction, protection and care, socialization, regulation of sexual behavior, affection

---

1 Bedar et al, *Social Psychology*, p205.
2 Azkamp, *Applied Social Psychology*, p581.
3 Myers, *Exploring Social Psychology*,p.239,281.
4 Bernards, *An Introduction to Family Studies*, p 74.

and companionship and also securing social status.[1] Murdock considered four sexual, economic, educational and production functions as the main functions of the family and Parsons regarded the children's socialization and the adult's personality stabilization as the main functions of the family in contemporary Western family.[2]

Parson believed that the extended family consisting of several family units which is one of the features of a simple and traditional society has been changed to be compatible with the necessities of the process of industrialization. Geographical, occupational and social mobility of human work force was in conflict with the kind of the extended family in which brothers, sisters and their children lived with the parents and grandparents, uncles, aunts and cousins together. Work force needs to have independence to change the job, move according to the location of industrial complexes and move within the large bureaucracy organizations. As a result, in an industrial society, members of a family are not at the same level in terms of specialization, power, income and responsibility. Breaking down of extended family in favor of the neolocal nuclear family consisting of father, mother and their children enables every member of the family to pursue his/her career path freely according to his/her talents, interests and opportunities and tastes This reform of family structure accompanied by the flexibility of social stratification which facilitates social and occupational mobility.[3]

Explaining the nuclear family, Parsons declares that modern nuclear family (which he considered as a feature of industrial societies and its emergence simultaneous with the decrease of functions of traditional family) maintains the function of socializing the children and providing a context for the growth and stability of the adults' personality.[4] In Parsons' opinion, the stabilization of the adults' personality refers to the role which the family performs in the cases of psychological pressures of daily life, the pressures which have the potential to destabilize the adults' personality. Stabilization of personality arises out of mutual emotional support that the married couples offer to each other as well as of parenting role. During the process of personality stabilization, the parents can go back to their childhood through playing with their children and consequently remove the tensions.[5]

Depending on a set of psychoanalytical findings, Parsons stated that an optimal form of gender division of labor between the wife and husband provides the ground for performing basic functions of the family in decisively shaping a solid adult personality   and socialization of the children and this issue has a fundamental role in the integration of the family and then in social stability. According to him, women's subordination in capitalist societies, functionally, is required to maintain family unity, and in turn family unity is essential for maintaining the class structure. Maintaining class structure is also essential to ensure the preservation of the established social structure.[6]

---

1 Schaefer,*Sociology*,p.324.
2 Bernards, *An Introduction to Family Studies*, p 74-75.
3 Roche, *Talcot Parson's Sociology* , p216.
4 Knuttila, *Introducing Sociology: A Critical Perspective*,p.266.
5 Harvey & MacDonald, *Doing Sociology*,p.196.
6 Ibid,p.197.

In contrast, if an unmarried woman be a breadwinner, the risk of competition with her husband will be created and this is very harmful for the family's solidarity and coordina-

-tion.[1]

13-3 Theory of symbolic interactionism

Theories of symbolic interactionism which have been originated from the works of philosophers and scientists such as Charles Darwin, William James, John Dewey and some early sociologists like Gorge Herbert Mead and Charles Cooley, emphasize the social patterns of interpretation and production of meaning. These theories revolve around the issue that humans share a set of signs (symbols, language and the like) about which there is a universal understanding and the creation and production of meaning is at the heart of the human social interactions.[2]

Symbolic interaction is associated with some basic assumptions:

- An understanding of human behavior is possible only based on the meaning that the actor assigns for it.
- The human infant is an unsocial creature at birth and he is exposed to a vast set of socializing messages over time which helps the production of meaning and social understanding. Therefore, all behaviors is acquired socially.
- Meanings in our mind are developed as a result of interaction with others and in turn influence our social interaction;
- During social interaction, people and society affect each other mutually. However, society precedes people; individual minds are a product of the society, but the society is not the product of individual minds.[3]

Some key concepts of the theories of symbolic interactionism are as follow:

- **Self**: self can be considered as a process of behavior whereby the individuals determine and control their own behavior. This concept requires an individual who makes a set of roles for himself and others. For example, the role of parent might be crucial for an individual's self-image but other person in this role considers it secondary compared to other roles. As a result, these two individuals will participate differently in the parenting activities;[4]
- **Sense of self**: self-awareness or sense of self arising out of social interaction reflects our experience of social interactions and our interpretation of how we are perceived by others through these interactions .This concept entails the point that some kind of awareness and sensitivity towards the others' understandings is formed in the individuals. Sense of self structured through social interactions provides a motivation for the behavior;
- **Identities**: Individuals relate their participation in social roles to identities or self-meanings .Identities are organized hierarchically according to the importance the individual attach to them. The more important these roles are,

1 Mitchell, *Sociology of Family and Marriage* ,p 122.
2 Chibucos & Leite , *Readings in Family Thoery*,p.237
3 Ibid , pp.237-238.
4 Ibid, p.239.

people associate themselves with them more and may reveal the individuals' stronger commitment to those specific roles;

- **Roles**: roles are common norms used for the people who obtain social positions. These common norms are formed as meaning systems which make it possible for individuals to predict others' actions and reactions. They also contribute to define the behaviors which people should do in social roles.
- **Interaction**: according to the theories of symbolic interactionism, interaction is not the content of social encounters rather the meaning levels existing in them. For example, a wife and a husband may use to say "I love you" at the end of the telephone conversation, but this sentence contains a deep meaning for one of them and merely a rote utterance for the other.[1]

These concepts and other related concepts such as socialization, looking-glass self, taking roles, primary group, reference group, significant others and symbolic relationship which are in the center of the theories of symbolic interactionism, often can be adapted to the family and family relationships and therefore, have provided strong tools for theorizing and research in this field of study.

13-4 Social conflict theory

Having its origin in the ideas of Marx, social conflict theory generally turns its attention towards the competition between social classes and patterns of competition in the society to access scarce resources. According to this theory, in such a competition, the groups holding greater power normally get access to more resources and at the same time, having access to more resources grants greater power to the group. Sociologists like Weber and Simmel adapted Marx's concepts to interpersonal interactions. Since then, the family institution was considered as the development of main patterns of social conflict and during last forty years, the concepts of this theory were used to examine different family issues;[2]

Some fundamental assumptions of social conflict theory are as follows:

- Self – interest is one of the main motivations of the human.
- The individuals and groups compete each other to access scarce resources (financial resources, dignity, power, authority or any other desired goods).
- There is no relationship free of competition and conflicting self - interests.
- There is no relationship in which all competitors win; all social relationships contain a " win- lose" relationship ;
- The competition between the individuals and groups to access scarce resources leads to conflict.
- The conflict between social groups is one of the main elements of social life and also inevitable.
- A conflict between the individual and group social interactions is deemed to be common; conversely, living in harmony and unity cannot be considered a natural state;

---

1 Ibid, p 238.
2 Ibid, p.183.

- Conflict not only is not regarded as negative, but also it is essential and often desired due to its impact on creating positive changes in favor of deprived individuals and groups.[2]

Some key concepts of social exchange are as follows:

- **Competition** : competition is a negative mutual dependence between the individuals in social situations;
- **Power**: Power in the families is reflected in the patterns of authority. Typically, the members with greater authority have greater power to influence other family members;
- **Negotiation** : Negotiation is a process during which all of the individuals and the groups involved accept the best possible solution though they don't approve of that solution in itself;
- **Bargain**: Bargain is a process during which the individuals look for a solution thereby they can maximize their self-interests. [1]

Based on these assumptions and concepts, social conflict theory explains the relationships within the family. It regards the families as power systems built upon sexual and age stratification. According to this theory, power is distributed unequally in the families; the children typically hold less power than adults, and the women have typically less power than men .As a result, self- interests of women and children are predominated by the men and adults of the families. The reflection of such fundamental differences appears in discriminatory participation in domestic labor, the patterns of abuse and negligence, influence and participation in decision makings.[2]

Generally speaking, the service that the family offers to men and capitalist class constitutes two main issues of the conflict theories. Regarding the first issue, Friedrich Engels in *the origin of the family, private property and the state*, regarded the emergence of monogamous family as a result of the tendency towards leaving the wealth and the succession of men's property among the children. According to him, marriage was the first form of class conflict in which the prosperity of a group (men) was based on the misery of other group (women) and their motivation for sexual domination was the economic exploitation of the women's work.[3]

Regarding second issue, i.e. the service that family offers to capitalism, conflict theorists declare that the contemporary nuclear family serves capitalism in several ways: production and re-production of workforce, providing a place to keep reserve army of labor (women who are hired in the market when it's necessary and are laid off when no longer needed) and facilitating the consumption of vast quantities of consumer goods.[4] Women's domestic labor serves capitalism both as a surplus profit which is finally returned to the capitalist and also by promoting livelihood status or maintaining it in a tolerable level which reduces political pressures (because it keeps the men satisfied with current conditions). It should be mentioned the effects of house chores and emotional

---

1 Ibid, pp.184-185.
2 Ibid, p.184.
3 Zanden, *Sociology: The Core*, p.261.
4 Knuttila , *Introducing Sociology :A Critical Perspective*,p.271.

support of women to reconstruct and refresh the husbands, older children and fathers to work in other working day.[1]

13-5 Feminist theory

The focus of feminist theories is examining how gender is perceived, gendered behavior patterns and gender inequalities. These theories consider gender as a prominent feature of family life and a source of subjugation or oppression in the families. In addition to understanding gender differences, the main goal of these theories is changing the conditions of family life and the women's experiences to empower them. Since social institutions such as family have fundamentally a patriarchal nature in contemporary societies and cause the women's inferiority, feminists feel a commitment to end this inferiority.[2] Fundamental assumption in feminist theories is that understanding social contexts is not possible except by considering the presence of gender and gendered patterns in those contexts. Accordingly, in order to understand the families as social units we have to perceive the women's experience in the families.[3]

Some key conceptions of feminist theories are as follow:

- **Sex and gender**: Unlike the concept of "sex" which implies biological differences between the man and woman, the concept of gender refers to socially constructed concept and it arises from the society's beliefs about the men and women and their different expectations of behaviors, values and attitudes. Gender is reflected in different participation of men and women in employment and domestic labor, different patterns of the boy and girl's socialization and even in linguistic categorization and labeling used about the men and women.[4]
- **Sex inequality**: Sex inequality as one of the social inequalities refers to the women's inferior status compared to men even in similar situations. The concept of sex discrimination is also another interpretation of sex inequality and refers to the man and woman's inequality in getting access to occupational, educational and other facilities.[5]
- **Sex oppression**: Generally, Webster's dictionary defines oppression as unjust or cruel exercise of power. Accordingly, sex oppression can be defined as unjust or cruel exercise of power by one sex against the other sex;
- **Patriarchy:** In feminist terms, patriarchy refers to the ideas and practices implying men's domination and ranging from the closest sexual encounters to major economic and ideological factors. Patriarchy was gradually used in the meaning that not only implied men's exercise of power over women in general terms , but also it included hierarchical characteristic of man's power and the

---

1 Bilton et al., *Introductory Sociology*, pp.351-352.
2 Chibucos & Leite ,*Readings in Family Theory*,p.209.
3 Ibid, p.209.
4 Ibid, p.209.
5 Lengerman & Brantely," Modern Feminist Theory", *Sociological Theory in Modern World*, p 475.

ideological legitimacy of this power as something natural, normal , right and just.[1]

Accordingly, each of the feminist approaches has provided its own specific theory in explaining sex inequality, particularly within the family. Liberal feminism believes that women's inferiority has its origin in the discriminatory laws and conventions against women and approved beliefs about "natural" differences between the man and woman which determines a different destiny for either sex. On the one hand, these discriminations prevent women from entering into public arenas and achieving success there and on the other hand, place the burden of the responsibilities of private arena on their shoulders. While real rewards of social life such as money, power, prestige, freedom and the opportunity to develop personally can only be found in the public arena.[2]

Marxist feminism regards class system and private property of production means as the origin of the women's inferiority and oppression which have been manifested in the form of capitalist system and accordingly believes that the women's inferior status is at the service of capitalist interests.[3]

Patriarchal system has been identified as the main cause of   the women's inferiority and oppression by Radical feminism, a system whose fundamental features are formed by power, authority, hierarchy and competition.[4] According to this approach, the women's oppression in a patriarchal society has a fundamental aspect and reflects the absolute power and authority which are exercised by the men over women. In such a society, the family as a primary social unit directly helps the women's oppression. Therefore, it should be abolished.[5]

Combining Marxist and Radical approaches, Socialist feminism regards two interwoven factors of patriarchy and capitalist means of production as the origin of the women's inferiority and oppression.[6] At last, Post-modernist feminism mainly deals with ideologies, customs and linguistic structures affecting the women's inferiority and oppression and the ways to break these structures.[7]

o **Abstract**

- The fundamental principle of social exchange theory is that humans in different social situations including family situations choose the behaviors which maximize the likelihood of meeting self- interests in those situations.
- Functionalist theorists identify different functions for the family including: reproduction, protection and care, socialization, regulation of sexual behavior, affection and companionship and also securing social status but Parsons

---

1 Sarokhani „*Social Science Encyclopedia*, p 672.

2 Ramazanoglu, *Feminism and the Contradictions of Oppression*,pp.33-34.

3 Lengerman & Berantely," Modern Feminist Theory", *Sociological Theory in Modern World*, p 475.

4 Abbott & Wallace, *An Introduction to Sociology of Feminist Approaches*, p 249.

5 Chibucos & Leite, *Readings in Family Theory*,p.210.

6 Abbott & Wallace, *An Introduction to Sociology of Feminist Approaches*, p 261.

7 Chibucos & Leite ,*Readings in Family Theory*, p.210.

considered socialization of children and the stability of adults' personality as two main functions of contemporary Western family.

- Theories of symbolic interactionism explain family relationships using the concepts such as socialization, looking-glass self, taking roles, primary group, reference group, significant others and symbolic relationship.
- Social conflict theory regards the families as power systems built upon gender and age stratification.
- Feminist theories consider sex as a prominent feature of family life and a source of subjugation or oppression in the families.

o **Self-Test**

1. How the fact that problematic marital relationships are not always dissolved but may be continued can be explained based on social exchange theory?
2. Explain Parsons' theory of family sociology.
3. Which of the concepts of the theories of symbolic interactionism is suitable for explaining the capacity of children to imitate their parents' behavior?
4. How do the theorists of conflict theory explain the service that family offers to capitalism?
5. How is sex inequality in the family explained according to each of the feminist approaches?

o **Research topic**

- Research the modern theories in the field of family sociology.
- Examine and criticize one of the theories of family sociology.
- Examine and criticize the anthropological foundation of the theories of family sociology by conducting a research.

CHAPTER 14
THE PHILOSOPHICAL AND IDEOLOGICAL BASICS
OF THE SOCIOLOGY OF FAMILY

Chapter 14

The philosophical and ideological basics of the sociology of family

Learning objectives of chapter 14

Getting familiar with the basic criticisms of the subjects in the field of the sociology of family

Based on stage objective of this chapter, the reader is expected to achieve the following learning objective and be able to:

- analyze and criticize some of the most important ontological and epistemological basics of the sociology of family.

Introduction

The sociological theories about family despite the contradictions between them have presented fairly strong and convincing explanations about various aspects of the institution of family and family ties and have greatly deepened our understanding and the experimental researches of this discipline have extended our knowledge of the realities of this institution and proved many of the past presuppositions false. Nonetheless, the findings of this scientific discipline just like any other human knowledge are by no means flawless and it is only through careful and scientific analysis that its defects can be recognized and attempts can be made to remedy them.

In this chapter, we will shortly consider the subject of the sociology of the family from a philosophical point of view and in the meantime we will introduce a criticism of some of the anthropological and epistemological assumptions of the theoreticians and authorities in this discipline. The mainstays of this study include: ignoring the element of innate nature, paying less attention to the natural differences between men and women, the secular mindset attitude, and relativism of values. It is worth saying that the criticisms discussed in this chapter generally address the dominant trend in the area of the sociology of the family which especially has been reflected in the Western books and articles and the exceptional cases opposed to this trend were not in mind and are left out.

14-1 ignoring the element of innate nature

One of the fundamental challenges of philosophy in ontological arguments is innate nature. The difficulties surrounding this issue due to inefficiency of rational and experimental methods in distinguishing between innate and non-innate issues [1]has led the Western philosophers to gradually discard the concept of innate nature). But because of the explicitness of the religious texts, particularly Surah Rome [Ayah 30], in providing confirmation for the idea of innate nature, this concept occupies a special position among the Muslim thinkers. Here there is not the opportunity to explore this topic in detail, but, it seems that by taking the idea of innate nature as a presupposition

---

1. Ahmadi, Innate Nature: *The Origin of Islamic Psychology*, p. 179

new horizons will be opened up for social sciences especially in important topics such as religion, ethics and family.

Specifically in the area of the sociology of the family the issue of the origin of the family can be put forward as an example. A group of theoreticians including Morgan,[1] Durkheim, and Levi Strauss who have investigated the historical evolution of the family posited a social-cultural origin for the institution of family and believe that it was only after the introduction of cultural factors such as prohibiting incest that family has come to be formed in the course of the history, but before the formation of the institution of family, there used to be a period of uncontrolled mixing of men and women or promiscuity[2] in which the relationships between the two sexes were not following any rules; the concept of legality is yet to be born; the cultural dimension of partnership in marriage was little and sometimes next to nothing and everything was revolving around natural drives and quenching them.[3]

These theories can be traced to the 19 century social Darwinists. They tried to incorporate the family in the evolutionary process by making the claim that it has gone through a process of evolution starting from a matriarchal group marriage to the patriarchal pattern and then to the modern monogamy. Marx and Engels also used this evolutionary approach in developing their theory which according to some Western scholars is totally speculative and ethnocentric. On the other hand, scholars such as Westermarck and Murdock, have emphasized the natural and instinctive origin of the family, and in more recent researches Gough, considered the efficiency of gender division of labor which has emerged since the early periods of human history as the cause of the genesis of the family.[4]

It seems that what this recent group of scholars mean by the natural causes is the sexual instinct or reproductive capabilities, but what has been ignored in these explanations is the element of innate nature which although has overlaps with the concept of instinct, it goes beyond that and includes cases which cannot be explained through the concept of instinct.[5]

Whereas Holy Quran emphasizes the role of nature in the emergence and strengthening of family where it states that:

---

1 H.L Morgan

2 The existence of the period of uncontrolled mixing of men and women or promiscuity is nothing more than a hypothesis and even considering it as true there is no reason to believe that in the history of man such a period has come to pass; because there is a significant claim in some of the religious tradition stating a lack of generational affinity the prehistoric homo-sapiens and the historical early humans. (refer to Tabatabayi, *Almizan fi Tafsir al-Quran*, vol4, pp. 144-146) and that the generational affinity of homo-sapiens and humans has not been proved by any anthropologist and archeologist. Whereas according to religious texts, marriage and family was in place since the time of Adam and Eve(AS).(Baqara, 35, Nesah, 1; Horr Ameli, Vasayel al-Shia, vol14, p. 2).

3 Sarokhani, *An introduction to the sociology of family*, p 147.

4 E.Westermarck

5 Ingoldsby,"*Family Origin and universality*", *Families in Global and Multicultural Perspective*, p.72

And one of his signs is that he created mates for you from yourselves that you may find rest in them, and he put between you love and compassion; most surely there are signs in this for a people who reflect.[1]

According to this noble verse, love and friendship between spouses have its origin in ingenuous invention and creation of God and this is a clear indication of the innate origin of family.

Denying or ignoring the element of innate nature, will make it difficult to explain the integrity of loving and affectionate marital relationships in many families considering the inequalities in terms of power between the husband and wife and the women being aware of this inequality and this problem is exactly what the conflict theory is facing. The critics of this theory say that: "Although the norms of family life demand that women despite having less sexual freedom to contribute a greater share of childcare and house chores, nonetheless, they find marriage and family life appealing". According to these critics, affection and cooperation can exist even when there is an imbalance of power, and that the theoreticians of the hostility school overestimate the people's tendency to achieve perfect equality.[2]

The same problem can be seen in feminist theories, because this theory is unable to present a convincing explanation of the unequal marriages which are nonetheless happy and joyful.[3] It seems that social exchange theory is also faced with the same problem; because although its theoretical framework using the concepts of "the value of alternative relationships "and "the degree of personal investment in the current relationships" holds the potential for explaining the reason behind the sustenance and not breaking up of unequal marriages,[4] but is inefficient in providing explanation for the happiness of the couples in these marriages.

14-2 Paying less attention to natural sex differences

In relation to natural sex differences, we can see an explicit inclination to deny or downplay the importance of these differences among sociologists. Despite plenty of biological and psychological evidences indicating the existence of natural differences between men and women which even in sociological texts more or less are discussed about, usually the subject of sex differences end with statements such as the following which suggest a denial, hesitation, or trivialization of these differences :

The fact that the differences between men and women have a natural or nurturing and social origin cannot be easily explained, however, even though there are natural differences they are neither so serious and important and nor so flexible to be able to account for the social inequalities.[5]

This inclination has two distinctive characteristics: First, attempting to gain prestige and validity by appealing to the findings of psychologists such as Carl Jung and Sandra Bem who have demonstrated the existence of masculine and feminine

---

1 Surah Rome, 21.
2 Curry et al., *Sociology for the Twenty-first Century*, p. 272
3 White, *Advancing Family Theories*, p.5.
4 Forsyth, *Our Social World*, p.435.
5 Stokes, *introduction to sociology*, p.243.

characteristics in both sexes and claimed that each person might possess a high or low degree of both types of characteristics and thus have recognized four types of characteristics including: masculine, feminine, androgyny, and uncertain[1] and also the findings of some anthropologists like Margaret Mead who found a discrepancy between the character and behavior pattern of men and women in some primitive societies and its common patterns in civilized societies.[2] Second, attaching labels such as ideological hypotheses and gender stereotypes whose aim is to strengthen double standards in sexual morality to the hypotheses indicating the existence of natural sex differences.[3]

Yet, it can be demonstrated that this approach itself is ideological; because if ideology is any unsupported claim which is based on uninformed justification or rationalization that instead of arguing based on a reason is based on a special cause and presents a distorted picture of reality,[4] then the claim for the insignificance of sex differences or denying them considering the following points can be regarded as ideological:

- This claim presents a distorted image of the realities of sex differences, and glosses over its fundamental and momentous effects on the structure of social systems. Of course, to be fair, we must differentiate between diverse examples of sex differences and accept the claim for insignificant differences at least about some of them including differences in terms of intelligence, but concerning some of the differences particularly, the difference in physical strength and sexual desires, the reality is that the social world in which these differences are absent will be so unlike the present social world that it will be difficult to even imagine it;

- This claim is unsupported and none of the psychological and anthropological evidences it uses as the basis for its proof, are inconsistent with natural sex differences; because the opposite position that holds the view that some of the sex differences are natural does not necessarily mean determinism and the impossibility of effecting change in them; therefore, arguing on the basis of these evidences is nothing other than rationalization;

- This claim rather than being based on "reason" or "argument" have its origin in some particular "causes" and it seems that among these causes the influence of feminism in academic settings and also the interests of the hegemonic systems that their support for feminism is based on ulterior motives is more pronounced. Regardless of radical feminists who believe in the naturalness of some of the sex differences, the more dominant and well-known feminist trend, which has been extended by liberal feminists, either denies natural sex differences or avoids it altogether and is in favor of leaving some questions unanswered in this regard; because it fears that the answers provided for these questions, will be used to justify the suppression and oppression of women.[5]

---

1 Forsyth, *Our Social World*, p.435.
2 Kanneyer et al., *Sociology: Experiencing Changing Societies*,p.331
3 Ibid,p.358
4 Soroush, *Lessons in the Philosophy of Social Science*, p. 294-297.
5 Tong , *Feminist Thought* ,p.32.

Concerning the issue of natural sex differences another important point needs to be mentioned and that is "the absence of a teleological approach" in modern sciences including sociology. The teleological approach due to the dominance of positivism in academic environments has been dispensed with long time ago; because it has been considered as not being scientific, and using the expression of logical positivists it lacked the criterion of significance, that is, falsifiability. Thus, human knowledge lost an important element in understanding and explanation of natural and social phenomena.

The point that concerns this subject, is that if we view the issue of natural sex differences from a teleological perspective, another aspect of disregard of social sciences for this issue will be revealed and that is the fact that the scientists and scholars of these disciplines and closed their eyes on the aim and purpose of the creation of these differences as a part of the larger divine design. When viewed from this perspective, it will no longer make any difference whether sex differences are great or minor, rigid or flexible; for the importance of these differences lies not in their intensity or rigidity or determinism, but rather in the fact that the order of Creation has ordained them for important purposes and ends. The following statement from Master Motahhari clearly expresses this type of approach to the issue of sex differences:

> Without including the principle of ultimate cause it will be impossible to interpret the phenomena in the universe. The great system of creation in order to achieve its end and preserve the species, has created the great reproductive system; constantly produces males and females in its factory and where the survival and continuity of the generations of the species requires the cooperation and mutual assistance of both sexes, particularly in the case of humans, in order to compel them to engage in this pursuit with each other's help, has devised the proper design for their unity and harmony… and to ensure that this design will be realized and to bond their body and soul, has established amazing physical and psychological differences between them and it is these differences that attracts them to each other strongly and makes them love and desire each other.[1]

Such an attitude will also definitely have strategic effects; including that we will no longer be justified in adopting strategies and policies in the area of sex issue by making the excuse that sex differences are insignificant, policies which will be inconsistent with the necessities of these differences and will possibly lead to their elimination.

14-3 Secular approach

The doctrine of secularism is not limited to the area of politics and it can emerge in all the areas in which religion claims to interfere and have an effect. Consequently, in the area of epistemology the tendency to exclude religion from the process of cognition and acquiring knowledge can be considered secular. Secularism particularly in the area of sociology of family acquires manifestations that we will point two of them here. The common feature of these two cases and similar ones, is ignoring the role of religion and specifically its components such as divine revelation, religious beliefs, ethics, rituals, behavior, and religious agents as explanatory factors:

---

1 Motahhari, *The system of Women's Rights in Islam*, p.110 and 211.

- A part of the subject of family sociology concerns the historical and prehistorical developments of family. In these studies topics such as the origin of marriage and family, the historical roots of rules such as mahramiyat and exogamy and also the causes of the growth of polygamy and gender division of labor are considered and usually the theories proposed can be generally referred to in two groups: theories that posit a natural and biological basis for these rules and phenomena and theories that explain these matters according to their social and economic functions. For instance, when explaining rule of mahramiyat or the forbiddance of marrying mahrams some theories have stressed the role of natural and instinctive factors, such as the humans' natural aversion to marry close relatives.[1] But, other theories have explained the emergence of this rule based on its social functions including paving the way for extending the kinship ties through the exchange of women between families and tribes.[2]

But, what is worth considering is that, none of these theories have pointed to the mere possibility of this rule and similar rules to have a religious origin and the fact that divine prophets have taught people to observe these rules, while according to the content of religious texts, divine prophets have had an undeniable role in the development of human civilization encompassing its cultural and material dimensions, of course, this subject needs to be addressed in another time and opportunity.

- Another manifestation of the secular attitude in the area of sociology of family can be seen in the disregard of the scholars in this field for the role of religious and moral shortcomings in explaining phenomena such as the disintegration of family, divorce, and domestic violence. Of course, a number of sociologists especially in recent researches have considered the effect of this factor, but they have not done justice to it; because at most they have considered it as a factor alongside other factors. Moreover, they have not analyzed this factor carefully and often contented themselves with stating the statistic correlations between religiosity and one of the aforementioned variables. For instance, based on experimental researches they state that "to be in close contact with church, which is a mark of social character and prestige, is in close correlation with compatibility in marital life while neglecting religion, has a major effect on disorders in marital life"[3] or "the highest divorce rate belongs to couples who are not associated with any religion",[4] but the fact that religiosity and religious devotion includes which influencing factors and through what mechanism supports the integrity of family and marital compatibility, is something that has not received much attention.

The realistic view necessitates that faith and religious ethics in comparison with many other factors receive a bigger share in maintaining the unity and integrity of family and reduction of domestic violence; because as it has already been mentioned, deficiency in religion even in the case that other destabilizing factors of family do not have a significant presence, alone can bring about the disintegration of family and on the contrary, the couples' devotion to religious beliefs and edicts and moral standards,

---

1 Kleinberg, *Social Psychology*, Vol 1.p.167.
2 Michelle, *the Sociology of Family and Marriage*, p.42 and 43.
3 King, *Sociology*, p.168
4 Goode, *The Family*, p.95.

despite the presence of other destabilizing factors of family will bring compatibility in marital life.

But the mechanism through which this factor comes into effect needs a detailed discussion and here we only review three points from the previous discussions:

1. The role of religious faith in making life meaningful and reducing its pains;

2. The effect of religious faith and morality on strengthening marital love and affection;[1]

3. Providing the religious person with an internal control or policing preventing him from resorting to any oppressive measures. Imam Hassan Mojtaba (AS) states this point in a hadith:

> Marry your daughter to a religious and pious man; for such a person if he loves your daughter he will treat her honorably and respectfully and in case he does not love her, he will not wrong and oppress her.[2]

14-4 Relativism of values

The relation between realities and values is one of the complex and difficult problems in the philosophy of social sciences. Generally, two viewpoints have been proposed in regard with this issue: first one is the objectivist view who believe in the logical distinction of these two areas and underscore the necessity of avoiding to mix scientific subjects with value judgments. Max Weber as one of the most influential supporters of this view has this to say about the negative consequences of engaging in value judgments in social sciences:

> It is true that in our sciences, personal value-judgments have tended to influence scientific arguments without being explicitly admitted. They have brought continual confusion and have caused various interpretations to be placed on scientific arguments even in the sphere of the determination of simple casual interconnections among facts according to whether the results increased or decreased the chances of realizing one's personal ideals, i.e., the possibility of desiring a certain thing. [3]

The second one is the view of the supporters of value partiality who consider science devoid of value system, assuming it possible, undesirable. The authorities on the side of the critical schools believe that explicit and self-conscious partiality should be included in the process of research.[4] However, in the works of the supporters of this view we do not find any clear value arguments concerning what values must be assumed in a research and what objectives it must serve. Instead, which camp to support is considered as something definite and predetermined as if, the world is made up of only good and evil with no in between.

---

1 About these two points refer to: This book, chapter 8, the discussion "emotional support in the relationship of couples"
2 Tabarsi, *Makarem-Al-Akhlaq*, p.214.
3 Weber, *Methodology of Social Sciences*, p.93.
4 Hammersley , *Taking sides in social Research*,pp.5-6.

What these two views have in common is the lack of a strong and reliable support, a problem which has arisen as a result of the demise of religious value system in the West and it's not having been replaced by an acceptable alternative value system and undoubtedly the prevalence of the views which deny the innate basis of values and stress the social origin of the moral and legal values was also an effective factor in this regard. As a result, we have come to witness an emergence of a kind of relativism of values in all the fields of humanities, including sociology of family.

Relativism of values appears in the works of many sociologists of family in the form of indifference to and avoiding value judgments and in the work of another group in the form of supporting deviant values, so that sometimes they adopt such extreme positions that no boundaries between values and counter values are left. The practical consequence of these two approaches is that in the works of the first group due to indifference to values, very few signs of accepting the reformist approach are detected and the works of the second group although are apparently inclined to the reform and improvement of social conditions, because of not being based on a justified and absolute and definite value system, only add to man's problems and pains. The above-mentioned claims will be further clarified by reviewing some examples that are found in abundance in the texts of the sociology of family.

Concerning the first approach, when the sociologist of family is considering the factors contributing to the increasing of marrying age, bearing in mind that in most cases he is not much concerned about the moral corruption and sexual perversity resulting from the increase in the age of marriage, he merely states the factors involved in this phenomenon such as employment of women, the growth of sexual freedoms and the possibilities and facilities of prevention of pregnancy[1] and not only does not offer any suggestions to reform the situation and reduce the age of marriage and in fact he does not feel obligated or duty-bound to do so, but because the reduction in the age of marriage affects an increase in the period of conception in women and consequently population increase, he will probably endorse delay in marriage. Also when he considers homosexual relationships and uses terms such as homosexual family or considers establishing laws in favor of these people as a "progress" in resolving their legal problems, or when he talks about the advantages of female homosexuality as compared to male homosexuality,[2] reveals his lack of obligation to values.

But the second approach is identifiable by its extreme and explicit value judgments and often can be seen in the works of the critical and feminist scholars. For example, Herbert Marcuse and Norman A. Brown two leftist thinkers turned Freud's psychoanalytical visions into a criticism of the limitations of the liberal society. These thinkers focused more on what they saw as the psychological repression of personal instinctive needs than on political and economic oppression and considered the goal of social change to be the freedom of desires, or as Marcuse expresses it, the free gratification of man's instinctive needs, the idea which has been used as a pretext for

---

1 Spanier ," Cohabitation: Recent Changes in the U.S." ,*Marriage and Family in Transition*,pp.98-99.

2 Curry et al., *Sociology for the Twenty-First Century* , p.260.

youth riots.[1] Also Simone De Beauvoir, the well-known feminist of 1950s, presenting a completely negative image of a woman's body, considered the activities pertaining to procreation particularly, pregnancy, childbirth, and suckling as purely natural and animalistic functions in contradiction to the possibility of woman's growth and refinement [2]And some other feminists use expressions such as slavery, legal rape, and unpaid labor about marriage.[3]

The more explicit form of relativism of values can be seen in the postmodernist view. John Bernards, based on this view states that:

> There are fierce debates about the morality of divorce, abortion, and …. The job of social science is not morality; we have another role to play. It is our job to study the reality of such situations rather than engage in moral debate. It is our task to understand how to minimize the pain, suffering and misery of family life and how to maximize the joy, pleasure and love of family life.[4]

Of course, it is true that it is not the job of social scientists to engage in in moral discussions, but this has been conflated with indifference and relativism of values. For example, he implicitly supported claims inconsistent with moral standards on the basis of the findings of feminist researches, for example the claim that "the fathers who have openly publicized their homosexuality, not only have caused no harm, but have caused easing and diffusing of tensions", or "the need does not exist for children to have a family with a heterosexual structure".[5]

He also explicitly suggests that sociologists of family take initiative in rejecting and burying "the ideology of family" and reconstructing a social environment in which different types of families can be respected.[6] In his view, the important thing is to preserve and protect family life, not its structure or official title, and families whether marital or non-marital can be good or bad; therefore, politicians must assign equal priority to marital or non-marital families.[7] The interesting thing is that this author acknowledges that although "new perceptions and understandings" about family life can be redeeming, but there is no guarantee that "the transformed perceptions" will not pose threats in other ways, or cause harm to them.[8]

One of the consequences of relativism of values is turning the sociology of family into a battlefield of clashes of values, so that even objective approaches by promoting relativism of and indifference to values, actually lead people to certain values, and thus, they add up to confusion and discordance and divide in ideas and opinions. Today, we can see in many topics in this discipline a confrontation of views which apparently are

---

1 Mintz &Kellogg ," Coming Apart: Radical Departures since 1960" *Marriage and Family in Transition*,p.110.
2 Hekman ,*Gender and Knowledge*,p.7.
3 Mintz &Kellogg ," Coming Apart: Radical Departures since 1960" *Marriage and Family in Transition*,p.110.
4 Bernards, *An Introduction to Family Studies*, p.114.
5 Ibid,p200.
6 Ibid , p112.
7 Ibid, p305.
8 Ibid, p 111.

presented based on experimental evidences, but in reality are based on different value and ideological foundations, and the acceptance of the opposing views rather than being based on experimental evidences is based on the acceptance of those tenets.

Now we can better understand the reason for Weber's concern about value judgments in social sciences. He had contemplated enough to conclude that experimental sciences including social sciences cannot perform any role in value judgments and in distinguishing between right and wrong values, and therefore he looked to find the reference for determining values outside of the domain of science. In his view, choice, agreement, the judgment of conscience and faith, are the things appropriate for playing this role.[1]

It is obvious that choice and agreement by themselves do not make an argument and must be supported by a valid and sound reference. Judgments of moral conscience are also confined to only a limited sphere of issues of value. Thus, the only valid reference for determining values is faith and that is religious faith, but what will that faith be? There is no doubt that the only religion fit to possess the absolute reference in human value judgments so that in addition to solid and strong philosophical support will be sufficiently comprehensive and complete, in the sense of having edicts and commands and establishing values in each and every area and domain of this-worldly life from the smallest to the biggest, and in our opinion no religion other than the true Islam that has been communicated to people by the Noble Prophet of Islam (pbuh) and His immaculate family possesses these qualities.

o **Abstract**

- The theories of the sociology of family because of denying or ignoring the factor of innate nature are facing difficulties in explaining the sustaining of loving and affectionate marital relationships in many families despite the inequalities in terms of power between the husband and wife and women's awareness about this inequality.
- There can be seen among the sociologists of family an explicit inclination to deny or downplay the importance of the natural sex differences.
- Taking into consideration the two factors of nature and natural gender differences in analyzing the sociology of family can exert a significant effect on enriching these analyses and also on the practical outcomes in this area.
- Employing the elements of religion and faith will enable the sociologists of family to strengthen and make more efficient their theoretical frameworks in explaining the problems of this field.
- The sociology of family either under the pretext of objectivism distanced itself from the domain of value judgments or when it has ventured into this area has provided a dark and ambiguous picture of value perspectives and this problem cannot be resolved except by reconciling this discipline and other scientific disciplines with the true teachings of Islam.

---

1 Weber, *the Methodology of Social Science*, p. 43, 50, 93.

o **Self-Test**

1. Explain the views of sociology and Islam about the origin of family.
2. Why the claim that natural gender differences are insignificant is an ideological claim? Explain.
3. How can religion be used as an explanatory element in sociological analyses? Illustrate with an example.
4. Provide one example for each one of these two approaches in sociology of family; indifference to values, and supporting deviant values.

o **Research topic**

- Conduct a research about the potentials of the concept of innate nature for enriching the subjects of sociology of family
- Focus your research on studying and analyzing postmodern perspectives about family.

CHAPTER 15

THE THEORY OF FAMILY IN THE THINKING OF ISLAMIC THINKERS

Chapter 15

The theory of family in the thinking of Islamic thinkers

Learning objectives of chapter 15

Getting familiar with a pattern of Islamic theorization in the area of sociology of family

According to stage objective of this chapter the learner is expected to achieve the following learning objective and be able to:

- explain the method by which the views of Islamic thinkers are used to construct explanatory theories in the area of sociology of family.

Introduction

In this chapter deriving inspiration from the ideas of the late Allamah Tabatabaie and Master Motaharri whose viewpoints to a great extent present the views of Islamic thinkers, a theory of family will be formulated. This theory which due to having its basis in the foundational principles of innate nature, is called the theory of innate bond is the product of rereading and re-organizing the ideas of these two well-respected and outstanding thinkers and this is not an attempt to develop an independent theory of family and even is not going to present a scientific theory, but only to present some disjointed subjects concerning women's rights and some related topics.

The point to be made here is that, in this discussion the term theory has been used in the usual exact sense of the word, that is, a set of concepts and propositions expressing the relation between those concepts which possess the characteristics of logical coherence, abstractness, testability, explanative capacity, predictability, falsifiability, the potential to be utilized in social policy making;[1] because all of the above-mentioned characteristics can be demonstrated in the theory of innate bond. It only remains to be pointed out that, this theory has not yet been used as a basis for experimental research, while the common theories-allegedly- achieve the status of a theory after going through the stage of experimental testing and, of course, this is itself a controvertible and claim and something that needs to be examined further.

According to the theory of innate bond, natural physical and psychological qualities and differences between men and women which are considered as innate issues, assume the central role in the genesis and strengthening of the institution of family and that other contributing factors play the supporting or complementary role.[2] Next, after pointing out the principle premises of this theory, I will expound its internal constituents and finally I will point out the application of this theory for explaining the disintegration of family in the contemporary era.

---

1 Refer to: Bostan (Najafi), *A Step Towards Religious Science: the Method of Using Religious Texts in Social Sciences*, Chapter 7.
2 The innate nature of every creature is its "special creation" and applying the adjective "innate" is due to the fact that these qualities have their origin in man and woman's special creation.

15-1 The assumptions of the theory of innate bond

The theory of innate bond is based on several assumptions which are as follows:

- The family life of human is basically natural, that is to say, man has been created naturally in a housed mould and if we have any supposed doubts about the natural basis of man's civilized life, the naturalness of his housed life and family life is beyond doubt.[1] This supposition sets the theory of innate bond in opposition to many theories of family that posit a social-historical origin for family. Clearly, this supposition concerns the principle of formation of family and it is not inconsistent with the diversity of family models in the diversity of societies and in the course of history.

- Contrary to false patriarchal beliefs that introduce marriage and family formation as entailing a sort of male possession of the female and unlike the dominant approach in contemporary Western societies that consider the nature of family life to be merely a partnership of human investments and a kind of mutual possession and ownership which has a contractual aspect to it, innate bond theory suggests that the nature of family life is a natural unity and oneness between man and woman which comes into existence in the form of the attraction between two opposite poles.[2]

- Contrary to the view of a great number of feminists who deny the natural gender differences and consider the basis of many differences between men and women to be environmental factors, [3] there are a wide range of natural physical and psychological differences between the two sexes including differences in the biology of reproduction, differences in sexual needs, differences in cognitive capacity, and emotional needs and differences in physical strength.[4] These differences establish a balance and well-suitedness between man and woman and they cannot be interpreted according to the concepts of imperfection and perfection.[5]

- The innateness of the tendency to family life does not necessitate its being determined, therefore there is always the possibility of suppression or deviation of this tendency,[6] as the people of Lot in the past and their modern followers put up a fight against it by preferring homosexuality.

- The changes undergone by the institution of family in the contemporary era is not a deterministic or inevitable process. As Master Motaharri expresses it, although industrial life and the progresses made in science and civilization and its consequences such as women's freedom, inescapably have had its effects on family relationships and will continue to have that effect, this does not mean that we have to allow for a historical determinism and thus for the Muslims of the East it is not an inevitable

---

1 Motahhari, *The System of Women's Rights in Islam*, p.188.

2 Tabatabaie, *Al-Mizan fi Tafsir al-Quran*, Vol.2, p.277 and 278; Motahhari, *the Notes of Master Motahhari*, Vol.5, p. 33 and 34.

3 Refer to, Bostan (Njafi), *Sex inequality from the viewpoint of Islam and feminism*. P. 74.

4 *Tabatabaie, al-mizan fi Tafsirr al-Quran*, Vol.2. p. 275; Motahhari, *the System of Women's Rights in Islam*, p.205 and 207; Ibid, The Notes of Master Motahhari, Vol.5. p. 154 and 179;Ibid, *A Collection of Works,(Vol 19): The Issue of Hijab*, p.436.

5 Motahhari, *the System of Women's Rights in Islam*, p.199-202.

6 *Tabatabaie, al-Mizan fi Tafesir al-Quran*, Vol.2, p. 273.

necessity to follow in the footsteps of the Westerners and to be dragged into any cesspool that they have been swallowed up in.[1]

15-2 The principle elements of the theory of innate bond

The theory of innate bond based on above-mentioned suppositions considers three sets of factors as affecting the integrity of family these factors are primary and secondary and supporting factors. These factors will be explained next:

a) The primary factors contributing to the integrity of family

The primary factors involved in the integrity of family designate the natural qualities of men and women which on the one hand play the central role in their bonding and on the other hand assuming the roles of parenting. The major share of these innate qualities is just the natural differences between men and women that produce a reciprocal dependence in the two sexes. Allamah Tabatabaie when expressing the significance of the differences between men and women in reproduction and its effect on the coming into being and strengthening of the family bonding writes:

> The man and woman each has been endowed with a peculiar reproductive system, so that in practice each completes the other's function and reproduction is the outcome of both of them combined; therefore each of them as a man and woman are in themselves incomplete and in need of the other and their coming together produces a complete whole that can result in the reproduction. It is because of this incompleteness and need that each one of them are attracted to the other so that they will achieve peace and tranquility; because every incomplete entity strives for its completeness and perfection and everything or everyone in need of some thing or someone tends to satisfy its/his need.[2]

Master Motaharri also about the role of this set of factors involved in strengthening family explains:

> The great system of Creation in order to achieve its end and preserve the species, has created the great reproductive system; constantly manufacturing males and females in its factory and where the survival and continuity of the generations of species requires the cooperation and mutual assistance of both sexes, particularly in the case of humans, in order to compel them to engage in this pursuit with each other's help, has devised the proper design for their unity and harmony... It has created them to be desiring to coexist with each other and to ensure that this design will be realized and to bond their body and soul, has established amazing physical and psychological differences between them and it is these differences that attracts them to each other strongly and makes them love and desire each other. If woman possessed masculine body and soul and temper it would be impossible for her to be able to render man as someone who will be at her service and charm him to desire to be united with her and if man possessed bodily and psychological qualities the same as

---

1 Motahhari, *the System of Women's Rights in Islam*, p.38.
2 Tabatabaie, *al-Mizan fi Tafesir al-Quran*, Vol.16, p. 166.

woman's, it would be impossible for the woman to regard him as the hero of her life and to consider winning man's heart as her highest art.[1]

One of the very effective natural qualities involved in strengthening the bond between husband and wife is sexual zeal. Zealotry does not belong to the category of jealousy or selfishness, but as a natural and innate quality in men with its reciprocal effect on husband and wife strengthens their bond. Zealotry on one hand, as a natural protective shield increases the sexual safety of the woman and on the other hand, prevents the man from engaging in adultery and illegal relationships and affairs with other women; because the zealous and honorable man as he feels a sense of honor and zeal toward his wife, averts his lustful eyes from other women too. The quote from Imam Ali (AS) which states: "An honorable person never commits adultery",[2] is indicative of the same point.

b) The secondary factors involved in strengthening the family

The secondary factors contributing to the strengthening of family which play a particular role in its strengthening and sustaining designate intentional, conscious and deeply-ingrained behavior that on the one hand have their origin in the innate qualities of men and women, or primary factors, and on the other hand, are influenced by social and cultural factors. Gender division of labor in family, the guardianship of the man in the family and avoiding extra-marital relationships and sexual pleasures outside of the family are considered the most important secondary factors. The effect of this set of factors on family unity is produced by two different mechanisms: 1) paving the way for the gratification of man and woman's mutual sexual and emotional needs. 2) Strengthening and intensifying man and woman's mutual needs covering the range of sexual, emotional and livelihood and sustenance needs.

To elaborate further this set of factors it can be said that gender division of labor in family (which to a great extent is based on different roles of men and women in the process of reproduction) and its components, namely performing the duties of motherhood and wifehood by women and bearing the expenses of life by men, has two important functions: first by reinforcing their mutual financial dependence intensifies the woman's sustenance need to man and reciprocally intensifies the man's need for woman's support in performing the household chores and secondly, lifts the burden of working outside the house from off the woman's shoulders and consequently provides the opportunity on the one hand to attend to her material and spiritual needs further and on the other hand to be more successful in providing emotional and sexual support for the husband. Master Motahhari has this to say about this issue:

> The maintenance of beauty and liveliness and pride in a woman requires less struggle and more comfort and peace of mind for her. If a woman is forced to be always struggling and striving to make money like a man, her pride will be hurt, the wrinkles that financial distress brings on a man's face will emerge in her face too. It is a commonplace fact that the Western woman who is forced to work in wretched conditions in sweatshops and factories and offices, longs

---

1 Motahhari, *the System of Women's Rights in Islam*, p. 210, 211.
2 Ibid, *A Collection of Works (Vol 19) The Issue of Hijab*, p.416, 417.

for the life of an Eastern woman. Evidently, a woman who lacks peace of mind will not find the opportunity to take care of her appearance and to bring joy and pleasure for her man… only a woman who is not exhausted and worn out and spent because of working outside the house can make family a center of peace and a place for forgetting the distresses and troubles.[1]

The guardianship role of man in family is also another secondary factor in strengthening family which is compatible with the natural differences between men and women, especially man's desire to possess woman's body and woman's desire to lean on and be supported by man and therefore it is in line with satisfying these mutual needs. Some even believe that woman according to her nature accepts man's dominance and control and likes her man to be commanding and authoritative unless when her character is humiliated.[2]

Restraint from extra-marital relationships and sexual pleasures is also another secondary factor that by intensifying the sexual and emotional needs of man and woman toward each other helps to further strengthen the family. Generally, a society in which the people are more strongly bound to this kind of restraint there will be stronger family bonds, and in reverse the more sexual freedom is advanced in a society family bonds will be weakened more. Master Motaharri explains the role of this thus:

> The underlying reason for women's covering and forbiddance of sexual fulfillment by someone other than the lawful wife in terms of family sociology is that the person's lawful wife be regarded as the only means of the man's psychological happiness, whereas in the system of sexual freedom the lawful wife is considered a nuisance and inconvenience and a warden or watchman and therefore the family is come to be based on enmity and hatred.[3]

It is worth saying that unlike the first two factors, that is, gender division of labor and man's guardianship in the family which have relatively clear innate origin, this is not so clear about the latter factor (restraint from extra-marital relationships); because it can't be denied that in humans, particularly in men, there is an instinctive propensity to unbounded pleasure-seeking. Therefore, if we consider an innate origin for the human's restraint from unlawful sexual relationships because of modesty, chastity, and zeal and sense of honor what we have in mind is human's innate inclinations, not his animalistic instinctive tendencies.

The effect of the secondary factors can be seen more conspicuously than any other time between husband and wife in their middle and old ages; the reason is that in this period one of the strongest primary factors involved in creating a family bond, that is, sexual desires have declined and at the same time, the sincerity and intimacy between them creates a very strong bond between them. In fact, it is these secondary factors specifically man's financial support and confining sexual pleasures only to the family that helps to create such a sincerity and intimacy progressively in the course of time and due to constant companionship and sharing the hardships and life's joys and sorrows

---

1. *Nahj al-balaqe* Vol.4, p. 73
2. Motahhari, *the System of Women's Rights in Islam*, p. 266.
3. Ibid, *the Notes of Master Motahhari*, Vol.5, p. 151.

and their states of mind being adapted to each other's.[1]

c) The supporting factors

The supporting factors designate those factors which are motivating or deterring and do not have a natural origin, but are educational and environmental and are directed toward strengthening family bonds, although in order for them to perform this role better they must be in coordination with the primary and secondary factors. The most important supporting factors include raising awareness, moral education, proper legislative strategies, social support and control in varied dimensions.

Raising awareness includes training of family rights, training about natural differences between men and women, communication skills training for couples and also training about a set a values about family, including values concerning the formation of family and protecting it, attending to marital roles, parenting, respecting and attending to parents and relatives.

About **moral upbringing**, the role of this factor in personal, family, and social reform is so clear in the framework of religious thinking that it can be considered as a premise for any religious thinker even though it is not explicitly stated. Gender upbringing as a pattern which in its objectives and methods allows for certain differences between girls and boys is also one of the strengthening factors of family in the theory of innate bond; because this model better prepares people for taking on their roles as husband and wife.

In terms of **legislative strategies** the role of state laws and regulations in strengthening or weakening family bonds has been corroborated by countless experiences. In analyzing this issue there is a general point to be mentioned and that is the consistency and compatibility of the legislative system to the system of Creation. On this basis, the more scrupulously this consistency is observed, in other words, the more natural differences between men and women are taken into account in terms of their rights and duties, the integrity of family will be better guaranteed. For instance, Islam recognizing the probability of the changes and fluctuations in sexual and emotional feelings of men, has adopted certain strategies to postpone divorce because this delay will probably lead to the husband reconsidering and changing his mind about divorce. But, divorce being forbidden by law and forcing the husband to keep living with a woman he does not like, because of being inconsistent with man and woman's natural characteristics cannot be an effective factor and that is why Islam contrary to the tradition of Christianity, does not approve of such a solution.[2]

Social support in its two official and unofficial forms has also a significant role in the integrity of family. In terms of official support the role of governmental institutions and organizations in providing educational, cultural and economic support for families and also in providing the ground for spending family leisure time. And in terms of unofficial support the effective role of some traditional models such as relationships between relatives, neighbors and friendly relationships between families in strengthening the family should be mentioned. Finally, **social control** in the form of

---

1 Ibid, *A Collection of Works (Vol 19): the Issue of Hijab*, p.437 and 438.
2 Ibid, *The System of Women's rights in Islam*, p. 330

positive intervention of relatives and acquaintances and also the intervention of state institutions to prevent domestic violence and in general all forms and types of supervision and control which are all included in the general Islamic principle of promoting virtue and preventing vice, can be effective in strengthening the bond between husband and wife. Based on what has been discussed earlier the following model for the theory of innate bond can be constructed:

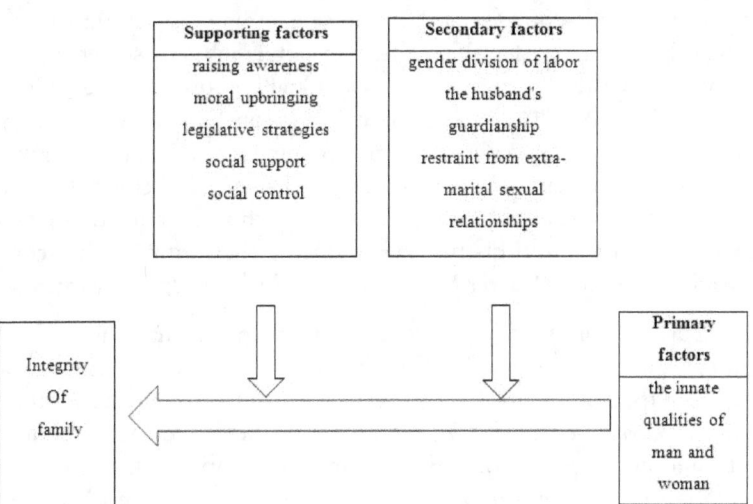

Supporting factors	Secondary factors
raising awareness	gender division of labor
moral upbringing	the husband's
legislative strategies	guardianship
social support	restraint from extra-
social control	marital sexual
	relationships

Diagram No.4: Theoretical model of the family's integrity

It is needed to be mentioned that in designing this theoretical model, only the factors which have relatively direct and immediate effect on the integrity of family have been taken into account. Without doubt, varied other factors can also be identified that indirectly affect family, but examining this type of factors was not in mind here.

15-3 An explanation of the disintegration of family in the contemporary era

The theory of innate bond not only presents an acceptable explanation of the factors involved in the genesis and strengthening of family, but it also has the potential to explain the changes in the institution of family. According to this theory, in explaining the disintegration of family in the contemporary era the emphasis more than anything else must be placed on the role of innate factors and the root cause of disintegration of family should be traced in the deviation from the necessities human nature or the aversion from innate nature in three levels of primary factors (personal qualities), secondary factors (the behavior of the couple) and some of the supporting factors (raising awareness and legislation). Furthermore, disturbances in some other supporting factors (moral upbringing and social control) have also had an effect on the disintegration of family.

Aversion from innate nature, on the level of primary factors, is not so widespread, because the determined natural differences between men and women have given them a relatively permanent and unchangeable character. But, as it has been said earlier, being natural does not necessitate being determined; therefore, there is the possibility of fading and disappearing of the innate and natural characteristics due to human intervention. For instance, characteristics such as sense of honor in men and modesty in women, despite being considered innate qualities due to behavior inconsistent with the necessities of these qualities might be weakened and eventually disappear. In any case, it is increasingly the case that men are losing their sense and zeal and women their modesty and there is a relative increase in the number of men with feminine attributes and women with masculine attributes.

About aversion from innate nature on the level of secondary factors, we see the distinctions between roles of men and women becoming less prominent and also the change in the role of the guardianship of man in family in many societies, a trend which has started in the Western societies and is gradually spreading over and permeating other societies.[1] The growth in extra-marital relationships and sexual pleasures is another manifestation of aversion from innateness in contemporary age. This phenomenon on the one hand by reducing couples' sexual and emotional needs to each other, has damaged the integrity of family and on the other hand by increasing the couples' mutual suspicion and distrust and reducing their intimacy has contributed to the disintegration of family. Master Motahhari explains this aspect by saying:

> The European lifestyle is such that the man and woman cannot be completely intimate and sincere with each other considering their being aware of each other's experiences prior to marriage and also seeing each other's betrayal during marriage especially the man who has been ordained and determined by nature to be the protector and guardian of the purity of his own generation and offspring cannot be intimate toward a woman whom he is not certain about her chastity.[2]

Ultimately, supporting factors are also weakened from different aspects which can be explained using the concept of aversion from innateness. Particularly, in terms of raising awareness the role of new deviant philosophies should be pointed out. Master Motahhari considers one of the decisive factors in weakening of family bonds to be the destructive and baseless ideas of philosophers who have not understood the philosophy of family life deeply and who have only viewed it from the perspective of two people establishing a partnership in life to be able to better enjoy the pleasures of life.[3] As a result of the dominance of such an attitude in Western societies we have come to witness the growth of a new morality in many families which some sociologists have called "market morality". Since this morality encourages us to view people as objects and relationships as opportunities to generate profits, it will ultimately lead to self-alienation.[4]

In this regard some humanistic philosophical and psychological schools can also be mentioned that underscore the importance of certain values such as independence, growth, and security and in general individualism and self-actualization. These theories have gradually come to dominate and supersede the previous theories which considered adaptation as the solution for personal problems and have come to play a significant

---

1. Refer to: This book, Chapters 5 and 6.
2. Motahhari, *the Notes of Master Motahhari*, Vol 5, p. 44.
3. Ibid, p.32.
4. Bahr & Bahr ," Families and Self-Sacrifice :Alternative Models and Meanings for Family Theory", *Social Force*,79(4)1234

role in changing values and attitudes about family, because considering the possibilities and opportunities provided for modern women to make personal growth and progress in many areas including education, many of them refuse to take on roles of motherhood and wifehood as the most important tasks of their lives and seek their self-actualization and success in gaining personal and social advantages usually following the male models of success and progress.

Another dimension of anti-family deviant philosophies can be seen in the theories defending pleasure-seeking. For instance, Herbert Marcuse, inspired by Freud's psychological vision criticizes the restrictions in liberal societies concerning psychological repression of instinctive needs and declares emancipation of desire as the target of social change.[1]

Furthermore, Feminists also furthered their destructive ideas against family to the point that some of them called marriage slavery, legal rape, and unpaid labor [2]and some of them explicitly talked about the necessity of out-datedness and obsoleteness of family and confined the path to freedom of woman in the following three edicts:1. The role of housekeeping woman must be abolished; 2. The institution of family must be abolished; 3. Gender roles must completely abolished.[3]

In terms of rights also aversion from innate nature has emerged in the form of endeavoring to expand the equal rights of men and women whose global version we have come to see in the disappearance of all forms of Discrimination against Women Convention. Undoubtedly, this has also played a significant role in the disintegration of family, as Master Motahhari points to this.[4]

At the end, the disruption to another two supporting factors, namely moral education and social control and its role in the disintegration of family should be mentioned. Of course, the disruption to these two factors has always been affecting the disintegration of family and is not confined to the present time, nevertheless some changes can be seen in it; including the decrease in the supervision of relatives due to the structure of family changing from extended to nuclear and also the changes in moral attitudes as a result of the phenomenon of conventionalization.

In addition to the three above-mentioned factors, there are also a set of mechanisms which play the role of intervening variables between primary factors and disintegration of family and without taking them into consideration the theoretical model can't be considered a complete model. Among these intervening variables which are numerous and varied, probably no other factor can be found to be more important and influential than the mass media, because the main part of transmission of knowledge, values and skills in the modern era takes place through these media especially in the form of films, soft wares, books, and magazines. One of the dimensions of the influence of the media on the disintegration of family is its hugely significant role in promoting sexual immorality and irresponsibility[5] and another

---

1 Ibid ,p.110.
2 Ibid,p.111.
3 Oakley ,*Woman's work: The Housewife ,Past and Present*,p.222.
4 Motahhari, *The System of Women's Rights in Islam*, p. 38.
5. Ibid ,294.

important aspect is their role in playing down the importance of men and women's natural differences and presenting as invalid or inefficient the gender role divisions.

It is evident that this theory calls for certain practical procedures to be adopted and positions to be assumed in varied educational, training, moral, legal, and social domains, but in short this statement by Master Motahhari can be deduced from it: "if society intends to strengthen the marital bonds, there is nothing to be done other than to pursue the path that has been proposed by Quran, that is, observing and respecting the laws of innate nature".[1]

o **Abstract**

- The theory of innate bond being based on the assumption that family life has a natural origin, accepting a broad set of natural physical and psychological differences between man and woman, rejecting the determinacy of family life and also rejecting the determinacy of the changes undergone by the institution of family in the contemporary age, considers three sets of primary, secondary and supporting factors influencing the genesis and integrity of family.
- The primary factors contributing to the disintegration of family designate natural differences between men and women that play the central role in their bonding and taking on the roles of parents.
- By secondary factors contributing to the disintegration of family we mean those intentional and conscious behaviors that have their origin in primary factors and which are influenced by social and cultural factors. Gender division of labor in family, the guardianship of man in family, and restraint from extra-marital sexual relationships and pleasures are considered the important secondary factors.
- Supporting factors designate those motivational or inhibitive factors that do not have natural origin, but are of educational and environmental character and are directed to the strengthening of family bonds although to better perform this role they must be in coordination with primary and secondary natural factors. Raising awareness, moral upbringing, proper legislative strategies, social support and control in varied dimensions are considered the most important among supporting factors.
- According to innate bond theory, the principle root cause of the disintegration of family in the contemporary era must be traced in deviation from the necessities of human nature on three levels of primary factors(personal qualities), secondary factors(the behavior of couples), and some of the supporting factors (raising awareness and legislation and rights).

o **Self-Test**

1. How does sexual zeal in men affect the bond between man and woman?
2. How does gender division of labor help strengthen the family?
3. What kind of training is needed for the couples to help them achieve a happy and long-lasting family life?

---

1. Ibid 244.

4. Mention some examples of aversion from innate nature on the level of primary factors (natural characteristics of man and woman).
5. Explain the role of new deviant philosophies in the disintegration of family in the contemporary era?
6. Mention two aspects of how media influences the disintegration of family?

o **Research topic**

- Conduct a research on the disintegration of family in contemporary Iran using the framework of innate theory.

Persian and Arabic sources

Holy Quran

Nahj-al-Balaghe.

Abercrombie Nicholas et al, *A Dictionary of Sociology*, translated by Hassan Pouyan, Tehran: Chapakhsh , 1988.

Abbot, Pamela and Wallace, Keller, *An Introduction to the Sociology of Feminist Approaches*, translated by Maryam Khorasani and Hamid Ahmadi, Tehran: Donyaye Madar, 1997.

Ahmadi, Ali Asghar, *Innate Nature: The Foundation of Islamic Psychology*, Tehran: Amir Kabir Institute, 1983.

Azkamp , Stewart, *Applied Social Psychology*, translated by Farhad Maher, Mashhad: Astan-e Ghods-e Razavi, 1991.

Eferfar , Ali "Sorat –al- Marat fi ketabate-al- Arabiat-al –moasera, *Reference bulletin: Feminism*, the Management of Islamic Studies and the Centre for International Cultural Studies, Tehran: the International Publishing House of Al-Mahdi, 1999.

Imam Khomeini, Seyed Rouhallah, *Tahrir al -Wasileh*, Qom: Journalist Institute of Ismailian, [Bita].

Imam Khomeini, Rouhallah, *Ketab-al Baye* (5 Volumes), Qom: Journalist Institute of Ismailian, [Bita].

Amani,Mahdi, *Fundamentals of Demography*, Tehran: Samt Publication, 1998.

Amir Khosravi, Arzhang, "An Introductory Review of Divorce Statistics of the Recent Decade in Iran", *population*, Pages. 35, 36. 2001.

Anderson Norman, *The Legal Developments of the Islamic World*, translated by Fakhr Al-Din Asghari et al, Qom: The Centre of Islamic Publications of Propagation of Islam Office in Qom Seminary, 1997.

Bohrani Esfahani, Abdollah, *Avalem-al-Oloom val Maaref val Ahval*, Qom: Al-Emam-al-Mahdi Institute, 2005.

Bedard Luke et al, *Social Psychology*, translated by Hamze Ghanji, Tehran: Savalan Publication, 2001.

Bernards, John, *Family Studies: An Introduction*, translated by Hussein Ghazian, Tehran: Ney Publications, 2005.

Bostan (Najafi), Hussein, *A Step Toward Religious Science (2): The Method of Using Religious Texts in Social Sciences*, Qom: The Research Centre of Emissary and University, 2011.

Bostan (Najafi), Hussein, Sex Inequality from the Islamic and Feminist Viewpoint, Qom: The Research Centre of Emissary and University, 2003.

Banihashemi Khomeini, Mohammad Hassan (Compiler), *Tozih-al-masael-al-maraje*, Qom: Islamic Publications Office, 1999.

Behnam, Jamshid and Rasekh, Shapour, *An Introduction to the Sociology of Iran*, Tehran: Kharazmi, 1969.

Parsa, Rolan, *Birth and Fertility, Population and Demography*, translated by Habiballah Zanjani, Tehran: The Centre for University Press, 1989.

Turner, Jonathan, H, *The Concepts and Functions of Sociology*, translated by Mohammad Fouladi and Mohammad Aziz Bakhtiary, Qom: Imam Khomeini Institute, 1999.

Jaggar Allison, "Four Interpretations of Feminism (1) and (2)", translated by S. Amiri, *Women*, Pages. 5, 28, 48-52, 31, 40-44, 1996.

Hejazi Banafsheh, *Woman in History: the Status of woman in Ancient Iran*, Tehran: Shahr-e Ashoub Publication, 1991.

Horr Amelli, Mohammad-ebn-al Hassan, *Wasael al-Shia*,(20 volumes), Tehran: Almaktab-al Islamiiah, [Bita].

Hamiri, *Abd-al Molk-ebn-al Hesham,Al-Sirat-al Nabaviah* (4 Volumes), Beirut, Dar ehya – al Tarath-al Arabi,1985.

Khoyi Seyed Ab-al Qasim, *Serat-al negat fi ajviah-al esteftaat*, Qom: Dar-al Etesam, 1996.

Khoyi Seyed Ab-al Qasim, *Menhaj-al Salehin*, (2 volumes), Qum: Medina-al Elm, 1990.

Durant, Will, *Pleasures of Philosophy*, translated by Abbas Zaryab, Tehran: Enghelab-e-Islami Publication and Education, 1992.

Durkheim, Emil, *On Social Division of Labor*, translated by Bagher Parham, Babol: Babol Book house, 1990.

Robertson, Yan, *An Introduction to Society*, translated by Hussein Behravan, Mashhad: Astan-e Ghods-e Razavi Printing and Publication Institute, 1995.

Rosenbaum, Heidi, *Family as a Structure against Society*, translated by Mohammad Sadeq Mahdavi, Tehran: University Press, 1988.

Ruche , *Sociology* of *Talcott Parsons,* translated by Abd-al Hussein Nik Ghohar, Tehran: Tabian Cultural and Publication Institute, 1997.

Sarokhani, Bagher, *Encyclopedia of Social Sciences*, Tehran: Keyhan Publication Organization, 1991.

Sarokhani, Bagher, *An Introduction to Family Sociology*, Tehran: Soroush, 1991.

Soroush, Abd-al Karim, *Lessons in the Philosophy of Social Science*, Tehran: Ney Publication, 1995.

Sega Len, Martin, *Historical Sociology of Family*, translated by Hamid Elyasi, Tehran: Markaz Publication, 1996.

Sistani, Seyed Ali, *Menhaj-al salehin*, (3 volumes), Qom: Maktab Ayat-al Ozma Sistani, 1416 lunar.

Syuti, Jalal-al Din Abd-al Rahman, *Addor-al Mansour*, Qom: Manshourat Maktanb Ayat-Allah Ozma Marashi Najafi, 1984.

Sherman Wood, *Modern Viewpoints on Sociology*, translated by Moustafa Azkia, Tehran: Keyhan, 1987.

Shahid Sani, Zei-al Din ebn Ali, *Al-Roza al-Bahya fi sharh-al lamah —al dameshghiyah* (10 volumes), Qom: Manshourat maktabah al-davari, 1990.

Shahid Sani, Zei-al Din ebn Ali, *Masalek-al afham*, (15 volumes), Qom: Maaref-e Eslami Institute, 1995.

Safaie, Seyed Hassan and Imamai, Asadallah, *Family Rights in Brief*, Tehran: Dadgostar Publication, 1999.

Tabatabaie, Yazdi, Seyed Mohammad Kazem, *Takammalah-al orvat-al vosgha* (4 volumes), Tehran: Matba-al-Heidari, 1959.

Tabatabaie, Seyed Mohammad Hussein, *Al-mizan fi tafsir-al Quran*, Qom: The Society of Teachers of Emissary in Qom, [Bita].

Tabarsi, Al-Hassan ebn Al-Fazl, *Makarem-al akhlagh*, Lebanon: Dar-al Havra, 1988.

French, Marlin, *War against Women*, translated by Touran Dokht Tamaddon, Tehran: Elmi Publications, 1994.

Freud, Sigmund, *Totem and Taboo*, translated by Iraj Pourbagher, Tehran: Asia, 1983.

Feiz-e Kashani, Al-Movla Mohsen, *Al-tafsir al-safi* (7 volumes), Tehran: Maktab-al Sadr, 1995.

Ghazi Tabatabaie, Mahmoud et al, *a National survey of domestic violence against women*, in collaboration with Higher Education Research and Planning Institute, the Presidential Centre for Women's Participation, Tehran: Ministry of the Interior, Social Issues Office, 2004.

Qotb, Seyed Mohammad, *Fi zalal-al Quran*, Lebanon and Egypt: Dar-al Shorough, 1988.

Kord Zanghaneh, Jafar, "A Survey of Dynamics of Marriage and Divorce in Iran Relying on the nation-wide census of 2007", Cultural Engineering Monthly, Pages. 3, 21, 22, 1999.

Klein Berg, Otto, *Social Psychology*, translated by Ali Mohammd Kardan, Tehran: Andisheh Publications, 1989.

King Samuel, *Sociology*, translated by Moshfegh Hamedani, Tehran: Simorgh Books, 1976.

Keynia, Mahdi, *The Fundamentals of Criminology* (3 volumes), Tehran: Tehran University, 1990.

Gordon, Michael, "Industrial Life and Family", Peter Worsley, *Modern Sociology*, translated by Hassan Pouyan, Tehran: Chapakhsh, 1994.

Giddens, Anthony, *Sociology*, translated by Manouchehr Saboori, Tehran: Ney Publication, 1995.

Lengerman, Patricia, Meadow and Berantley, Gil Nib Roug, "Contemporary Feminist Theory", George Wrightser, *The Theory of Sociology in Contemporary Period*, translated by Mohsen Salasi, Tehran: Elmi Publications, 1995, Pages.459-526.

Majlesi, Mohammad Bagher, *Behar-al Anvar*, Beirut: Dar Ahya –al Terath-al Arabi, 1982.

Mohseni, Manouchehr, *A Survey of Social-Cultural Awareness*, Attitudes, and Behaviors in Iran, Tehran: Public Cultural Council, 2000.

Mosavati, Azar, Majid, *Social Pathology of Iran (Sociology of Deviations)*, Tabriz: Nobel, 1995.

Motahari, Morteza, *A Collection of Works (Vol. 19): The Issue of Hijab*, Tehran and Qum:

Motahari, Morteza, *the System of Woman's Rights in Islam*, Tehran and Qom: Sadra, 1990.

Motahari, Morteza, *Notes of Master Motahari*, Vol.5, Tehran: Sadra, 2003.

Mendras, Henry, Gorvic, George, *Fundamentals of Sociology*, translated by Bagher Parham, Tehran: Amirkabir, 1990.

Montesquieu, Charles de Secondat, Baron de, *The Spirit of Laws*, translated by Ali Akbar Mahtadi, Tehran: Amirkabir, 1983.

Michelle, Andre, *Fighting against Sex Discrimination*, translated by Mohammad Jafar Pouyandeh, Tehran: Neghah, 1997.

Michelle, Andre, *the Sociology of Family and Marriage*, translated by Farangis Ardalan, Tehran: Faculty of Social Sciences and Cooperation, 1975.

Nouri, Mirza Hussein, *Mostadrak-al vasayel*, Lebanon: Al-al Bayt le Ehya-al Tarath Institute, 1988.

Nahj-al balagheh, (4 volumes), Mohammad Abdeh, Qum: Dar-al Zakhaer, 1991.

Weber, Max, *On the Methodology of the Social Sciences*, translated by Hassan Chavoshian, Tehran: Markaz Publications, 2003.

Heller, Agnes, "*Women, Civil Society, and Government*", transaletd by Sahar Sajjadi, Second Sex, (Vol.3), Noushin Ahmadi Khorasani, Tehran: Tousee Publication, 1999, Pages. 50-66.

Heywood, Andrew, "Four Essential Discussions in Feminism" translated by Rosa Eftekhari, Women, 5, 32, 1996, Pages.30-33.

English Sources

Adams, Bert N. (2004), " Families and Family Study in International Perspective ", *Journal of Marriage and Family 66*, December.

Allan, Graham & Crow, Graham (2001), *Families, Households and Society*, New York : Palgrave.

Almquist, Elizabeth M. et al. (1978), *Sociology : Women, Men and Society*, St. Paul : West Publishing Company.

Aronson, Elliot (1991), *The Social Animal*, New York : Freeman and Company.

Bahr, Howard M. & S. Bahr, Kathleen (2001), " Families and Self-Sacrifice : Alternative Models and Meanings for Family Theory ", *Social Forces*, 79(4).

Baron, R. A. & D. Byrne (1997), *Social Psychology*, Boston : Allyn and Bacon.

Bengtson, Vern L. et al. (eds.) (2005), *Sourcebook of Family Theory & Research*, Thousand Okas and London : Sage Publications, Inc.

Berk, Laura E. (1994), *Child Development*, Boston & London : Allyn and Bacon.

Bilton, Tony et al. (1981), *Introductory Sociology*, London & Basingstoke : McMillan Press LTD.

Bradley, Harriet, " Changing Social Structures : Class and Gender ", Stuart Hall and Bram Gieben (eds.) (1992), *Formations of Modernity*, Cambridge : Polity/Open University Press.

Burr, Vivien (1998), *Gender and Social Psychology*, London & New York : Routledge.

Carlson, Neil R. (1993), *Psychology : The Science of Behavior*, Boston : Allyn.

Charles, Nickie & Kerr, Marion (1999), " Women's Work ", *The Sociology of The Family*, Graham Allan (ed.), Oxford : Blackwell Publishers.

Chibucos, Thomas R. & Leite, Randall W. (2005), *Readings in Family Theory*, Thousand Okas and London : Sage Publications.

Chodorow, Nancy (1997), " The Psychodynamics of the Family ", *The Second Wave*, Linda Nicholson (ed.), New York & London : Routledge.

Cotgrove, Stephen (1972), *The Science of Society : An Introduction to Sociology*, London : George Allen and Unwin LTD.

Curry, T.; R. Jiobu & K. Schwirian (1997), *Sociology for the Twenty-First Century*, Upper Saddle River and New Jersey : Prentice Hall.

De Beauvoir, Simone (1989), *The Second Sex*, New York : Vintage Books.

Despres, R. & L. Griffin (2005), *The Truth about Family Life*, New York : Facts On File, Inc.

Firestone, Shulamith (1997), " The Dialectic of sex ", *The Second Wave*, Linda Nicholson (ed.), New York & London : Routledge.

Forsyth, Donelson R. (1995), *Our Social World*, Pacific Grove : Book/Cole Publishing Company.

Fox, Bonnie J. (ed.) (1993), *Family Patterns, Gender Relations*, Oxford : Oxford University Press.

Goode, William J. (1960), " The Sociology of the Family ", *Sociology Today*, Robert K. Merton et al., New York : Basic Books, INC.

Goode, William J. (1964), *The Family, Englewood Cliffs*, New Jersey : Prentice-Hall, Inc.

Grusec, J. E. & H. Lytton (1988), *Social Development : History, Theory and Research*, New York : Springer-Verlag.

Halbwachs, Maurice (1978), *The Causes of Suicide*, (Trans. By Harold Goldblatt), London & Henley : Routledge & Kegan Paul.

Hammersley, Martyn (2000), *Taking Sides in Social Research*, London & New York : Routledge.

Harvey, Lee & Morag McDonald (1993), *Doing Sociology*, London : The McMillan Press LTD.

Hekman, Susan J. (1992), *Gender and Knowledge*, Boston : Northeastern University Press.

Hendrick, Susan S. & Hendrick Clyde (1992), *Romantic Love*, Newbury Park & London : Sage Publications.

Huber, Joan & Glenna Spitze (1988), " Trends in Family Sociology ", *Handbook of Sociology*, Neil J. Smelser (ed.) NewBury Park : Sage Publications.

Ingoldsby, Born B. (2006), " Family Origin and Universality ", *Families in Global and Multicultural Perspective*, Ingoldsby & Smith (eds.), Thousand Oaks : Sage Publications, Inc.

Ingoldsby, Born B. (2006), " Marital Structure ", *Families in Global and Multicultural Perspective*, Ingoldsby & Smith (eds.), Thousand Oaks : Sage Publications, Inc.

Ingoldsby, Born B. (2006), " Mate Selection and Marriage ", *Families in Global and Multicultural Perspective*, Ingoldsby & Smith (eds.), Thousand Oaks : Sage Publications, Inc.

Jaggar, Alison M. (1994), " Human Biology in Feminist Theory : Sexual Equality Reconsidered ", *Knowing Women*, Helen Crowley & Susan Himmelweit (eds.), Cambridge : Polity Press.

Kammeyer, K. C. W.; G. Ritzer & Norman R. Yetman (1989), *Sociology : Experiencing Changing Societies*, Boston & London : Allyn & Bacon.

Kendall, Diana (1999), *Sociology in our Times*, Belmont, CA : Wadsworth Publishing Company.

Klein, Renate C. A. (ed.) (1998), *Multidisciplinary Perspective on Family Violence*, London & New York : Routledge.

Knuttila, Murray (1996), *Introducing Sociology : A Critical Perspective*, Toronto, New York & Oxford : Oxford University Press.

Komter, Aafke (2001), " Hidden Power in Marriage ", *Self and society*, Ann Branaman (ed.), Massachusetts : Blackwell Publishers Inc.

Kuper, Adam & Jessica Kuper (eds.) (1985), *The Social Science Encyclopedia*, London & Boston : Routledge & Kegan Paul.

Lawson, Tony & Joan Garrod (2001), *Dictionary of Sociology*, London & Chicago : Fitzroy Dearborn Publishers.

Le Gall, Didier (1998), " Family Conflict in France Through the Eyes of Teenagers ", *Multidisciplinary Perspective on Family Violence*, Renate C. A. Klein (ed.), London & New York : Routledge.

Lee, David & Howard Newby (1995), *The Problem of Sociology*, London & New York : Routledge.

Lenski, G.; P. Nolan & J. Lenski (1995), *Human Societies*, New York : McGraw-Hill, Inc.

Lindsey, Linda L. & Stephen Beach (2000), *Sociology : Social Life and Social Issues*, Uper Saddle River & New Jersey : Prentice Hall.

Lott, Bernice (1993), *Women's Lives*, Pacific Grove and California : Cole Publishing Company.

McConnell, J. V. & R. P. Philipchalk (1992), *Understanding Human Behavior*, Orlando : HBJ Publishers.

McLoughlin, Jane (1991), *The Demographic Revolution*, London & Boston : Faber and Faber.

McRae, Susan (1999), " Cohabitation or Marriage ? - Cohabitation ", *The Sociology of the Family*, Graham Allan (ed.), Oxford : Blackwell Publishers.

Mintz, Steven & Susan Kellogg (1991), " Coming Apart : Radical Departures Since 1960 ", John N. Edwards & David H. Demo (eds.), *Marriage and Family in Transition*, Boston & London : Allyn and Bacon.

Mitchell, G. Duncan (ed.) (1977), *A Dictionary of Sociology*, London & Henley : Routledge & Kegan Paul.

Morris, Lydia (1999), " The Household and the Labour Market ", *The Sociology of the Family*, Graham Allan (ed.), Oxford : Blackwell Publishers.

Myers, David G. (2000), *Exploring Social Psychology*, Boston : McGraw Hill.

Nazroo, James (1999), " Uncovering Gender Differences in the Use of Marital Violence : The Effect of Methodology ", *The Sociology of the Family*, Graham Allan (ed.), Oxford : Blackwell Publishers.

Oakley, Ann (1976), *Woman's work : The Housewife, Past and Present*, New York : Vintage Books.

Oliver, Kelly (1997), *Family Values*, New York & London : Routledge.

Parsons, Talcott (1965), *Man and Civilization,* New York : McGraw-Hill Book Company.

Peach, Lucinda Joy (ed.) (1998), *Women in Culture,* Massachusetts : Blackweel Publishers.

Perlmutter, Marion & Elizabeth Hall (1992), *Adult Development and Aging,* New York : John Wiley & Sons INC.

Ramazanoglu, Caroline (1989), *Feminism and the Contradictions of Oppression,* London & New York : Routledge.

Russo, Sandra L. & Suzanna D. Smith (2006), " Women in the Two-Thirds World ", *Fimilies in Global and Multicultural Perspective,* Ingoldsby and Smith (eds.), Thousand Oaks : Sage Publications Inc.

Sabini, John (1995), *Social Psychology,* New York & London : W. W. Norton & Company.

Santrock, J. W. & S. R. Yussen (1989), *Child Development : An Introduction,* Dubuque & Iowa : Wcb Publishers.

Schaefer, Richard (1989), *Sociology,* New York : McGraw-Hill Book Company.

Sears, D. O.; A. Peplau; J. L. Freedman & S. E. Taylor (1988), *Social Psychology,* Englewood Cliffs : Prentice-Hall Inc.

Seidler, V. J. (1998), " Masculinity, Violence and Emotional Life ", *Emotions in Social Life,* Gillian Bendelow and Simon J. Williams (eds.), London & New York : Routledge.

Shepard, Jon M. (1999), *Sociology,* New York & Boston : Wadsworth.

Shorter, Edward (1977), *The Making of the Modern Family,* New York : Basic Books, INC.

Siegel, Larry J. (1997), *Criminology,* Belmont : Wadsworth Publishing Company.

Spanier, Graham B. (1991), " Cohabitation : Recent Changes in the U.S. ", *Marriage and Family in Transition,* John N. Edwards & David H. Demo (eds.), Boston & London : Allyn and Bacon.

Sterba, James P. (1998), " Is Feminism Good for Men and Are Men Good For Feminism ? ", *Men Doing Feminism,* Tom Digby (ed.), New York & London : Routledge.

Stokes, Randall (1984), *Introduction to Sociology,* Dubuque & Iowa : Wcb Publishers.

Taylor, S. E.; L. A. Peplau & D. O. Sears (2000), *Social Psychology,* New Jersey : Prentice Hall Inc.

Tong, Rosemarie (1997), *Feminist Thought,* London : Routledge.

Vogler, Carolyn & Jan Pahl (1999), " Money, Power and Inequality in Marriage ", *The Sociology of the Family,* Graham Allan (ed.), Oxford : Blackwell Publishers.

Ward, D. A. & L. H. Stone (1998), *Sociology for the 21th Century,* Dubuque & Iowa : Kendall/Hunt Publishing Company.

White, James M. (2005), *Advancing Family Theories,* Thousand Oaks and London : Sage Publications.

Wilkie, Jane Riblett (1991), " Marriage, Family Life, and Women's Employment ", *Marriage and Family in Transition,* Edwards and Demo (eds.), Boston & London : Allyn and Bacon.

Winch, Robert F. (1971), *The Modern Family,* New York : Holt, Rinehart and Winston, Inc.

Zanden, James W. Vander (1993), *Sociology : The Core,* New York : McGraw-Hill, Inc.

Web Addresses :

1. "Center of Iranian Statistics" ,"Managing Socio-economic Statistics of Households".

2. www.U.S.Bureau of the Census.

3. www.IranElika.com

Narration index

قُلْتُ لِأَبِي عَبْدِ اللَّهِ ع إِنَّ أَبِي قَدْ كَبِرَ جِدّاً وَ ضَعُفَ فَنَحْنُ نَحْمِلُهُ إِذَا أَرَادَ الْحَاجَةَ فَقَالَ إِنِ اسْتَطَعْتَ أَنْ تَلِيَ ذَلِكَ مِنْهُ فَافْعَلْ وَ لَقِّمْهُ بِيَدِكَ فَإِنَّهُ جُنَّةٌ لَكَ غَداً ، 99

قِيلَ لَه: إنا نُزوج صبياننا وهُم صغار فقال :إذا زوجوا وَ هُم صغار لَم يَكَادو أن يأتلفو(يأتلفوا خ ل)، 8

كانَ عَلِي(ع) يَقول:لَولاماسَبَقَنِى به ابنِ الخِطاب يعنى عمر ما زنا الاشقى،كتب على بن أسباط الى أبى جعفر(ع) فى أمر بناته وأنه لا يجد أحدا مثله، فكتب اليه أبوجعفر(ع) : فهمت ما ذكرت من أمر بناتك و أنك لا تجد أحدا مثلك، فلا تنظر فى ذالك رحمك الله، فان رسول الله (ص) قال: اذا جاءكم من ترضون خلقه ودينه فزوجوه الا تفعلوه تكن فتنه فى الأرض و فسادكبير، 30

كتبت الى أبى الحسن (ع) : رجل زوج ابنته من رجل فرغب فيه ثم زهد فيه بعد ذالك، واحب ان يفرق بينه وبين ابنته وابى الختن ذالك، ولم يجب الى طلاق، فأخذه بمهر ابنته ليجيب الى الطلاق و مذهب الاب التخلص منه، فلما اخذ بالمهر أجاب الى الطلاق، فكتب (ع) : ان كان الزهد من طريق الدين فليعمد الى التخلص، و ان كان غيره فلا يتعرض لذالك، 150

لو أنكم اذا بلغكم عن الرجل شى تمشيتم اليه فقلتم: يا هذا اما أن تعتزلنا و تجتنبا، و اما أن تكف عن هذا، فان فعل و الا فاجتنبوه، 140

ما أحب للرجل المسلم أن يتزوج اليهوديه و لا النصرانيه مخافه أن يتهود ولده أو يتنصر، 26

ما أظن رجلا يزداد فى اليمان خيرا الا ازداد حبا للنساء، 107

ما زنى غيور قط، 201

ما من شى مما أحله الله اليه أبغض من الطلاق وان الله عز وجل يبغض المطلاق الذواق، 149

ما من لبن رضع به الصبى ءعظم بركه عليه من لبن أمه، 95

مر رسول الله(ص) برجل فقال : ما فعلت امرأتك؟ قال : طلقتها يا رسول الله، قال: من غير سوء؟ قال: من غير سوء.قال: ثم ان الرجل تزوج فمر به النبى (ص) فقال: نعم، ثم مر به، فقال ما فعلت امرأتك؟قال : من غير سوء.فقال رسول الله (ص) ان الله عزوجل يبغض أو يلعن كل ذواق من الرجال و كل ذواقه من النساء، 150

من حق الولد على والده ثلاثه: يحسن اسمه و يعلمه الكتابه و يزوجه اذا بلغ، 14

من خطب اليكم فرضيتم دينه و أمانته فزوجوه، 30

من شرب الخمر بعد ما حرمها الله على لسانى فليس بأهل أن يزوج اذا خطب، 30

من قبل ولده كتب الله له حسنه، ومن فرحه فرحه الله يوم القيامه، 109

225

Author Index

Subject index

www.ingramcontent.com/pod-product-compliance
Lightning Source LLC
Chambersburg PA
CBHW081206280526
45787CB00006B/2349